The ideas of the Russian theorist Lev Vygotsky and his followers have provided rich ground for research in the West. Now that those influential ideas have saturated the literature, researchers and theorists are asking themselves how to push the research beyond Vygotsky's intentions. The contributors to this volume strive to develop a cross-disciplinary "language" in which to deal with today's complex problems.

Sociocultural Studies of Mind addresses the primary question: How is mental functioning related to the cultural, historical, and institutional settings in which it exists? Although the contributors speak from different perspectives, a clear set of unifying themes runs through the volume: (1) One of the basic ways in which sociocultural setting shapes mental functioning is through the cultural tools employed. (2) Mediation provides a formulation of how this shaping occurs. (3) In order to specify how cultural tools exist and have their effects, it is essential to focus on human action as a unit of analysis.

This landmark volume defines a general approach to sociocultural psychology – one that will be debated and redefined as the field moves forward. *Sociocultural Studies of Mind* is crucial reading for researchers and graduate students in developmental and educational psychology, cognitive science, philosophy, and cultural anthropology.

Sociocultural studies of mind

Learning in doing: Social, cognitive, and computational perspectives

GENERAL EDITORS: ROY PEA
JOHN SEELY BROWN

The construction zone: Working for cognitive change in school
Denis Newman, Peg Griffin, and Michael Cole

Plans and situated actions: The problem of human–machine interaction
Lucy Suchman

Situated learning: Legitimate peripheral participation
Jean Lave and Etienne Wenger

Street mathematics and school mathematics
Terezinha Nunes, Analucia Dias Schliemann, and David William Carraher

Distributed cognitions: Psychological and educational considerations
Gavriel Salomon (editor)

Understanding practice: Perspectives on activity and context
Seth Chaiklin and Jean Lave (editors)

The computer as medium
Peter Andersen (editor)

Sociocultural studies of mind
James V. Wertsch, Pablo del Río, and Amelia Alvarez (editors)

Sociocultural studies of mind

Edited by

JAMES V. WERTSCH
Clark University

PABLO DEL RÍO
Universidad de Salamanca

AMELIA ALVAREZ
Fundación Infancia y Aprendizaje

CAMBRIDGE
UNIVERSITY PRESS

Published by the Press Syndicate of the University of Cambridge
The Pitt Building, Trumpington Street, Cambridge CB2 1RP
40 West 20th Street, New York, NY 10011–4211, USA
10 Stamford Road, Oakleigh, Melbourne 3166, Australia

First published 1995

Library of Congress Cataloging-in-Publication Data
Sociocultural studies of mind / edited by James V. Wertsch, Pablo del
Río, Amelia Alvarez.
p.   cm. – (Learning in doing)
ISBN 0-521-47056-0 (hbk.). – ISBN 0-521-47643-7 (pbk.)
1. Ethnopsychology.   2. Social psychology.   I. Wertsch, James V.
II. Río, Pablo del.   III. Alvarez, Amelia.   IV. Series.
GN502.S65   1995
155.8 – dc20   94-34685
                                                                          CIP

A catalog record for this book is available from the British Library.

ISBN 0-521-47056-0 Hardback
ISBN 0-521-47643-7 Paperback

Transferred to digital printing 2002

Contents

Series Foreword

This series for Cambridge University Press is becoming widely known as an international forum for studies of situated learning and cognition.

Innovative contributions from anthropology; cognitive, developmental, and cultural psychology; computer science; education, and social theory are providing theory and research that seeks new ways of understanding the social, historical, and contextual nature of the learning, thinking, and practice emerging from human activity. The empirical settings of these research inquiries range from the classroom, to the workplace, to the high-technology office, to learning in the streets and in other communities of practice.

The situated nature of learning and remembering through activity is a central fact. It may appear obvious that human minds develop in social situations, and that they come to appropriate the tools that culture provides to support and extend their sphere of activity and communicative competencies. But cognitive theories of knowledge representation and learning alone have not provided sufficient insight into these relationships.

This series is born of the conviction that new and exciting interdisciplinary syntheses are underway, as scholars and practitioners from diverse fields seek to develop theory and empirical investigations adequate to characterizing the complex relations of social and mental life, and to understanding successful learning wherever it occurs. The series invites contributions that advance our understanding of these seminal issues.

Roy Pea
John Seely Brown

Contributors

Amelia Alvarez
Fundación Infancia y
 Aprendizaje
Carretera de Canillas
Madrid, Spain

Jean-Paul Bronckart
Université de Genève
Place de l'Université
Switzerland

Michael Cole
Laboratory of Comparative
 Human Cognition
University of California
La Jolla, California

Pablo del Río
Universidad de Salamanca
Facultad de Ciencias Sociales
Salamanca, Spain

Maria Cecília R. De Goes
Department of Educational
 Psychology
Faculdade de Educaco
UNICAMP
Campinas, Brazil

David R. Olson
Centre for Applied Cognitive
 Science
Ontario Institute for Studies in
 Education
Toronto, Ontario, Canada

Angel Pino
Department of Educational
 Psychology
Faculdade de Educaco
UNICAMP
Campinas, Brazil

Barbara Rogoff
Psychology Department
University of California
Santa Cruz, California

Ana Luiza B. Smolka
Department of Educational
 Psychology
Faculdade de Educaco
UNICAMP
Campinas, Brazil

Tadanobu Tsunoda
Tokyo Medical and Dental
 University
Chiba, Japan

James V. Wertsch
Frances L. Hiatt School of
 Psychology
Clark University
Worcester, Massachusetts

Vladimir P. Zinchenko
Moscow Institute of Engineering,
 Electronics, and Automation
Moscow, Russia

Sociocultural studies: history, action, and mediation

James V. Wertsch, Pablo del Río, and Amelia Alvarez

Perhaps it is the fate of every generation to believe it experiences a period of crisis, or at least rapid social change. In the twentieth century alone, several events have been nominated as major crises with their attendant cultural and psychological dimensions. For example, Fussell (1975) has eloquently shown how World War I fundamentally changed poetry and literature along with the general worldview of the English, and Elder (1974) has documented the lasting psychological impact of the Great Depression on Americans. In both cases the focus is on the cultural and psychological dimensions of great social crises, and the assumption is that these dimensions are as central to understanding such events as are economic, political, or other dimensions.

Although armed conflict and economic deprivation remain an all too familiar part of the news today, we are fortunately not in the midst of a world war or a world depression. However, we are in the midst of other major social changes and crises. For example, instead of bringing the prosperity and tranquility expected by many, the end of the Cold War has unleashed a host of major social and political forces that are changing our lives in ways few had anticipated: The forces of globalization have accelerated in a variety of arenas such as finance, economic production, and communication, while simultaneously and somewhat paradoxically, new forces of localism, especially in the form of nation-

The authors wish to express their appreciation to Michael Cole and Julia Hough for their helpful comments on an earlier draft of this chapter. The writing of this chapter was assisted by a grant from the Spencer Foundation to the first author. The statements made and the views expressed are solely the responsibility of the authors.

1

alism, have emerged with their attendant and often brutal consequences. These sequelae of the Cold War were not generally
anticipated. Indeed, many theories in the social sciences even imply
that this paradoxical combination *could not* happen.

In the context of these unsettling and often tragic transformations,
it is disheartening that the human sciences have seemed to contribute
so little to understanding, let alone addressing, the issues at hand. Instead of dealing with such issues, it seems that a great deal of effort
continues to be focused on answering narrowly defined questions that
drive the discourse within the confines of a particular discipline or
subdiscipline. There are certainly exceptions to this, reflecting either
intellectually motivated attempts to escape the constraints of a particular discipline or the demands of funding agencies and foundations to
address today's complex problems in an interdisciplinary way. These
exceptions, however, are best understood as struggles against the dominant trend of academic discourse as usual with its narrow disciplinary
focus and its resulting irrelevance to major social issues.

Even when there is a will, there often seems to be little way to
address complex problems with today's human sciences. The contributors to this volume believe that this is not solely, or even primarily,
the result of some unwillingness or perversity on the part of researchers
in the human sciences. Instead, we see this largely as resulting from
the use of inadequate or inappropriate "languages" for talking about
these problems – specifically, theoretical and methodological languages
that encourage or even force speakers to isolate various dimensions and
issues in such a way that it is nearly impossible to communicate with
one another or to formulate intelligent integrative pictures of complex
phenomena. There are languages of psychology, anthropology, linguistics, history, sociology, and so forth, and it is usually extremely difficult
if not impossible to translate the account of a phenomenon from one
of these languages into another. Even more dismaying is the fact that
there are many mutually untranslatable languages *within* any of these
disciplinary categories. In psychology, for example, it is very difficult
for a behaviorist to speak to a cognitivist or for either to speak to a
psychoanalyst, and within each of *these* subdisciplines there are further
incommensurable differences.

What we have to say in this volume will not solve all these issues.
However, it is motivated, at least in part, by a desire to make the human

sciences more capable of addressing today's major social issues. And since these social issues come in complex forms rather than in presliced disciplinary fragments, we believe that a starting point for doing this is to find a common language that makes it possible to communicate effectively across artificially drawn academic boundaries.

This is not to say that everyone must speak only one language, something that would undoubtedly be detrimental to all (on the dangers of such an approach see Zinchenko, chapter 1, this volume). Instead of such a reductionistic, totalizing goal, we envision a kind of multilingualism with the caveat that one of the languages each of us uses should serve as a common tongue for communicating with at least some other parties, linking our various efforts together into a richer and a more general whole. This should not be mistaken as an attack on specialized expertise. We view such expertise as essential as long as there is a way for each specialization to be linked with others in a forum of common discourse.

A "sociocultural" approach

In this volume, proposals for how to address these problems are framed in terms of what we call a sociocultural approach. This is hardly the first time the term "sociocultural" has been used in the human sciences. Indeed, it has been employed by several authors from a variety of disciplines – for example, Dewey (1938), who used it when discussing issues of logic and inquiry, and Kress (1985), who has used it in his studies of language and discourse. In these cases, however, there has been no special significance attached to the term in the sense of designating an approach or method. One of the goals of this volume is to use this term to signify a general approach in the human sciences, hopefully one that can contribute to the development of the common language just mentioned.

At the risk of homogenizing some of the multivoicedness in this volume, we can begin by stating that the goal of a sociocultural approach is to explicate the relationships between human mental functioning, on the one hand, and the cultural, institutional, and historical situations in which this functioning occurs, on the other. We shall come to modify this formulation, especially with regard to the place of "mental functioning" in it. However, the explicit mention of mental func-

tioning is appropriate at the outset because it reflects the fact that, to
date, a great deal of writing that either has given rise to sociocultural
research or has been explicitly labeled as such has been concerned with
psychological issues. In particular, these efforts have been concerned
with bringing psychology back into closer contact with other areas of
the social sciences and humanities.

Historical antecedents

A search for the historical antecedents of sociocultural research
can lead down many paths. At certain points these antecedents are
thoroughly intertwined, but at many others they have evolved somewhat independently. We shall now review some of the historical precursors that we find particularly relevant for understanding the chapters
in this volume.

The first antecedent to sociocultural research we shall outline is what
Cole (1990) has called the "once and future discipline" of *cultural psychology*. In trying to situate this discipline in the academic landscape
of the past and present, Cole writes:

Cultural psychology is different from specialized branches of psychology in that it did
not evolve as a subdiscipline after the founding of experimental psychology; the idea
of cultural psychology predates experimental psychology and was present at its birth.
(1990, p. 279)

One of the implications of Cole's formulation of cultural psychology
is that it is not to be confused with, or reduced to, the subdiscipline
of cross-cultural psychology. Instead, the origins of cultural psychology
that he has in mind are to be found in Wundt's writings. It is, of
course, possible to trace the roots of cultural psychology back several
centuries as Jahoda (1993) has done, but Cole's point is that Wundt,
the figure generally considered to be the "father of psychology," clearly
saw a role for a version of cultural psychology that was on a par with
other areas of the discipline oriented more toward the natural sciences.
In recounting how the pieces to the overall picture emerged, Wundt
wrote:

In the year 1860 I conceived the idea of adding a kind of superstructure to experimental
psychology, which by the nature of its aims and methods has to confine itself to the
facts of individual mental life. Although this superstructure is bound to rest on

the foundation of these facts, it has to go beyond them and take its departure from the phenomena of human social life. Soon this began to appear to me as the higher task of psychology, and truly its proper completion. (1920, p. 201, as cited in Jahoda, 1993, p. 133)

Wundt's definition of the nature and role of "Volkerpsychologie" is taken by many as one of the major precursors of today's efforts to create, or re-create, a cultural psychology.

Other contemporary formulations of cultural psychology do not mention Wundt but rely on a variety of ideas from other disciplines of the human sciences. For example, Shweder (1990) draws heavily on figures from anthropology, psychology, and psychological anthropology. His hope is that cultural psychology will "synthesize, or at least combine, some of the virtues" of such disciplines "while seeking to disencumber itself from their vices" (p. 17). The intended result will be a cultural psychology, which, among other things, will be "an interdisciplinary human science" (p. 3). As is often the case when talking about cultural psychology, it turns out to be easier to state what it is *not* than what it is, and in this vein Shweder notes that it is not general psychology, cross-cultural psychology, psychological anthropology, or ethnopsychology.

In yet another formulation of cultural psychology, Bruner (1990) sees it as being engaged in a much broader and more fundamental task than that of cross-cultural psychology. This is the task of attacking head on "a widely held and rather old-fashioned fallacy [about the relationship between biology and culture] that the human sciences inherited from the nineteenth century" (p. 20). Instead of viewing culture as some kind of " 'overlay' on biologically determined human nature" in which "the *causes* of human behavior were assumed to lie in that biological substrate," Bruner argues that we should take the perspective that "culture and the quest for meaning within culture are the proper causes of human action" (p. 20).

Although the formulations of cultural psychology we have reviewed share certain basic themes, they hardly present a unified picture. One indication of the differences involved is the failure of many of the authors mentioned to cite each other, or even common sources (on this, see Wertsch, 1992). At least part of this difference can be traced to the role played in the various contemporary accounts by a second major source of sociocultural research we shall examine: the writings of the Soviet psychologist, semiotician, and pedagogical theorist Lev Semenovich Vygotsky and his followers. Bruner (1990) and Cole (1990) have drawn on the ideas of Vygotsky in formulating their accounts of cultural psychology, but it remains the case that many contemporary scholars concerned with cultural psychology cite nothing from the Vygotskian tradition, and those writing from the Vygotskian perspective often seem to know nothing of cultural psychology. This shortcoming is addressed to some degree in this volume, but many questions remain about how this has come about and whether it must remain so.

"Cultural-historical" versus "sociocultural"

Perhaps the first point to make about the Vygotskian foundations of a sociocultural approach is that Vygotsky himself seldom, if ever, used the term "sociocultural." Instead, he and his followers usually spoke of a "sociohistorical" (e.g., Luria, 1981) or "cultural-historical" (e.g., Smirnov, 1975) approach. If this is the case, why should we feel justified in appropriating many of his ideas under the heading of "sociocultural" research? As Cole (pp. 212–13 n1, this volume) notes this is a terminological issue worth considering seriously. He uses the term "socio-cultural-historical psychology" in the title of his chapter to index his concern and argues that to switch to the term "sociocultural" may do "a disservice to the historical record and fails to add conceptual clarity" to the discussion. The term used in his Chapter 8 is, therefore, "cultural-historical" or "cultural-historical activity theory." Zinchenko (Chapter 1) is the contributor to this volume who is most concerned with the history of these ideas in Soviet psychology, and he also uses the term "cultural-historical" psychology when referring to the schools of Vygotsky, Leont'ev, and Luria.

We would agree that "cultural-historical" and "sociohistorical" are more appropriate terms when referring to the *heritage* we recognize from Vygotsky, Leont'ev, Luria, and many other Soviet psychologists. However, we believe that "sociocultural" is a better term when it comes to dealing with how this heritage has been *appropriated* in contemporary debates in the human sciences, at least in the West. The reason for this has to do with how culture is understood by the various parties involved.

As dedicated participants in the effort to carry out the first grand socialist experiment in the form of the Soviet Union, Vygotsky as well as his students and colleagues in the 1920s and 1930s were committed to formulating a psychology grounded in Marxism. To be sure, major divisions emerged over the years among those involved in this effort (see Zinchenko, Chapter 1, this volume). However, one of the fundamental tenets for all was a belief in some form of universal human rationality and progress. The rationality involved was viewed as being accessible to all humans, though some groups and individuals might lag behind others in their mastery of it.

Based on this assumption, Vygotsky and his colleagues made many distinctions within the "genetic domains" (Wertsch, 1985) of sociocultural history and ontogenesis between "higher" and "lower" forms of mental functioning. For example, with regard to sociocultural history, Vygotsky argued in *Studies on the History of Behavior: Ape, Primitive, and Child* (Vygotsky & Luria, 1993) that "cultural" peoples are distinct from "primitive" peoples in the forms of language and thinking they employ. This was not to say that primitive languages were viewed as simpler or less adequate in all ways. Indeed, in certain respects precisely the opposite was being argued:

Primitive man differs from cultural man not simply because his language turns out to be more meager in means, cruder, and less developed than the language of a cultural man. All this, of course, is so; but at the same time, with respect to the language of primitive man, we are struck precisely by the huge wealth of vocabulary. All the difficulty of understanding and studying these languages first and foremost stems from their superiority over the languages of cultural peoples because of the degree of wealth, abundance, and luxury of their various nomenclatures, which is totally absent in our language. (1993, p. 108)

However, even while recognizing certain respects in which the languages of primitive people seem to be superior to those of "cultural man," Vygotsky viewed properties such as the "huge wealth of vocabulary" to be impediments to developing the "psychological tools," or "mediational means" (Wertsch, 1985) for higher mental functioning:

The primitive man does not have concepts; abstract, generic names are completely alien to him. He uses the word differently than we do. . . . All the characteristics of primitive thinking can be reduced to this main fact, that is, to the fact that instead of [conceptual] notions, it operates with complexes. . . . The main progress in thought development affects a shift from the first mode of using a word as a proper name to the second mode, where the word is a sign of a complex, and finally to the third mode, where a word is a tool or means for developing the concept. . . . the cultural development of thinking is found to have [a] close connection with the history of the development of human language. (pp. 118–121)

In making such claims about thinking and language, Vygotsky was making strong assumptions about universal human rationality and progress. "Primitive thinking" in general differs from modern forms in that the former does not rely on abstract concepts. Such abstract concepts are viewed as emerging at a later historical point. One of the results of this formulation is that what we would today call cross-cultural differences were for Vygotsky and his colleagues "cross-historical" differences (see Wertsch, 1985).

As Scribner (1985) pointed out, this does not mean that all of Vygotsky's comments on history can be neatly categorized in a monolithic way. On the one hand, it would seem that Vygotsky's understanding of history was very much in line with the Enlightenment idea of universal human progress, a view that interprets difference in terms of levels on a single line of development or evolution. On the other hand, however, Scribner (1985) noted that there are many points in Vygotsky's writings where he evidenced a wider set of ideas than might be anticipated. For example, he did not posit a single, globalizing set of stages of the sort outlined by Spencer (1876) for categorizing social formations.

Instead, Vygotsky seemed to recognize a complex relationship between history as change and history as universal human progress. This comes out in his account of the particular aspect of history that was of most interest to him, "the symbolic-communicative spheres of activity in which humans collectively produce new means for regulating their behavior" (Scribner, 1985, p. 123). Among other things, the fact that he seems to have recognized historical processes other than those that fall under the heading of universal human progress led him away from simple comparisons between historical development and ontogenesis and the resulting pitfalls of recapitulationism. Indeed, as Scribner noted, Vygotsky argued that "only 'sloth' would assimilate his theory to recapitulationist or parallelist positions" (1985, p. 138).

It is less clear, however, that all of Vygotsky's students and followers made such a distinction between history as change and history as universal human progress, something that may reflect the pressures of the different political contexts in which they lived and worked (see Zinchenko, Chapter 1, this volume). For example, the account provided by Luria (1976) of differences between the performance of Central Asian peasants and urban Europeans on various reasoning tasks would seem to be more consistent with the very kind of recapitulationist position that Vygotsky rejected.

The tendency to view history as universal human progress is linked with what Shweder (1991) terms "evolutionism":

Confronted with the apparent diversity of human understandings, evolutionists rely on a powerful three-stage rule for ordering that variety into a sequence of lower to higher (primitive to advanced, incipient to elaborated) forms: (1) locate a normative model . . . ; (2) treat the normative model as the endpoint of development; (3) describe diverse beliefs and understandings as steps on an ideational Jacob's ladder moving progressively in the direction of the normative endpoint. . . . Variations in thought are ranked in terms of their degree of approximation to the endpoint. (pp. 117–118)

One of the problems with such a view has been outlined by Goody (1977). In his view, the approximation to the end point envisioned by evolutionists has often reflected an implicit dichotomy between "us" and "them." Goody sees this as emerging in anthropological literature in its use of dichotomies such as that between "savage" and "domesticated," or "Neolithic" and "modern" cultures. In Vygotsky's writings, versions of this dichotomy appear in the distinctions between "rudimentary" and "higher" mental functioning, or "eidetic" and "logical" memory, and his statement that "*he* [primitive man] uses the word differently than *we* do" (Vygotsky & Luria, 1993, p. 118; italics added) is particularly telling in this regard.

It was precisely a critique of evolutionism and the dichotomies that so often accompany it that gave rise to much of the thinking in contemporary cultural anthropology and cultural psychology. In contrast to grounding cultural and psychological analyses in assumptions about "psychic unity" (Jahoda, 1993) and the evolution thereof, figures such as Boas (1911, 1920) focused on the qualitative differences among cultures and argued that each has its own historical, psychological, and social configuration and must be understood in its own terms (see Lucy & Wertsch, 1987). The critique and ensuing theoretical framework outlined by Boas and such students of his as Sapir (1931) and Whorf (1956) provided the basic framework for much of today's cultural anthropology.

Our reason for going into these issues is to identify a basic incompatibility between assumptions that Vygotsky's followers (if not Vygotsky himself) held and those that guide the thinking of contemporary scholars concerned with culture, culture theory, cultural psychology, and so forth. Vygotsky's followers assumed a notion of culture that is clearly in line with universalist assumptions about the psychic unity of humankind and evolutionist claims often associated with these assumptions. Given that some of the most productive recent appropriations of Vygotsky have been made by scholars (e.g., Rogoff, Chapter 6, this volume) whose notion of culture derives from the tradition of Boas, some clarification is in order about where one agrees and disagrees with Vygotsky and his Soviet students and followers. It seems to us that the evolutionist assumptions indexed by the terms "sociohistorical" and "cultural-historical" are one place where most authors in this volume part ways with Vygotsky's followers, if not Vygotsky himself. It is for this reason that we prefer the term "sociocultural."

Having said all this about the problems associated with the ideas of Vygotsky and his followers, it might be assumed that sociocultural research is best formulated without invoking his name or ideas at all. This is clearly not the case for the authors included in this volume, however, and the reasons for this have to do with at least two fundamental themes running throughout sociocultural research that derive to a large extent from the writings of Vygotsky and his followers. The two themes we have in mind concern *human action* and *mediation*. Indeed, these two themes can be considered to be the defining moments of sociocultural research as presented in this volume.

Human action

One of the fundamental claims of sociocultural research as outlined herein is that its proper focus is human action. As understood here, action may be external as well as internal, and it may be carried out by groups, both small and large, or by individuals. The fact that the notion of action is applied as naturally to group as to individual processes means that it need not be constrained by the problematic assumptions of individualistic reductionism that limit so much of contemporary psychology (see Wertsch, 1991; Chapter 2, this volume).

Of course, this is not to say that action does not have a psychological moment or dimension. It clearly does. Even action in its most mundane motor form has its psychological dimension. The point is that we should think of this as a *moment* of action rather than as a separate process that exists somehow in isolation. This is what motivated our comment in the preceding section that the preliminary formulation of a sociocultural approach, one that spoke of mental functioning, would need to be revisited. It could now read: The goal of a sociocultural approach is to explicate the relationships between human action, on the one hand, and the cultural, institutional, and historical situations in which this action occurs, on the other.

The issue of action is explicitly addressed in a general way in the chapters by Bronckart and Wertsch. In his analysis, Bronckart argues that while there are several existing notions of action in psychological research, most of them fail to take into account the fact that "the structuring of human activity is of a *sociocultural* nature" (p. 76, this volume). Instead, "for a wide range of theoretical approaches, undoubtedly a majority, human activity is first and foremost an *externalization of the biological characteristics* of an organism" (p. 76, this volume), precisely the problem Bruner warned against in his comment cited earlier. Throughout Bronckart's analysis and in most other chapters of this volume as well, the emphasis on action reflects a rejection of the "mechanistic materialism" (Taylor, 1985) that has guided so much of psychology in the past and is a call to replace the study of what Kenneth Burke calls "sheer motion" (Gusfield, 1989, p. 53) with the study of meaningful human action. These are precisely the kinds of issues Bruner had in mind when he asserted that "a cultural psychology, almost by definition, will not be preoccupied with 'behavior' but with 'action,' its intentionally based counterpart" (1990, p. 19).

There are several theoretical traditions to which one can turn when formulating an account of action. In his Chapter 3, Bronckart notes the importance of figures such as Habermas, Ricoeur, and Weber. In an analogous way, Wertsch (Chapter 2, this volume) notes the importance of Dewey and Burke. For the majority of authors in this volume, however, the figures whose ideas about action play a particularly important role are Leont'ev (1959, 1975, 1981) and Vygotsky (1978, 1987). Zinchenko (Chapter 1, this volume) has provided what is perhaps the clearest exposition to date of the relationship between Leont'ev's and Vygotsky's ideas. In his exposition he argues that there are several complex interconnections between Leont'ev's "theory of activity" and

Vygotsky's "cultural-historical" psychology. He notes that while there are grounds for asserting that some of the roots of activity theory can be found in Vygotsky's writings, it seems on balance most appropriate to recognize important elements of evolution and differentiation that distinguish the writings of Leont'ev from those of Vygotsky.

Zinchenko argues that a search for the roots of activity theory in Vygotsky's writings is fraught with personal, political, and intellectual issues. However, there are two points of compatibility between Vygotsky's and Leont'ev's ideas that seem reasonably clear. First, even though Vygotsky did not explicitly formulate his ideas in terms of a theory of activity, his analyses of mental functioning, semiotic mediation, and other issues consistently focus on processes that have most if not all of the attributes of what later came to be called action by Leont'ev and others.

The very title of his last volume, *Thinking and Speech* (Myshlenie i Rech'), is a reflection of this. Vygotsky's focus throughout that volume was on the emerging interfunctional relationships between speaking and thinking as one example of a kind of action dynamic that characterizes the development of consciousness more generally (see Lee, 1985; Wertsch, 1985). The essential point for our purposes is that in all cases the formulations of "functions" (e.g., speaking, thinking, remembering) are inherently compatible with notions of action that later became the focus of research in Soviet psychology. As an example of this, consider the fact that the linguist and psychologist A. A. Leont'ev (1965) interpreted several of Vygotsky's claims about speech in terms of "speech activity."

The fact that *myshlenie* (thinking) and *rech'* (speech, or speaking) have sometimes been mistranslated into English as "thought" and "language," respectively, has served to obscure the action orientation in Vygotsky's writings. For him, speech is a *process, if not a form of action*, that uses language as a *means*. Language, as distinct from speech, is a semiotic means that certainly has the power to shape speaking and thinking, as several authors in this volume argue, but it is not itself a form of action in Vygotsky's terminology. The distinction Vygotsky was using has parallels in the philosophy of language, where distinctions such as that between "utterance" and "sentence" are commonplace.

Vygotsky's tendency to focus on speech, as opposed to language, reflects the general orientation of his Russian colleagues of the time.

For example, Bakhtin (1986) not only distinguished language from speech and sentence from utterance; he privileged the notion of utterance to the degree that he viewed the study of it ("metalinguistics") as having a kind of primacy over linguistics.

The second point we would make with regard to Vygotsky and a notion of action goes beyond potential compatibilities others may see between his formulation of functions and other processes, on the one hand, and action, on the other. It concerns concrete reinterpretations of his claims in terms of some notion of action. Zinchenko (1985) has argued that action – rather than the item nominated by Vygotsky, word meaning – is the appropriate unit of analysis in Vygotsky's theoretical framework. In particular, Zinchenko argues that "tool-mediated action" is a preferable analytic unit for Vygotsky in light of theoretical advances since the latter's time. Wertsch (1985, 1991) has similarly argued that "mediated action" is the appropriate unit of analysis for a Vygotskian-derived sociocultural approach. Both Zinchenko's and Wertsch's lines of reasoning draw on accounts of action developed after Vygotsky's death in 1934, but they are also based on the recognition that Vygotsky's formulation is quite compatible with taking action as a basic unit of analysis.

As already noted, there are several accounts of action on which one can draw to formulate a Vygotskian sociocultural approach. The one most often used to date is from the writings of Leont'ev (1981). The notion of action formulated by Leont'ev qualifies as a form of what Habermas (1984) terms "teleological action." This is a form of action that "may be evaluated on the criterion of truth . . . and on the criterion of effectiveness" (Bronckart, p. 78, this volume):

Since Aristotle the concept of *teleological action* has been at the center of the philosophical theory of action. The actor attains an end or brings about the occurrence of a desired state by choosing means that have promise of being successful in the given situation and applying them in a suitable manner. The central concept is that of a *decision* among alternative courses of action, with a view to the realization of an end, guided by maxims, and based on an interpretation of the situation. (Habermas, 1984, p. 85)

As Wertsch (1991) has noted, this notion of action is in some respects compatible with Vygotsky's theoretical framework, given its concern with planning and executing problem-solving efforts. However, as the ideas of other figures such as Bakhtin and Habermas have entered the discussion of how to formulate sociocultural research, the notion of teleological action becomes less tenable as a unit (at least as the *only* unit) of analysis. To be sure, the focus is still on action, as opposed to behavior or "events" (Bronckart, Chapter 3, this volume) or any other analytic unit that does not take issues such as meaning, interpretation, and "self-interpretation" (Taylor, 1985) into account. However, the formulation that would be compatible with the various forms of action explored in the sociocultural analyses of this volume needs to be quite broad, more along the lines of Burke's (1966) formulation of "symbolic action." While Burke is seldom mentioned in this volume, his ideas can nonetheless provide a useful framework for understanding how various claims about action and mediation are related, and for this reason we shall turn to him at several points in what follows.

In his account of symbolic action, Burke begins with the distinction between "action" and "sheer motion." For him, " 'action' is a term for the kind of behavior possible to a typically symbol-using animal (such as man) in contrast with the extrasymbolic or nonsymbolic operations of nature" (Gusfield, 1989, p. 53). Hence, action is in all cases symbolic action for Burke:

There can be no action without motion – that is, even the "symbolic action" of pure thought requires corresponding motions of the brain. . . . There can be motion without action. (For instance, the motions of the tides, of sunlight, or growth and decay.) . . . Action is not reducible to terms of motion. For instance, the "essence" or "meaning" of a sentence is not reducible to its sheer physical existence as sounds in the air or marks on the page, although material motions of some sort are necessary for the production, transmission, and reception of a sentence. (Gusfield, 1989, pp. 53–54)

The differences between Burke's notion of action and the teleological account found in Leont'ev or Vygotsky become more evident as one looks further into Burke's (1969) "dramatistic" analysis. As Gusfield (1989) notes, "The concept of 'drama' implies action rather than motion" and "action is dramatic because it includes conflict, purpose, reflection, and choice" (p. 10). Burke (1969) outlined his notion of dramatic action in terms of his "dramatistic pentad":

Dramatism centers on observations of this sort: for there to be an *act*, there must be an *agent*. Similarly, there must be a *scene* in which the agent acts. To act in a scene, the agent must employ some means, or *agency*. And it can be called an act in the full sense of the term only if it involves a *purpose* (that is, if a support happens to give way and one falls, such motion on the agent's part is not an act, but an accident). These five terms (act, scene, agent, agency, purpose) have been labeled the dramatistic pentad; the aim of calling attention to them in this way is to show how the functions which they designate operate in the imputing of motives. (p. 445)

The goal in introducing this pentad was not to provide a set of formal, static categories that could be used to produce a frozen description of an action and its motives. Instead, Burke's goal was to outline a set of elements that exist in dynamic tension, or dialectical opposition. In this view action is often, if not always open to further interpretation because there are ambiguities that emerge in taking the dialectically interacting elements into account. Indeed, "instead of considering it our task to 'dispose of' ambiguity by merely disclosing the fact that it is an ambiguity, we rather consider it our task to study and clarify the *resources* of ambiguity" (1969, p. xix).

The advantage of introducing Burke into our discussion of action is that his framework makes it possible to consider a wide range of actions, with an accompanying wide range of motivations, rather than focusing on one basic form such as teleological action. Thus, while his account specifically includes the construct of "purpose" (a fact that makes it compatible with Leont'ev's goal-directed action), it allows for other forms of action as well. It does this by allowing for various elements or combinations of elements in his "pentad" to be the forces that shape action and the motives associated with it. Throughout, Burke emphasizes that these elements of the pentad exist in dialectical relationships that organize action in complex ways. Among other things this means that instead of restricting ourselves to an understanding of the person as a goal-directed problem solver, we can entertain alternatives such as the "oratorical" and "rhetorical" images of the person envisioned by figures such as Burke (see Gusfield, 1989, pp. 17–23) and Billig (1987).

In their Chapter 7, Smolka, De Goes, and Pino raise a set of issues closely related to this point. Their analysis has to do with how the "subject" is constructed through the kind of social processes that have been at the core of many Vygotsky-inspired empirical studies. Specifically, they have in mind studies that examine ways in which "intermental" processes give rise to "intramental" ones, and in connection with the former, they examine the construct of "intersubjectivity" as it has been employed by authors such as Rogoff (1990), Rommetveit (1979, 1985), and Wertsch (1985, 1989).

Smolka et al. do not focus on the forms of action involved, but an assumption that frames many of the studies they review is that some form of teleological action is at issue. Thus, in studies by Rogoff and Wertsch, the focus is on planning, constructing an object, or some other form of goal-directed action. Furthermore, an implication of such studies is that socialization is largely a matter of mastering forms of goal-directed action deemed appropriate in a sociocultural setting for a task and taught in one way or another by its experienced members. In this formulation, the student or apprentice is asked to participate actively, something that has been stressed by authors such as Rogoff (1990); but even with this emphasis, the focus remains on forms of action in which there is generally assumed to be a single, most effective and efficient outcome.

In such a context, socialization comes to be viewed largely in terms of how tutees "appropriate" the existing strategies of others and hence reproduce an existing cognitive and social order. From the perspective of the dynamics of intermental functioning, this is viewed as involving an increasing intersubjectivity between teachers, tutors, or masters, on the one hand, and students, tutees, or apprentices, on the other. One of the main points raised by Smolka et al. is that such intersubjectivity – at least the harmonious, symmetrical form usually posited – does not seem to be characteristic of many settings, and this raises essential questions about accounts of intermental processes, intramental outcomes, and, eventually, the nature of action in general.

In contrast to the intersubjectivity of "mutual understanding" and "symmetrical dialogue" envisioned by others, Smolka et al. argue that other forms of social interaction, such as "divergent perspectives, opposition of ideas, resistance to communication, and other disharmonious [episodes]" (p. 172, this volume), are often to be found and should not be viewed simply as failed attempts at intersubjectivity. Indeed, they see interaction that does not conform to this usual notion of intersubjectivity as being ubiquitous and playing an essential role in the formation of the subject:

If in the texture of human relations we cannot always find the ideal or desired "symmetry" and "harmony," we can certainly identify simultaneous, even *reciprocal*, processes whereby subjects are constituted in relation to some definite or assumed social positions. This reciprocity does not, however, have the same harmonious meaning as "mutuality," which pervades the notion of intersubjectivity. Here, "reciprocal" is used in the sense of being inversely related, as the empowering of one subject disempowers the other. But yet, in a deeper sense, we can say that "reciprocal" means "constitutively related." The process of individual consciousness formation, or subject constitution, happens not only "intersubjectively" but also dialectically in interpsychological functioning. (p. 178, this volume)

Such statements strongly suggest that the basic notion of action involved in sociocultural studies needs to be expanded beyond that of teleological action. This would certainly appear to be the case when it comes to examining issues such as the formation of the subject, but we would argue that it extends further. Many instances of reasoning, problem solving, or "arguing and thinking" (Billig, 1987) are more appropriately conceptualized in terms of fundamental opposition, rhetorical encounter, or "polyphonic concert" (Smolka et al., Chapter 7, this volume), rather than in terms of harmonious intersubjectivity and the appropriation of strategies already existing in a sociocultural setting. As Smolka et al. note, this claim is consistent with the ideas of Bakhtin and with some of the claims Vygotsky made in his aesthetic analyses, but it is also worth noting that it stands in opposition to the assumptions about an evolving, universal rationality that run throughout so much of Vygotsky's writings and those of his followers such as Leont'ev.

Like Billig (1987), we would not want to deny the importance, even centrality, of rational and teleological action in formulating an account of human action. However, again like Billig we would also stress that this is only part of the story. In the formation of the subject and mental processes, we eventually must consider the various other forms of action suggested by Burke's dramatistic analysis. Chapter 7 by Smolka et al. provides an important introduction on how this might be done.

While we are suggesting the need to go beyond Leont'ev's notion of teleological action in sociocultural analyses, we continue to see other aspects of his overall theoretical framework as useful. Specifically, we agree with his claims about the need for multiple levels of analysis to account for how action is situated in activity, or an activity setting (Leont'ev, 1975, 1981). In his formulation, the Marxist category of labor was viewed as the prototypical activity, though other activities were recognized as well, and various "leading activities" were viewed as playing an essential role in organizing ontogenesis (El'konin, 1972; also see Cole, this volume).

It is in connection with this notion of activity that we find another useful counterpart to Leont'ev's ideas in Burke's writings, a counterpart that preserves a basic insight but does so in terms of a more general formulation that allows other voices to enter the discussion. The counterpart to activity in Burke's dramatic analysis that we have in mind is "scene." Burke's main goal was by no means to formulate a Marxist psychology, but he was concerned with how Marxist claims could be interpreted from a dramatistic approach, and in this connection he argued that the key was to be found in the role given to scene. In Burke's (1969) formulation:

Using "scene" in the sense of setting, or background, and "act" in the sense of action, one could say that "the scene contains the act." And using "agents" in the sense of actors . . . one could say that "the scene contains the agents." It is the principle of drama that the nature of acts and agents should be consistent with the nature of scene. . . . Or, if you will, the stage-set [i.e., scene] contains the action *ambiguously* (as regards the norms of action) – and in the course of the play's development this ambiguity is converted into a corresponding *articulacy*. The proportion would be: scene is to act as implicit is to explicit. (pp. 3–7)

For the purposes of formulating a sociocultural approach, we would argue, therefore, that the notion of scene can serve as a more general counterpart to Leont'ev's account of how the level of analysis having to do with activity is related to the level of analysis concerned with action. We would again note that drawing such parallels is not a simple matter of using a fully compatible, but more inclusive theoretical framework (i.e., Burke's) to expand on the insights of another (i.e., Leont'ev's). There clearly are incompatibilities as well. However, we continue to see the more global dramatistic approach of Burke as providing a useful framework for considering the range of issues raised in this volume.

The issue of how an activity setting or scene "contains the action ambiguously" is a topic taken up by Cole and Rogoff (Chapters 8 and 6, respectively). Rogoff outlines a sociocultural approach involving three planes of analysis corresponding to "personal," "interpersonal," and "community processes." The developmental processes corresponding to these three analytic planes are "participatory appropriation," "guided participation," and "apprenticeship," respectively. She emphasizes the need to incorporate all three planes into sociocultural research:

Without an understanding of such mutually constituting processes, a sociocultural approach is at times assimilated to other approaches that examine only part of the package. For example, it is incomplete to focus only on the relation of individual development and social interaction without concern for the cultural activity in which personal and interpersonal actions take place. And it is incomplete to assume that development occurs in one plane and not in others (e.g., that children develop but that their partners or their cultural communities do not) or that influence can be ascribed in one direction or another . . . (e.g., parent to child or child to parent; culture to individual). (p. 141, this volume)

Cole approaches the issues of scene or activity setting in a slightly different way, but many compatibilities can be found with Rogoff's ideas as well. Assuming the need to approach the issues involved developmentally, Cole outlines a " 'mesogenetic' approach to cultural mediation, one whose time scale falls between the microgenetic scale employed in classical studies . . . [of children's problem solving] and the macrogenetic scale implied by the historical difference between peasant and industrialized societies" (p. 194, this volume). In this genetic framework, as well as in his other accounts of the institutional settings or scenes within which action takes place, Cole manifests a concern quite similar to Rogoff's about the need to consider psychological and social interactional processes as part of a larger package that takes activity setting, or scene, into account. In addition to many of the figures we have already mentioned, Cole notes the importance of Bronfenbrenner (1979) in the formulation of these notions.

Mediation, mediational means, and mediated action

In addition to providing a general framework for understanding action and its relationship to activity setting, or scene, Burke's dramatistic analysis provides a useful organizing framework for sociocultural research in connection with the notions of "mediation," "mediational means," and "mediated action." In general, the chapters of this volume rest on an assumption that the notions of action and mediation are inherently related, so to distinguish them as we are doing here is somewhat artificial. We do so for the sake of clarity of presentation, but we also do so with the understanding that what is at issue is an *analytic* distinction, not one that somehow exists in external reality.

The inherent relationship between action and mediation is reflected in Burke's writings, where the notion of symbol is mentioned in the very definition of action (see earlier). Similarly, it is reflected in the reinterpretations of Vygotsky's writings by Zinchenko (1985), where the notion of "tool-mediated action" is the centerpiece, and by Wertsch (1991), where "mediated action" plays a similar role.

The counterpart of mediation in Burke's framework is "agency," or instrumentality. In his view the clearest example of how a philosophical school privileges this item in the pentad over the others can be found in pragmatism:

Pragmatism philosophies are generated by the featuring of the term, Agency. We can discern this genius most readily in the very title, *Instrumentalism*, which John Dewey chooses to characterize his variant of the pragmatist doctrine. Similarly William James explicitly asserts that Pragmatism is "a method only." And adapting Peirce's notion that beliefs are rules for action, he says that "theories thus become instruments," thereby stressing the practical nature of theory. (Burke, 1969, p. 275)

In addition to Dewey and the pragmatists more generally, one can point to several other progenitors of the idea that mediation is a key to understanding human action and human nature. Cole does exactly that under the heading of "the common starting point of all socio-cultural-historical viewpoints" (p. 190, this volume). The quote he uses from Henri Bergson (1911/1983) is particularly striking in this regard:

If we could rid ourselves of all pride, if, to define our species, we kept strictly to what the historic and prehistoric periods show us to be the constant characteristic of man and of intelligence, we should say not *Homo Sapiens* but *Homo Faber*. In short, *intelligence, considered in what seems to be its original feature, is the faculty of manufacturing artificial objects, especially tools for the making of tools, and of indefinitely varying the manufacture.* (p. 139)

In Vygotsky's writings the construct of mediation – especially semiotic mediation – played a central theoretical role, becoming increasingly important during the last years of his life and career. A year before his death he wrote that "the central fact about our psychology is the fact of mediation" (1982, p. 166). In contrast, Leont'ev's theory of activity focused on activity and action. This was framed by the intellectual and political disputes of the time (see Zinchenko, Chapter 1, this volume), especially as they involved accusations of "idealism," but it had to do with deep-seated intellectual issues as well. Drawing selectively on the insights of both Vygotsky and Leont'ev, the notions of "mediational means" and "mediated action" have emerged today as essential building blocks in the formulation of sociocultural research.

An underlying assumption of such research is that humans have access to the world only indirectly, or mediately, rather than directly, or immediately. This applies both with regard to how humans obtain information about the world and how they act on it – two processes that are usually viewed as being fundamentally intertwined. In the view of Leont'ev, this stands in stark opposition to classic two-part theoretical schemes such as those involving stimulus–response associations because the latter are grounded in the "postulate of immediacy" (1981, p. 45). In place of such a postulate, Leont'ev argued that some intermediate term (his candidate was activity) is essential for an adequate theoretical formulation. Zinchenko (Chapter 1, this volume) outlines some of the major differences between Leont'ev and Vygotsky with regard to how alternatives to the postulate of immediacy could be formulated, but at a general level these two figures share the assumption that this postulate provides a fundamentally misleading basis for psychological theorizing.

The theme of mediation as understood by Vygotsky is perhaps more pronounced than any other in this volume, which reflects the pervasive assumption that mediational means, or cultural tools (terms we shall use interchangeably), must play an essential role in the basic formulation of sociocultural research. In particular, they provide the link or bridge between the concrete actions carried out by individuals and groups, on the one hand, and cultural, institutional, and historical settings, on the other. The central role played by mediation in this volume suggests that in addition to mediating the human action that is the object of sociocultural studies, the analysis of these cultural tools occupies a kind of mediating position in the sociocultural theoretical framework itself. Specifically, this analysis serves as a kind of bridge making it possible to reconnect some of the areas of the human sciences that modern disciplinary fragmentation have so often kept apart.

There are several variations on this theme that can be found in the chapters that follow. This is not so much because the authors disagree, at least explicitly, about mediation as it is that they are focusing on different aspects of this broad topic. In most cases, the claims about mediation and mediated action made by one author would be viewed by others not as being incompatible with what they have said, but as reflecting a different perspective or emphasis. Alongside these variations, there are a few basic similarities in the treatment of mediation that run throughout these chapters. In many cases, these similarities take the form of assumptions, and in others they surface as explicit claims.

The active nature of mediation

The first point about mediation that emerges in several chapters is that it is an active process. While the cultural tools or artifacts involved in mediation certainly play an essential role in *shaping* action, they do not *determine* or *cause* action in some kind of static, mechanistic way. Indeed, in and of themselves, such cultural tools are powerless to do anything. They can have their impact only when individuals *use* them. The point of all this is to remind us that the study of mediation and mediated action cannot focus solely on the cultural tools involved. Even the most sophisticated analysis of these tools cannot itself tell us how they are taken up and used by individuals to carry out action. Instead, mediation is best thought of as a *process* involving the potential of cultural tools to shape action, on the one hand, and the unique use of these tools, on the other.

One way of differentiating these analytically distinct, yet inextricably linked moments of mediated action can be found in Bakhtin's discussion of the production of an utterance or text:

Every text presupposes a system of signs understandable to everybody (that is, conventional, valid within the limits of a given collectivity), a "language". . . . To this system belong all the elements of the text that are repeated and reproduced, reiterative and reproducible. . . . At the same time, however, every text (by virtue of constituting an utterance) represents something individual, unique, nonreiterative, and therein lies all its meaning (its intention, the reason why it has been created). . . . In relation to this aspect, all that is reiterative and reproducible turns out to be raw materials and means. To that extent, this second aspect, or pole goes beyond the boundaries of linguistics and philology. It is inherent to the text, but becomes manifest only in concrete situations and within sequences of texts (within verbal communication in a given realm). This pole is not tied to the (reiterative) elements of the system of language (that is, to signs), but to other (nonreiterative) texts by particular relations of a dialogical nature. (1979, pp. 283–284)

Those aspects of an action that are "reiterative and reproducible" are associated with the mediational means (in this case the conventions of a language) invoked to carry out the action, whereas the "nonreiterative" moments are contributions of the unique appropriation of these mediational means. To focus exclusively on the former would be to violate the basic tenets of Burke's analysis of human action and motives by considering one element in the pentad, namely, agency, or instrumentality, in isolation. To focus exclusively on the unique, nonreiterative aspects (Burke's "act"), on the other hand, would be to ignore the power of cultural tools to shape action. Furthermore, in addition to agency and act, it is necessary at some point to consider the contributions of the other elements of the pentad.

Transformatory capacities of mediation

If the first point we would make about mediation is that it is an active process, the second is that the introduction of a new cultural tool into this active process inevitably transforms it. In this view, mediational means such as language and technical tools do not simply facilitate forms of action that would otherwise occur. Instead, "by being included in the process of behavior, the psychological tool alters the entire flow and structure of mental functions. It does this by determining the structure of a new instrumental act, just as a technical tool alters the process of a natural adaptation by determining the form of labor operations" (Vygotsky, 1981, p. 137).

Such a perspective contrasts with many others in psychology. For example, as Olson (Chapter 4, this volume) points out, it contrasts with some basic tenets of Piaget:

For Piaget, as I understand him, children's mastery of the symbolic world – the world of representations – was not basically different from their mastery of the natural world. Language did not create a representational or symbolic function; rather the representational function that was based on the ability to hold objects in mind in their absence made language learning possible. Similarly, learning to read was seen as an exercise in the use of existing cognitive resources rather than the creation of new resources for thinking. (pp. 96–7, this volume)

The central claim of Olson's chapter is that "we come to think about our speech, indeed to hear our speech, in terms of the categories laid down by our scripts" (p. 98, this volume). In this formulation, the emergence of the new cultural tool of writing systems is seen as transforming, if not giving rise to an entirely new form of mediated action. This occurs because "writing systems provide the concepts and categories for thinking about the structure of spoken language" (p. 100, this volume). Similar arguments are made in this volume by Wertsch in connection with other cultural tools and forms of mediated action.

Tsunoda (Chapter 5, this volume) carries this argument into yet another area in his analyses of how mastery of human language in general, and specific languages in particular, affect brain functioning. He views the "automatic switching mechanism" that has been at the focus of so many of his studies as being responsible for distinguishing verbal from nonverbal information, but he goes on to make the even more interesting claim that the switching mechanism for speakers of Japanese is different from that characteristic for speakers of other languages.

Tsunoda's claims about how the functional organization of the brain reflects and facilitates the use of particular systems of cultural tools raise what may be extremely exciting issues for future sociocultural investigations. Some of these possibilities occur in the writings of Mecacci (1979) and, of course, Luria (1973, 1981), but the area of studies that might be dubbed "sociocultural neuropsychology" is still far from being well developed.

Mediation as empowering and constraining

The third point we would make about mediation is that it always involves constraint as well as empowerment. Most of the chapters in this volume that deal with mediation view it as empowering, opening up new avenues of action. While this is a legitimate focus of studies of mediated action, it is also essential to keep in mind that any form of mediation involves some form of limitation. When analyzing or planning for new forms of mediation, the focus is typically on how these new mediational means will overcome some perceived problem or restriction inherent in existing forms of mediated action. However, one of the points that follows inescapably from the view of mediated action outlined in these chapters is that even if a new cultural tool frees us from some earlier limitation of perspective, it introduces new ones of its own. Mitchell's (1990) aphorism about there being "no representation without taxation" (p. 21) is quite apropos here.

The kind of constraints we have in mind are often recognized only in retrospect. It is only with the appearance of new, further empowering (and constraining) forms of mediation that we are likely to recognize the limitations of earlier ones. As noted by one of the progenitors of sociocultural research, John Dewey:

When we look back at earlier periods, it is evident that certain problems could not have arisen in the context of institutions, customs, occupations and interests that then existed, and that even if, *per impossible,* they had been capable of detection and formulation, there were no means available for solving them. If we do not see that this conditioning, both negative and positive, exists at present, the failure to see it is due to an illusion of perspective. (1938, pp. 487–488)

We certainly can and must be willing to reflect on, criticize, and change the cultural tools we find to be inadequate for whatever reason. However, the notion of mediation that underlies most of the chapters entails not being able to free ourselves of the constraints imposed by the cultural tools we use to act. We can never "speak from nowhere," given that we can speak (or more broadly, act) only by invoking mediational means that are available in the "cultural tool kit" provided by the sociocultural setting in which we operate (Wertsch, 1991). As already noted, this does not mean that we are mechanistically determined by, or are mere puppets of, the mediational means we employ, but it does mean that constraints of some kind always exist. How to understand and overcome them are questions that concern virtually all the contributors to this volume.

Mediation as "spin-off"

A fourth point we would make about mediation is that cultural tools usually emerge for reasons other than to facilitate many of the kinds of action they in fact end up shaping. When considered from too narrow a psychological perspective, the implicit assumption is often made that cultural tools such as language somehow emerged in the service of the forms of mental functioning they mediate. However, this is seldom the normal course of events. Instead, mediational means often emerge in response to a host of forces typically unrelated to the form of mental functioning at issue. Then these means are incorporated into action in unanticipated ways. The implication of such a claim, of course, is that human action, including mental functioning, is shaped by forces that have little to do with an ideal design.

Several authors in this volume touch on this point in one way or another. It is examined as an explicit claim in Chapter 2 by Wertsch, and it underlies much of the line of reasoning put forth in Chapter 9 by del Río and Alvarez. Furthermore, it serves as a background assumption for Cole and Rogoff (Chapters 8 and 6, respectively). In the last two cases, the assumption emerges in connection with the fact that action and the mediational means that it employs exist in the real world in complex cultural, institutional, and historical settings, and these settings inevitably shape the cultural tools that are invoked in carrying out action.

For example, in Cole's study we see that different forms of mediation (as reflected in his "crude variable of 'noise level' ") are characteristic of different institutional contexts. While Cole does not go into specifics about the mediational means involved, he does provide ample illustration of the claim that sociocultural context shapes the selection of cultural tools (e.g., "speech genres" [Wertsch, 1991] – as reflected by noise level), and this of course shapes the form of mediated action we see. For our current purposes, the main point is that the mediational means used were not somehow specifically or ideally designed to benefit the "guided participation" or the "participatory appropriation" outlined by Rogoff. Instead, the cultural tools were selected, or even dictated, by other sociocultural forces, and any benefits they might have had for guided participation or participatory appropriation were more or less accidental and unanticipated.

These accidental and unanticipated effects are what might be called "spin-offs," to employ contemporary jargon about the benefits, alleged or real, that accrue to the civilian sector from military research and development. The spin-off process is also a central issue in Olson's Chapter 4 on the development of writing and its effects on mind. As noted earlier, the effects he posits are that "writing systems provide the concepts and categories for thinking about the structure of spoken language" (p. 100, this volume). Sounding much like Dewey when he spoke of the "illusion of perspective," Olson argues that instead of mapping onto preexisting models of language, such models typically come into existence as a result of the imposition of writing systems, a process whose sequence is often subsequently misinterpreted:

Awareness of linguistic structure is a product of a writing system, not a precondition for its development. If true, this will not explain the evolution of writing as the attempt to represent linguistic structures such as sentences, words, or phonemes for the simple reason that prewriters had no such concepts. (p. 100, this volume)

The implications of Olson's claims for what we are calling spin-off take two basic forms. The first of these has to do with the processes that give rise to a cultural tool. In this connection Olson argues that writing systems generally do not evolve in response to the need to reflect on language and thought. Instead, their emergence is largely a response to the demands of mnemonic and communicative processes, and the role they play in reflection is largely an unanticipated consequence. Hence, this is a case in which a cultural tool is harnessed for a purpose other than the one that shaped its evolution. This suggests that at least in some instances, the tool we use to reflect on and model language and thought may not be ideally designed for that purpose.

This point comes across even more strongly when we turn to a second, related claim by Olson having to do with instances in which one language community borrows another's writing system. He argues that it is a common historical occurrence for the graphic system that has evolved and is used in connection with one language (for which it is, thereby, reasonably well suited) to be employed in another language for which it is not well suited:

It is now recognized that the development of the alphabet, like that of the syllabary, was a rather straightforward consequence of applying a script that was suitable for one language to a second language for which it was not designed, namely, of applying a script for a Semitic language in which vocalic differences were relatively insignificant to a Greek language in which they were highly significant. . . . But equipped with such signs representing vowel sounds, the Greeks were in a position to "hear," perhaps for the first time, that those sounds also occurred within the syllables represented by the Semitic consonant signs. In this way syllables were dissolved into consonant–vowel pairings and the alphabet was born. (p. 111–12, this volume)

Other chapters herein do not address this point as explicitly or directly, but two implications of Olson's argument that are generally consistent with all of them are that (a) most or all of the cultural tools that mediate human action did not evolve for many of the purposes they have come to take on, and (b) in many cases the cultural tools we use are borrowed from quite distinct contexts. In a sense, then, we often "misuse" tools, and this may have the consequence that our action is shaped in ways that are not helpful or are even antithetical to our expressed intentions and assumptions about the design of the tools we employ.

The phenomenon of spin-off we have outlined can be profitably considered in terms of some of the issues of history raised earlier. In particular, it is worth considering in connection with the history of cultural tools. Del Río and Alvarez (Chapter 9, this volume) raise several major points in this connection. In their view, many forms of everyday action can be understood only by taking into consideration how they are shaped by complex cultural tools. The complexity they envision results from the fact that cultural tools have a history that typically leaves its traces on mediational means and, hence, on mediated action at later points.

Of particular relevance in this respect is the argument del Río and Alvarez outline with regard to "vestigial systems of representation." In their view, the cultural tools (e.g., language) that we employ today with the assumption that they serve certain modern purposes often shape our action in ways that reflect the quite different demands of the settings in which they emerged. In this view the " 'primitive' . . . has never ceased to play a role" (p. 234, this volume); it has never ceased to be a fundamental force shaping human action. Like Cassirer (1944), del Río and Alvarez are intrigued with what happens when old cultural tools are put to new uses.

This historical orientation is one that leads del Río and Alvarez to see fundamental connections rather than discontinuities between earlier forms of mediated action and those of today. One of the reasons for this is that in their analysis of human action and consciousness, they insist on considering both cognitive and "directive" processes, the latter having to do with "the affective-moral action of consciousness and conduct" (p. 219, this volume). For example, in their analysis of the "encultured nature" of a traditional rural Castilian setting, they cite the continuing influence of traditional forms of rituals and forms of speech on individuals' overall "psychological architecture," an architecture that involves both rational and "nonrational" (Shweder, 1984) aspects of human action and consciousness.

Design and intervention

A final issue that is of concern to several of the authors in this volume is the belief that sociocultural studies should be involved in *changing* and not just examining human action and the cultural, institutional, and historical settings in which it occurs. This of course echoes the comments we made at the outset of this chapter. The process we and others envision amounts to much more than a call for applying existing insights from sociocultural studies to real-world problems, however. It is also a call to recognize that intervention efforts often provide the best setting for carrying out research.

Cole (Chapter 8, this volume) follows this line of reasoning in outlining his "mesogenetic" approach, an approach whose time scale falls between microgenesis and sociocultural history. The basic task of this mesogenetic approach is to "create a system of activities with its own standing rules, artifacts, social roles, and ecological setting, that is, its own culture" (p. 194, this volume). Cole's proposal for how to do this is one that has involved him in creating and maintaining a new kind of sociocultural system, the "Fifth Dimension." He does not view this system simply as an intervention effort based on existing theoretical and empirical research, although such research has obviously guided much of his thinking. Instead, he views it simultaneously as generating a wealth of new research opportunities and challenges. If the distinctions between intervention and research, as well as between theory and practice, at least in their traditional senses, are not always clear in Cole's formulation, this is no accident. Indeed, following the line of reasoning that Luria (1979) employed to formulate so many of his efforts, Cole wants to transcend these distinctions.

Cole also does not view the Fifth Dimension simply as a stable experimental context within which the socialization of elementary school children takes place. Instead of taking an approach that implicitly presupposes a notion of unidirectional causality, his approach calls for recognizing the developmental dynamics of the sociocultural system itself, dynamics that are interrelated with the socialization processes of the individuals in it. For example, he examines processes whereby new "generations" of professional researchers, undergraduate students acting as teachers, and elementary school children are incorporated into the system and how this process transforms individuals as well as the system in which they are operating. In all of this, the need to employ multiple, interrelated levels of analysis is obvious, a point that is a hallmark of sociocultural research according to Rogoff (Chapter 6, this volume).

Of course, one of the keys to doing this kind of multilevel intervention/research is to overcome the limitations imposed by traditional disciplinary divisions. Questions about whether a research effort falls in psychology, sociology, anthropology, or whatever are not part of the motivating framework. It is precisely the desire to address complex issues without being hamstrung by traditional disciplinary boundaries that lies behind Rogoff's formulation (Chapter 6, this volume) of a research methodology involving different interrelated planes of inquiry. In this view intervention/research inherently calls for interdisciplinary, or perhaps nondisciplinary, thinking.

The issue of intervention in sociocultural studies also emerges in Chapter 9 by del Río and Alvarez. Their introduction mentions issues such as urbanization, mass migration, the elimination of old belief and identity systems, drug dependency, as well as conflicts of national and cultural identity and is almost overwhelming in its implications. Their point is not that sociocultural studies should take on all these issues, let alone that it has addressed any one of them satisfactorily. Instead, it is that massive institutional, cultural, historical, and psychological changes characterize today's landscape and that investigators in the human sciences have made all too few contributions to understanding and directing these changes. Like other authors in this volume, del Río and Alvarez assume that the problem at the heart of this connection is not so much a lack of interest as it is a lack of theoretical and methodological tools.

Such claims bring us back to an issue we raised at the outset of this introduction, the problem of the "languages" used to formulate issues such as those listed by del Río and Alvarez. As noted earlier, we do not claim to have answers for most of the social and political issues that motivate many of our efforts. Given the dearth of contributions by the human sciences discussing these issues, our goal is much more modest and preliminary. Specifically, it is to outline some of the theoretical and methodological tools (e.g., languages) that would make it possible for human scientists to address these issues more effectively.

We hope that this volume will contribute broad outlines of what will be productive sociocultural research. In particular, we believe that the authors have provided a specification of what "sociocultural" research is, why action – specifically, mediated action – must be at the heart of it, and how issues of intervention are related to the research agenda. The reader will have to judge whether or not we have succeeded, but we will judge this volume a success if it pushes the debate forward, even in ways that we cannot foresee.

References

Bakhtin, M. M. (1979). *Estitika slovesnogo tvorchestva* [The esthetics of verbal creativity]. Moscow: Iskusstvo.

Bakhtin, M. M. (1986). *Speech genres and other late essays* (C. Emerson & M. Holquist, Eds., V. W. McGee, Trans.). Austin: University of Texas Press.

Bergson, H. (1911/1983). *Creative evolution*. New York: Henry Holt.

Billig, M. (1987). *Arguing and thinking: A rhetorical approach to social psychology*. Cambridge University Press.

Boas, F. (1911). Introduction. In F. Boas (Ed.), *Handbook of American Indian languages* (Bureau of American Ethnology Bulletin 40, Part I, pp. 1–83). Washington, DC: Smithsonian Institution.

Boas, F. (1920). The methods of ethnology. *American Anthropologist, 22,* 311–321.

Bronfenbrenner, U. (1979). *Experimental human ecology*. Cambridge, MA: Harvard University Press.

Bruner, J. (1990). *Acts of meaning*. Cambridge, MA: Harvard University Press.

Burke, K. (1966). *Language as symbolic action: Essays on life, literature, and method*. Berkeley: University of California Press.

Burke, K. (1969). *A grammar of motives*. Berkeley: University of California Press.

Cassirer, E. (1944). *An essay on man: An introduction to a philosophy of human culture*. New Haven, CT: Yale University Press.

Cole, M. (1990). Cultural psychology: A once and future discipline? In J. J. Berman (Ed.), *Nebraska symposium on motivation, 1989: Cross-cultural perspectives* (Vol. 37, pp. 279–335). Lincoln: University of Nebraska Press.

Dewey, J. (1938). *Logic: The theory of inquiry*. New York: Holt, Rinehart, & Winston.

Elder, G. H. (1974). *Children of the great depression*. Chicago: University of Chicago Press.

El'konin, D. B. (1972). Toward the problem of stages in the mental development of the child. *Soviet Psychology, 10,* 225–251.

Fussell, P. (1975). *The Great War and modern memory*. London: Oxford University Press.

Goody, J. (1977). *The domestication of the savage mind*. Cambridge University Press.

Gusfield, J. R. (Ed.). (1989). *Kenneth Burke on symbols and society*. Chicago: University of Chicago Press.

Habermas, J. (1984). *The theory of communicative action: Vol. 1, Reason and the rationalization of society.* (T. McCarthy, Trans.) Boston: Beacon.

Jahoda, G. (1993). *Crossroads between culture and mind: Continuities and change in theories of human nature.* Cambridge, MA: Harvard University Press.

Kress, G. (1985). *Linguistic processes in sociocultural practice.* London: Oxford University Press.

Lee, B. (1985). Intellectual origins of Vygotsky's semiotic analysis. In J. V. Wertsch (Ed.), *Culture, communication, and cognition: Vygotskian perspectives* (pp. 66–93). Cambridge University Press.

Leont'ev, A. A. (1965). *Slovo v rechevoi deyatel'nosti* [The word in speech activity]. Moscow: Izdatel'stvo Nauka.

Leont'ev, A. N. (1959). *Problemy razvitiya psikhiki* [Problems in the development of mind]. Moscow: Izdatel'stvo Moskovskogo Gosudarstvennogo Universiteta. Published in English as *Problems in the development of mind.* Moscow: Progress Publishers, 1982.

Leont'ev, A. N. (1975). *Deyatel'nost', soznanie, lichnost'* [Activity, consciousness, personality]. Leningrad: Izdatel'stvo Politicheskoi Literaturi. Published in English as *Activity, consciousness, and personality.* Englewood Cliffs, NJ: Prentice-Hall, 1978.

Leont'ev, A. N. (1981). The problem of activity in psychology. In J. V. Wertsch (Ed.), *The concept of activity in Soviet psychology* (pp. 37–71). Armonk, NY: Sharpe.

Lucy, J. A., & Wertsch, J. V. (1987). Vygotsky and Whorf: A comparative analysis. In M. A. Hickmann (Ed.), *Social and functional approaches to language and thought* (pp. 67–86). Orlando, FL: Academic.

Luria, A. R. (1973). *The working brain: An introduction to neuropsychology* (B. Haigh, Trans.). New York: Basic.

Luria, A. R. (1976). *Cognitive development: Its cultural and social foundations* (M. Lopez-Morillas and L. Solotaroff, Trans.; M. Cole, Ed.). Cambridge, MA: Harvard University Press.

Luria, A. R. (1979). *The making of mind: A personal account of Soviet psychology* (M. Cole & S. Cole, Trans.). Cambridge, MA: Harvard University Press.

Luria, A. R. (1981). *Language and cognition.* (J. V. Wertsch, Ed. and Trans.). New York: Wiley Intersciences.

Mecacci, L. (1979). *Brain and history: The relationship between neuropsychology and psychology in Soviet research* (H. A. Buchtel, Trans.) New York: Brunner/Mazel.

Mitchell, W. J. T. (1990). Representation. In F. Lentricchia & T. McLaughlin (Eds.), *Critical terms for literary study* (pp. 11–22). Chicago: University of Chicago Press.

Rogoff, B. (1990). *Apprenticeship in thinking: Cognitive development in social context.* New York: Oxford University Press.

Rommetveit, R. (1979). Deep structure of sentence versus message structure: Some critical remarks on current paradigms, and suggestions for an alternative approach. In R. Rommetveit & R. Blakar (Eds.), *Studies of language, thought and verbal communication* (pp. 17–34). London: Academic.

Rommetveit, R. (1985). Language acquisition as increasing linguistic structuring of experience and symbolic behavior control. In J. V. Wertsch (Ed.), *Culture, communication, and cognition: Vygotskian perspectives* (pp. 183–204). Cambridge University Press.

Sapir, E. (1931). Conceptual categories in primitive languages. *Science, 74,* 578.

Scribner, S. (1985). Vygotsky's uses of history. In J. V. Wertsch (Ed.), *Culture, communication, and cognition: Vygotskian perspectives* (pp. 119–145). Cambridge University Press.

Shweder, R. A. (1984). Anthropology's romantic rebellion against the enlightenment, or there's more to thinking than reason and evidence. In R. A. Shweder & R. A. LeVine (Eds.), *Culture theory: Essays on mind, self, and emotion* (pp. 27–66). Cambridge University Press.

Shweder, R. A. (1990). Cultural psychology – What is it? In J. W. Stigler, R. A. Shweder, & G. Herdt (Eds.), *Cultural psychology: Essays on comparative human development* (pp. 1–43). Cambridge University Press.

Shweder, R. A. (1991). *Thinking through cultures: Expeditions in cultural psychology.* Cambridge, MA: Harvard University Press.

Smirnov, A. N. (1975). *Razvitie i sovremennoe sostoyanie psikhologicheskoi nauki v SSSR* [The development and present status of psychology in the USSR]. Moscow: Izdatel'stvo Pedagogika.

Spencer, H. (1876). *The principles of sociology* (3 vols.), London: Williams & Norgate.

Taylor, C. (1985). *Human agency and language: Philosophical papers, I.* Cambridge University Press.

Vygotsky, L. S. (1978). *Mind in society: The development of higher psychological processes* (M. Cole, V. John-Steiner, S. Scribner, & E. Souberman, Trans.) Cambridge, MA: Harvard University Press.

Vygotsky, L. S. (1981). The instrumental method in psychology. In J. V. Wertsch (Ed.), *The concept of activity in Soviet psychology* (pp. 134–143). Armonk, NY: Sharpe.

Vygotsky, L. S. (1982). *Sobranie sochinenii. Tom pervyi: Problemy teorii i istorii psikhologii* [Collected works: Vol. 1, Problems in the theory and history of general psychology]. Moscow: Izdatel'stvo Pedagogika.

Vygotsky, L. S. (1987). *The collected works of L. S. Vygotsky: Vol. 1, Problems of general psychology. Including the volume Thinking and speech* (N. Minick, Trans.). New York: Plenum.

Vygotsky, L. S., & Luria, A. R. (1993). *Studies on the history of behavior: Ape, primitive, and child* (V. I. Golod & J. E. Knox, Eds. and Trans.). Hillsdale, NJ: Erlbaum.

Wertsch, J. V. (1985). *Vygotsky and the social formation of mind.* Cambridge, MA: Harvard University Press.

Wertsch, J. V. (1989). Semiotic mechanisms in joint cognitive activity. *Infancia y Aprendizaje, 47,* 3–36.

Wertsch, J. V. (1991). *Voices of the mind: A sociocultural approach to mediated action.* Cambridge, MA: Harvard University Press.

Wertsch, J. V. (1992). Keys to cultural psychology. *Culture, Medicine and Psychiatry, 16,* 273–280.

Whorf, B. L. (1956). *Language, thought, and reality: Selected writings of Benjamin Lee Whorf* (J. Carroll, Ed.). Cambridge, MA: MIT Press.

Zinchenko, V. P. (1985). Vygotsky's ideas about units of analysis for the analysis of mind. In J. V. Wertsch (Ed.), *Culture, communication, and cognition: Vygotskian perspectives* (pp. 94–118). Cambridge University Press.

Part I

**Human action:
historical and theoretical
foundations**

1 Cultural-historical psychology and the psychological theory of activity: retrospect and prospect

Vladimir P. Zinchenko

Vygotsky's account of cultural-historical psychology emerged just when the silver age, or renaissance, of Russian culture was in decline. During this age there were no sharp divisions of labor among science, art, aesthetics, philosophy, and even theology. Gustav Shpet, Aleksei Losev, Mikhail Bakhtin, Pavel Florenskii, and the major founder of cultural-historical psychology, Lev Vygotsky, were simultaneously scholars and connoisseurs of these spheres of human activity. The ideas of Vladimir Solov'ev about the "unity in all" of rational and spiritual knowledge were still alive. The remarkable poets Boris Pasternak and Osip Mandel'shtam were deeply schooled in philosophy and the sciences.

A major characteristic of cultural-historical psychology was its tendency to integrate knowledge about humans by drawing on various approaches and methods. In its first stages, the genetic method of research was dominant. Subsequently, other methods such as functional-genetic and functional-structural analyses (including microgenetic, macrostructural, and microdynamic) emerged to complement the genetic method. This amounted to an extension and enrichment of the initial ideas of Vygotsky and an attempt to address a mass of empirical material.

During the development of cultural-historical psychology, there were not only additions, but losses, or simplifications, in the original corpus of ideas. The spiritual component of the "unity in all" was lost, which amounted to its destruction. There was a narrowing of the idea of

This chapter was translated by James V. Wertsch.

37

mediation. In Vygotsky we find three main mediators: sign, word, and symbol. In the course of the development of his school of thought, the symbol was lost. The role of sign and word in the development of higher mental functions was studied above all. Vygotsky and his followers almost never studied the role of a fourth mediator in development – myth, although investigators such as Vygotsky and Aleksandr Zaporozhets did examine the role of fairly tales in children's development as a kind of surrogate.

One of the issues that any account of the cultural-historical school in Russian and Soviet psychology must address is how it is related to the theory of activity. Among other things, this means that we must examine the relationship between the ideas of Vygotsky and those of Aleksei Leont'ev. Such an examination by no means constitutes a complete analysis of the relationship between cultural-historical psychology and the theory of activity, but the story of the relationship between the ideas of these two figures is sufficiently rich and complex that it deserves attention in its own right.

Leont'ev started his career at the Institute of Psychology, which was headed by G. Chelpanov and was part of Moscow University. After Chelpanov's expulsion from the institute he had created, Leont'ev began collaborating with Vygotsky and Aleksandr Luria, and he made a major contribution to the cultural-historical psychology created by Vygotsky. In 1931 Leont'ev published his first major volume, *The Development of Memory*, in which he showed that the foundations of human memory, and of certain aspects of consciousness, reside in signs (as well as tools and instruments). No less important is the fact that in this work one can find a brilliant experimental demonstration of Vygotsky's ideas about the mediated structure of higher mental functions. In addition, Leont'ev demonstrated the role of internalization in the emergence and development of higher forms of memory and attention.

In the early 1930s, Leont'ev moved from Moscow to Khar'kov, where he was joined by Luria and Zaporozhets. In Khar'kov, Leont'ev created his own scientific school, which later was called the "activity approach" in psychology or the "psychological theory of activity." In the Khar'kov school of psychology, whose clear leader was Leont'ev, the connection with Vygotsky was not severed, but it was weakened despite the fact that Vygotsky visited Khar'kov several times.

The motives of Vygotsky's students and colleagues for moving from

Moscow have remained unclear to this day. This is the case for his pupil Lidiya Bozhovich, who moved to Poltava, for Leont'ev and Luria, two of his most impressive colleagues, and for Zaporozhets, whom he viewed as his most able pupil. We need to remember that the ideological atmosphere in Moscow had become not only unbearable, but life-threatening. There were attacks on Vygotsky, and some of the work he and Luria were doing was banned. In addition, his colleagues wished to put their own strengths to the test and return to their research. In any event, the Khar'kov school of psychology changed its focus to activity from what had been a focus on consciousness, the central problem for the cultural-historical school. I think this was done quite consciously.

Leont'ev always seemed to be aware of the difference between his own and Vygotsky's line of research, with one notable exception. In his obituary of Vygotsky, which was published in 1934, Leont'ev stated

Vygotsky's treatment of the mediated structure of human psychological processes and of mental functioning as human *activity* serves as the foundation stone, the basis for all the rest of the psychological theory he elaborated – a theory of *social-historical* ("cultural" in contrast to "natural") development of the human mind. (Leont'ev, 1983, p. 19)

It does not seem that in this or other segments of this obituary, Leont'ev was reading into Vygotsky his own thoughts or his treatment of psychology as a Marxist discipline, even though such things were often done both for the defense of a deceased scientist and for self-defense. On the next page of this obituary we read about a series of Vygotsky's theoretical positions comprising the foundations of his "study of the *systemic and meaning based [symslovoi] structure of consciousness*" (Leont'ev, 1983, p. 20).

Some 20 years later, in 1954, Leont'ev (1983) wrote:

Even if Vygotsky did not arrive in his own works at a consistent materialist understanding of mental processes as the product of the development of complex forms of human activity (this position was developed later in Soviet psychology), the significance of the propositions outlined above for how to move beyond ideas about invariant "mental functions" are extremely important. (p. 11)

The reader might notice that Vygotsky's role in founding the activity approach in psychology is evaluated somewhat differently here. And 10 years after that, in 1964, Leont'ev writes that consciousness comprised the inner context of Vygotsky's works: "The problem of consciousness is the alpha and omega of Vygotsky's creative path" (1983, p. 23).

Paraphrasing Leont'ev, we can say that the problem of activity is the alpha and omega of his own creative path. This is not to say that Leont'ev himself or his colleagues, first in the Khar'kov school, and later in the Moscow school of psychology, completely ignored the problem of consciousness. They periodically returned to it but limited themselves primarily to the analysis of the historical and ontogenetic roots of consciousness.

I have already had the opportunity to write about the fact that the reorientation of the leading members of Vygotsky's school was obviously needed and served to preserve, if not their lives, their freedom and, possibly, their morality (Zinchenko, 1989, p. 11). Nonetheless, one cannot simply ignore certain criticisms of Vygotsky coming from Leont'ev and Luria. This criticism also came from my father, Petr Zinchenko, in his "activity" period. It is true that my father also criticized the work of his teacher – Leont'ev – quite severely. One can say that this criticism was carried out, if not in a strictly academic form, then at least in a decent form, meaning without political accusations.

It is necessary to be reminded of these points since it is time for us to realize that today we are dealing with two scientific paradigms: cultural-historical psychology and the psychological theory of activity. It is also time to realize that what is involved here are two strands of research, but not two schools. This is so even though it goes without saying that most students of Leont'ev, Luria, Bozhovich, Zaporozhets, P. Zinchenko, L. Zankov, Danil El'konin, and others either worked directly with Vygotsky or subsequently participated in the creation and development of the activity paradigm. The paradigms exist, but acknowledging the existence of separate schools today would be inappropriately optimistic.

We also must not forget one additional circumstance. In the post-Stalin era, practically everyone involved in the activity paradigm voluntarily accepted a kind of personal code of conduct regarding criticism of others. Both research strands were marked as the scientific school of Vygotsky, Leont'ev, and Luria. This was done by advocates as well as opponents. For advocates, one can think that this personal code of conduct represented the discharge of a moral debt to Vygotsky. Apparently part of the truth is to be found here, but not all of it. Even opponents kept "birth marks" of cultural-historical psychology, and this explains many of the successes of the psychological theory of activity. For several decades this was one of the most authoritative strands in Soviet psychology. We should not exclude yet another variant. This code of conduct against criticism extended to Vygotsky, though, in the post-Stalin era, not directly to his theory, but rather that of Leont'ev. This contributed both to the rehabilitation of Vygotsky and to the increased authority of Leont'ev's school.

Nonetheless, the psychological theory of activity was distinguished from cultural-historical psychology in essential ways, even though both of them were created by one and the same set of scholars. (We will proceed from the initial thesis by Leont'ev that Vygotsky also made a contribution to the foundations of a psychological theory of activity.) These scholars successively or in parallel worked in both strands, consciously or unconsciously enriching both. This is true to the extent that if we look at the overall scientific biography of Vygotsky and Leont'ev, it is difficult to attribute something to one or the other in isolation. The difficulties in self-definition that I myself have are also connected with this.

In what follows I will try to characterize briefly the differences between cultural-historical psychology and the psychological theory of activity. The main difference is that for cultural-historical psychology, the central problem was and remains the mediation of mind and consciousness. For the psychological theory of activity, the central problem was object-orientedness, in both external and internal mental activity. Of course, in the psychological theory of activity the issue of mediation also emerged, but while for Vygotsky consciousness was mediated by culture, for Leont'ev mind and consciousness were mediated by tools and objects.

Correspondingly, the two strands have different philosophical, historical, and cultural roots. Cultural-historical psychology is connected with what Solov'ev called the "spiritual vertical," what Pasternak called "spiritual equipment," what Mandel'shtam called the "vertical section" of time, what Aleksandr Ukhtomskii and Bakhtin called the "chronotope," and so forth. In other words, cultural-historical psychology is connected with the analysis of the role of mediators (according to Losev: signs, words, symbols, myths). It was this orientation by Vygotsky that provided the foundations for many scholars, including myself, to reproach him at one or another time for idealism, for an absence of a connection between his theory and Marxism. When speaking of the origins of cultural-historical psychology, I am intentionally not dealing with the influence on Vygotsky of the European philosophical and psychological tradition. This influence was very great, but it requires separate treatment.

Leont'ev apparently took into consideration the criticism aimed at Vygotsky and derived his own ideas about the nature of mind and consciousness, as well as their development directly from the well-known theses of Marx on Feuerbach and from *German Ideology*, where one finds discussions about the tendency to ignore object-oriented activity. Of course, the psychological theory of activity had other sources as well. In the 1920s the idea (and the problem) of activity was in the air. In 1922 Sergei Rubinshtein transplanted the philosophical category of "activity" into psychological soil. Somewhat earlier Vladimir Bekhterev and V. Myasishchev tried to create "ergology" (ergonology), with the aim of carrying out the complex study of labor activity. In the same strand one can find the psychotechnic research of I. Shpil'rein and S. Gellershtein, as well as the investigations in the area of physiology, psychophysiology, and biomechanics by Ukhtomskii and Nikolai Bernshtein. In the context of pedology, Mikhail Basov outlined an approach to personality as an active actor. Cultural-historical psychology was formed in a way that is parallel to the psychotechnic movement construed in the broad sense. One must not forget that Vygotsky participated in the psychotechnic and pedological movements, and of course he was familiar with the problematics of activity and action. But the basic focus of his interests was on consciousness and higher mental functions. It was specifically into this problematic that Leont'ev began to fit a new "activity" key.

In the psychological theory of activity, it was argued that all mental processes, including personality (cf. Asmolov, 1990), have an object-activity nature. This is what comprises the merit of this strand. Its proponents used experimental methods to examine sensory, perceptual, executive, memory, cognitive, and affective actions. Action, both in concept and in essence, emerged not only as the object of research, but also as the unit for analyzing mental processes. The focus was specifically on action and not on meaning, as it was for Vygotsky. However, action as a unit for analyzing mind fulfilled all the requirements set out by Vygotsky in his formulation of such units (Gordeeva & Zin-chenko, 1982; Zinchenko, 1985). Action, as a unit of analysis, emerged in Zaporozhets's studies of sensation, perception, intellect, and the emotions; in P. Zinchenko's research on memory; in V. Asnin's and K. Gurevich's studies of volition; and in Petr Gal'perin's analysis of the formation of concepts and thinking. It was also then used by Vasili Davydov in his analysis of the formation of generalizations.

But Leont'ev himself, in moving away from a notion of meaning as a unit for analyzing mind, made the statement that sense is such a unit, and in his last book, *Activity, Consciousness, Personality,* he confronted future researchers with the problem of identifying a unit of analysis. There is absolutely no doubt that this unit of analysis is action. Action was the unit for analyzing mental processes, including emotion, about which Rubinshtein wrote in 1941. I believe that Leont'ev chose this unit in part due to the research carried out by the Khar'kov school of psychology in the 1930s. With the help of various claims in the psychological theory of activity, it has been shown, for example, that a motive is an object and that a need (after encountering an object) also becomes object-oriented.

All this resulted in the reproach (which was the opposite of reproaches addressed to Vygotsky) that the psychological theory of activity ignores or oversimplifies the spiritual world of humans, reducing it to object-oriented activity and thereby treating it mechanistically and without regard to any spiritual dimension. This reproach is accurate, but only in part. Of course, in the three-level scheme that Leont'ev used to describe the structure of activity (activity-motive, action-goal, operation-condition) there is no direct indication of the place of meaning, sense, mediators, consciousness, personality, and so forth. All these terms lie, as it were, outside the boundaries of the approach, and indeed the very structure of the approach may be perceived only as a way to decipher the very elementary scheme: goal–means–result.

In general I think that the three-level scheme is not the most successful of Leont'ev's inventions. But one must always remember that his background was cultural-historical psychology and that meaning (including object-oriented and operational meaning, as well as verbal meaning) and sense were present in the body, but not in the scheme of his theory of activity. In this approach, sense, which is derivative of the relationship between motive and goal, permeates the two upper levels of the organization of activity. This corresponds with the logic of Bernshtein, according to which movement at the object level leads to a semantic (*smyslovoi*), rather than a spatial image. It is also important to remember the quite similar position of Shpet, who wrote that sense is grounded in being, or existence. All of this testifies to the claim that sense constitutes not only consciousness, but also object-oriented activity. In this we can see the definite continuity between cultural-historical psychology and the psychological theory of activity. In any case Leont'ev did not search for sense in ideology, although he submitted to it.

Being the basic object of the first strand of research, consciousness was preserved in the second strand as well, although as noted earlier it was preserved in the form of studying the historical and ontogenetic roots of consciousness. In this second strand, consciousness was not freed from the short rein of activity. Rather than giving rise to activity, consciousness was a secondary, though not a second-rate, reflection of it.

If for the sake of clarity we completely simplify the picture, we can say that cultural-historical psychology was concerned with the problem of ideal mediators that exist between humans and between humans and the world. It included the obligatory references to real tools of labor, which Losev refrained from mentioning, noting that the sense of the word *techne* in antiquity indicated handicrafts or art. In passing, it is worth noting that the problem of the interrelationship of external tools with spiritual tools and instruments is far from a simple one. Bakhtin did no more than mention that the tool does not have meaning but has purpose. This thesis is in need of further development.

However, in cultural-historical psychology there was not and there could not be a discussion about the "metaphysical religious verticals" (M. Mamardashvili), about the true intermediaries between humans and God. Instead, reflecting the influence of Marxist philosophy, Vygotsky called mediators "psychological instruments."

The psychological theory of activity was concerned with the problem of real (i.e., concrete) tools and objects that humans, also in accordance with Marxism, place between themselves and nature. In other words, what makes humans human? Symbol or thing? The crucifix or the hammer and sickle? If it is the symbol, then this is idealism. If it is the thing, then this is materialism or perhaps dialectical materialism. True, the dialectic did not help us understand Florenskii's thought that the transition from thing (instrument) to idea and from idea to thing is always mediated by a symbol, inasmuch as the latter is simultaneously an idea and a thing. It is clear that the decision to focus on things was predetermined by the context, especially given that the use of Vygotsky's name was forbidden, although not forgotten, during the 1930s. I remember that in his book *The Development of Memory*, Leont'ev (1931) traced how a thing takes on sign-related (*znakovye*) properties and that these make internalization possible. After all, what is internalized is not the thing, but the sign-related (i.e., ideal) properties and procedures for using these properties that the thing acquires.

The problem of mediators in all its dimensions has not been posed in cultural-historical psychology either, although it may be more precise to say that it is still to be explicated. El'konin began this work but did not complete it. He began by focusing on Vygotsky's ideas about the presence of the ideal form that gives rise to children's development. Second, he paid attention not only to Vygotsky's treatment of problems connected with the role of symbolic/sign-related systems in the formation of human consciousness. These issues were thought and written about both before and after Vygotsky. In analyzing Vygotsky's volume *The Psychology of Art* (1925), El'konin concluded that the general intention of all of Vygotsky's work was to show how affective-sense formations emerge, how the whole subjective world of the individual human arises upon meeting affective-sense formations that already exist objectively in the world of art, understood in the widest sense of the word. In this conceptualization, art includes all forms of mediators – that is, the sign, the word, the symbol, myth, and even techniques in the ancient sense of this word. This made it possible for El'konin to view Vygotsky as the founder of nonclassical objective psychology (El'konin, 1989). It is another matter that of the wide range of known mediators, Vygotsky concentrated primarily on the sign, the word, and, to a much lesser extent, the symbol, while not touching on myth to any extent at all.

Let us return to the psychological theory of activity. Vygotsky's students and colleagues who made the transition to working on this strand did not simply camouflage their earlier views. Instead, they enthusiastically worked in a new direction. The niche they selected turned out to be safe. Not long ago Italian and German colleagues told me that in their countries totalitarian regimes made no pretense of trying to develop research analogous to the theory of activity. The main requirement for colleagues in those countries was to study activity with curtailed consciousness, with consciousness only as a secondary property, or without consciousness at all. This touches on a kind of personality (if it was personality at all?) whose characteristics were completely inoffensive to totalitarian regimes (see the novel *Man Without Properties* by Muzil'). The main characteristics of this personality are collectivism, conformity, and an inability to act. This was a misfortune not only for the theory of activity, but for the psychology of our people. It occurred despite the fact that the last book of the leader of the psychological theory of activity concerned activity, consciousness, and personality (Leont'ev, 1975).

One's first school of thought is like a first love. A great deal of research flows from the junction of the two strands, and it is difficult to attribute to either one of them much that has been neatly classified. (This is an interesting topic for philosophers and historians of science.) It is important to remember that the psychological theory of activity was created in the Soviet Union, not in some empty place. (I have in mind here not cultural-historical psychology, but those trends of studying activity about which I spoke earlier.) Leont'ev, the creator of the theory of activity, and his followers utilized cultural-historical psychology in their work. Without this connection, it is possible that the theory of activity might still have emerged, but it would have been different.

Today, the most intelligent course we can follow is to refrain from trying to select one of these strands as the main or, God forbid, the correct one. Instead, we should look at them as mutually amplifying one another, as enriching each other. Such work has already begun, and not just yesterday, and it must be continued in the interest of developing both strands.

The intermediate position some scholars occupy between the two paradigms is explained by their "existence" in a social situation of "palpable darkness." Having to observe the laws of the "ideological community," they cast about between mind and reflex, consciousness and brain, consciousness and a proper world view, determinism and spontaneous development (already articulated in the Book of Genesis), genesis (creation) and reflection (signalization), external and internal (internalization and externalization), personality and "the New Man," deed and physiological and technological act, and development and the "appropriation" of social experience (appropriation being a term of Marx's that has been exploited in the psychological theory of activity). The number of such oppositions can be multiplied. External prohibitions and taboos were internalized and became one's own, which was far from always realized by scholars themselves.

I do not know whether it is true that when speaking to his disciples, Christ said, "When you do the same in your heart as in your action, then you will enter the Kingdom of Heaven" (in the Sermon on the Mount), but even discussing such a view on the problem of external and internal was punished during Soviet times. Our teachers had to mask their personalities, put a veil over them, and it is necessary to give them their proper due when they sometimes, even publicly, opened this curtain a little way. Indeed, what could they do in the situation in which Don Aminado (1991) foresaw, saying: "A handful of pseudonyms, 180 million anonymous authors. The handful will rule, the anonymous authors will keep silent" (p. 223). Yes, it is only now that the individual in the crowd is beginning to be distinguished.

But nonetheless, our teachers did not become "impostors of thought" (Mamardashvili), "merchants of the sense of life" or "mournful composers of prepared meaning" (Mandel'shtam). They managed to preserve their personal meaning in life and to do a great deal in science. We must not forget that the rebirth of psychology that is now beginning is to no small degree due to the fact that they introduced generations of psychologists to the taste and love for science and to the fact that they gave these generations a cultural psychological code, including a personal code.

Today it is very important to our own and to younger generations of psychologists to recognize what came from the two strands of research I have outlined and what was stolen from both of them. In addition to these two strands, it is of course important to recognize a host of other productive and interesting directions of our psychology. Here I will note only the school of differential psychology, in which the rich phenomenological experimental talent of its creator, B. Teplov, was fulfilled only to a small degree, and the school of the psychology of set in which the philosophical views of its creator, D. Uznadze, have gone almost completely unused.

We have been talking about how psychologists found for themselves several relatively safe niches in which they could work. But homes (let alone cathedrals) cannot be constructed out of niches. Isn't this why we do not have a university textbook? In the current situation in Russia, it would seem that the task of building a home is premature. (I will be quite happy if I am mistaken.) We need to begin with the reconstruction of the cultural field (space) that existed in the beginning decades of our century. In this field there were strong and weak interactions. Local voices were fused into a special choir together with an organ. There was a reality of polyphonic and dialogic consciousness that characterized the Russian renaissance. Let me clarify what this means.

The ideas of Solov'ev about the overarching unity of human knowledge, about the Absolute, had an influence on the ideas of Florenskii about the spiritual sphere or "pneumosphere," the ideas of V. Vernadskii about the noosphere, the ideas of Uznadze about the biosphere, the ideas of A. Severtsev about mind as a factor in evolution, and possibly the ideas of A. Gurvich about the biological field. Florenskii's ideas about organic projection had an influence on Ukhtomskii and, I think, on Bernshtein, in their formulation of functional organs. It is also possible that Florenskii's ideas influenced Mandel'shtam, who labeled the image and representation as organs of the individual. Finally, these same ideas were developed by Leont'ev in a context of the psychological theory of activity. Solov'ev's ideas about the spiritual vertical were also interpreted by Losev in his study of mediators (sign, word, symbol, myth).

At the same time it is possible that Solov'ev and Losev had an influence on Vygotsky, the creator and founder of cultural-historical psychology, and on his selection of mediators (sign, symbol, word). I think that an equally important influence on the development of ideas about mediation came from Shpet's analyses of the internal form of the word. Bakhtin recognized that he borrowed the idea of the "chronotope" (which by the way is close to the ideas of the Absolute, the biosphere, and the noosphere) from Ukhtomskii. And Bakhtin himself undoubtedly had an influence on cultural-historical psychology, which does not exclude the possibility that he in turn was influenced by it. Losev's ideas about the energetic self-assertion of personality possibly influenced Gurvich's idea about the dynamically preformed morph (essentially entelechy). It is true that Gurvich then rejected (or was required to reject?) this idea. Without any stretch of the imagination, we can also say that Vygotsky's idea about the ideal form that precedes human ontogenesis is close to the ideas about the Absolute, the biosphere, the noosphere, and the chronotope and in turn is close to the ideas developed by V. Nalimov about the semantic universe.

I certainly do not wish to idealize everything that occurred in the silver age of Russian culture. Everything was possible. There were utopian ideas about humans, their consciousness, and their future. It is possible to connect them (and they are being connected) with the deadly futurology called "scientific communism." But there were also anti-utopias. One must add acmeism to the well-known versions. S. Averintsev recently noted in a negative way his anti-utopian tendency. Wasn't this because all the participants in this artistic movement had met with such a tragic fate? The Bolsheviks, after all, cannot deny satanic insight as well.

Much of what I have said about the interacting influences cannot be proved. And indeed, must it be proved? The field did exist after all. In any case it is important not to forget that at the end of the 1920s, citations of others' work became dangerous. When he cited lines from N. Gumilev and Mandel'shtam in *Thinking and Speech*, Vygotsky (1934) did not refer to the authors. It was much less dangerous to cite Western authors. But all the ideas that I have enumerated lived in the air. They were absorbed through the skin.

This field is now destroyed. The period of stagnation and the time of favoritism managed to annihilate intelligent matter and decreased the thinking space, shrinking it down to nothing. But the conditions for its reconstruction exist once again (in large measure thanks to publications in the journal *Voprosy Filosofii* [Problems in Philosophy] and its remarkable supplements). Many of the concepts and ideas that I have been discussing were developed by A. Lyubishchev, B. Kuzin, S. Meienom, E. Yudin, and Mamardashvili. These ideas continue to be developed by Vyacheslav Ivanov, S. Averintsev, S. Khoruzh, Yuri Lotmam, A. Pyatigorskii, Georgi Shchedorvitskii, V. Toporov, Nalimov, Davydov, Asmolov, Vladimir Lefevr, Fedor Vasilyuk, Boris El'konin, A. Kop'ev, A. Puzyrei, G. Tsukerman, and many others. Unfortunately these are still local voices who have not today come together to form a harmonious whole.

The preceding analysis of the interrelationships between cultural-historical psychology and the psychological theory of activity lead me to the conclusion that the first gave birth to the second. Moreover, the development of the psychological theory of activity to a significant degree is tied to the process of assimilating and reinterpreting achievements of cultural-historical psychology. Of course, the psychological theory of activity substituted a new object of research and units for analyzing higher mental functions. Unlike cultural-historical psychology, it did not focus on meaning, but on object-oriented, tool-mediated action. However, the logic of the development of the psychological theory of activity led to a situation in which transmuted forms of object-oriented action – sensory, perceptual, memory, cognitive, affective, and so forth – were increasingly drawn into its sphere of analysis. In these forms of object-oriented action, ideal attributes were prevalent along with the preservation of object-oriented qualities. Another way of putting this is that the psychological theory of activity progressively approached the analysis of what we provisionally call cultural action. Of course, this does not mean that object-oriented action is necessarily without cultural dimensions or is acultural. Objects themselves are condensations of one or another culture.

It is interesting that we can observe a similar evolution in the work of James Wertsch (1985, 1991). He began with an analysis of Vygotsky's cultural-historical psychology and then turned to Bakhtin, while conducting a parallel analysis of investigations carried out in the context of the psychological theory of activity. Most recently he has turned more frequently to action as a unit of analysis of higher mental functions. My evolution is in the opposite direction. I began with perceptual, memory, and executive actions, and have recently turned increasingly to the problem of mediators (signs, words, symbols, myths). I think the zone of proximal development of the psychological theory of activity will involve the study of individual and personal actions and deeds. According to Bakhtin such actions and deeds are the only thing that allow no human alibi in being. But investigating the deed is impossible outside of an analysis of consciousness. The deed does not derive directly from object-oriented action and does not result in it.

I do not want to say that the psychological theory of activity was generally without a subject, but communist ideology constantly pushed it toward such an understanding of activity. This ideology was alien to the doubts of Karl Marx, who wrote, "We have fallen into a difficult position owing to the fact that we examined persons only as personified categories and not as individuums" (1961, p. 169). From the point of view of this ideology, the human was nothing more than a function, an organ, or a functional organ that served as a means for carrying out activity that had been ordered.

What I have said is to some degree also true of cultural-historical psychology, which was not unacquainted with the idea of the formation of the "new man." True, during Vygotsky's life Russian culture had still not been transformed into the code of communism, but it already was beginning to manifest significant aggressive characteristics. It was being increasingly transformed from an anthropocentric to a culturocentric position.

All of this is connected with the orientation in our society toward the so-called socialization of the personality. It was called this because it was poorly understood and was carried out as a counterbalance to, or at the expense of, the individualization of the personality. In this context the spontaneity of development was completely ignored or even negatively evaluated. The presence in humans of an individual, as opposed to a societal, essence was denied. The central problem today for our society is the task of individualizing development. The development of the amorphous, conformist collectivism has led us to bankruptcy. True, we talk a lot about and even participate in demonstrations for sovereignty, but the problems of personal growth and the formation of a sovereign personality in our society are being recognized only very slowly.

What I have said indicates that there are *vital* (i.e., *life-giving*) *contradictions* between cultural-historical psychology and the psychological theory of activity and that these contradictions are a point of growth for both directions. They may be resolved or overcome, but they also may be made deeper, which is completely natural. If we return to the problem of self-definition, then in concluding I will refrain from deciding to which strand I belong. I am inclined to try to go beyond the boundaries of both, to look at them from a wider point of view and to understand their role and place in psychology in general. In other words there is a need to overcome a childhood (or student) disease and to understand that neither one of these strands represents all of psychology or can aspire to formulate an exhaustive explanatory principle, be it culture or activity.

It is possible that I am now making an illogical move in my argument, but it is hard for me to refrain from being reminded of the external circumstances in which both strands emerged, existed, and developed. It is impossible to forget that cultural-historical psychology emerged during the dismemberment of Russian culture and that its very emergence was a miracle. The psychological theory of activity emerged against a background of the enslavement of the peasants and the organization of slave-based production (not only in the gulag, but in the country as a whole) that was unprecedented in history. Therefore, its appearance was no less miraculous. We must remember this when we evaluate both strands or when we discuss them in a critical way.

It is no surprise that in neither strand was there any kind of full presentation of the problems of freedom, fate, and death. In addition neither one of them broached the issues of values and the ethical aspects of existence. (What I have said applies in a significantly lesser degree to the works of Rubinshtein published during the post-Stalinist period.)

Returning to the problem of an explanatory principle in psychology, it must be said that the concepts of set and consciousness have no less a right to the role of such a principle. Everyone is already tired of the monism that flows from Prutkov's project to introduce a conformity of ideas in Russia, be they from Marxism or from the Orthodox Church.

It would be useful for those who follow (or continue) both strands to think over the interconnections between ontology and phenomenology in human development, as well as the interrelationships in psychology of objective and subjective methods. It is time to stop being afraid of or avoiding the latter in each case. It would be better to turn them to the benefit of science. Without this we will not arrive at any kind of intelligent and valued understanding of humans. Such work must be directed at overcoming the schematisms of consciousness and also at enriching scientific strands in the context of which we have grown up and according to which we move. If such work will be carried out not by lone individuals but together with colleagues of like spirit, then real possibilities for reclaiming lost time and thinking space will appear.

Let me say a few words about the future. In our country both culture and activity are in a depressing state. This makes the task of the development and mutual enrichment of the two strands of thought I have outlined all the more pressing. There is no doubt that human activity is the main source of culture and civilization. There is also no doubt that it is the main way to destroy them. It is mainly activity that has given birth to many of the global problems of the contemporary world. This should not be surprising since in human history the organization and management of activity have dominated the culture of reflecting on and studying that activity, on its results and consequences. Humanity still remembers the boy in experiments carried out by the Khar'kov school who became very upset in the problem situation in which he was trying to get a piece of inaccessible candy. In response to a command to think, he answered that he did not need to think, he simply needed to get it.

In order for the results of activity (which occasionally are difficult to call human activity) not to be so monstrous or worthless, the development of a cultural-historical psychology of consciousness and activity may introduce a modest contribution. This is an initial or at least a verbal form of the possible unification of the two remarkable strands of our country's psychology.

References

Asmolov, A. G. (1990). *Psikhologiya lichnosti* [The psychology of personality]. Moscow: Izdatel'stvo Moskovskogo Universiteta.

Don Aminado, G. (1991). Poetry. *Almanacs,* no. 59, Moscow.

El'konin, D. B. (1989). *Izbrannye psikhologicheskie trudy* [Selected psychological works]. Moscow: Pedagogika.

Gordeeva, N. D., & Zinchenko, V. P. (1982). *Funktsional'naya struktura deistviya* [The functional structure of action]. Moscow: Izdatel'stvo Moskovskogo Universiteta.

Gordeeva, N. D, & Zinchenko, V. P. (1991). Model' predmetnogo deistviya: Sposoby postroeniya, struktura organizatsii i sistema funktsionirovaniya [A model of object-oriented action: Means of construction, structural organization, and functioning system]. *Sistemnye issledovaniya. Ezhegodnik 1989–1990* [Systems research: Yearbook, 1989–1990]. Moscow: Nauka.

Gordon, V. M., & Zinchenko, V. P. (1976). Metodologicheskie problemy psikhologicheskogo analiza deyatel'nosti [Methodological problems of the psychological analysis of activity]. *Sistemnye issledovaniya. Ezhegodnik 1975* [Systems research: Yearbook, 1975] (pp. 82–127). Moscow: Nauka.

Leont'ev, A. N. (1931). *Razvitie pamyati* [The development of memory]. Moscow: Gosizdat.

Leont'ev, A. N. (1975). *Deyatel'nost', soznania, lichnost'* [Activity, consciousness, personality]. Moscow: Izdatel'stvo Politicheskoi Literatury.

Leont'ev, A. N. (1983). *Izbrannye psikhologicheskie proizvedeniya. Tom 1* [Selected psychological works, Vol. 1]. Moscow: Pedagogika.

Marx, K. (1961). *Kapital* [Capital]. Vol. 1. Moscow: Gospolitizdat.

Vygotsky, L. S. (1925). *Psikhologiya iskusstva* [The psychology of art]. Moscow: Izdatel'stvo Moskovskogo Iskusstva.

Vygotsky, L. S. (1934). *Myshlenie i rech': Psikhologicheskie issledovaniya* [Thinking and speech: Psychological investigations]. Moscow: Gosudarstvennoe Sotsial'no-Ekonomicheskoe Izdatel'stvo.

Vygotsky, L. S. (1956). *Izbrannye psikhologicheskie proizvedeniya* [Selected psychological works]. Moscow: Izdatel'stvo Akademii Pedagogicheskikh Nauk RSFSR.

Wertsch, J. V. (1985). *Vygotsky and the social formation of mind.* Cambridge, MA: Harvard University Press.

Wertsch, J. V. (1991). *Voices of the mind: A sociocultural approach to mediated action.* Cambridge, MA: Harvard University Press.

Zinchenko, V. P. (1983a). A. N. Leont'ev i razvitie sovremennoi psikhologii. Ocherk o A. N. Leont'ev [A. N. Leont'ev and the development of contemporary psychology: An essay on A. N. Leont'ev]. In A. N. Leont'ev, *Izbrannye psikhologicheskie proizvedeniya. Tom 1* [Selected psychological works; Vol. 1] (pp. 3–47). Moscow: Pedagogika.

Zinchenko, V. P. (1983b). Ot genezis oshushchii k obrazu mira [From the origins of sensation to an image of the world]. In A. N. Leont'ev, *A. N. Leont'ev i sovremennaya psikhologiya* [A. N. Leont'ev and contemporary psychology] (pp. 74–117). Moscow: Izdatel'stvo Nauka.

Zinchenko, V. P. (1985). Vygotsky's ideas about units for the analysis of mind. In J. V. Wertsch (Ed.), *Culture, communication, and cognition: Vygotskian perspectives* (pp. 94–118). Cambridge University Press.

Zinchenko, V. P. (1988). Problema obrazuyushchikh soznaniya v deyatel'nostnoi teorii psikhologii [The problem of the formation of consciousness in an activity theory in psychology]. *Vestnik Moskovskogo Universiteta. Seriya 14. Psikhologiya* [Moscow University Record: Series 14, Psychology], No. 3. pp. 119–151.

Zinchenko, V. P. (1989). Poslednee interv'yu A. N. Leont'eva [A. N. Leont'ev's last interview]. *Nauka v SSSR* [Science in the USSR], No. 5. Pp. 3–17.

Zinchenko, V. P. (1990). Psikhologicheskaya teoriya deyatel'nosti i psikhologiya deistviya [The psychological theory of activity and the psychology of action]. *Deyatel'nostnyi podkhod v psikhologii: Problemy i perspektivy* [The activity approach in psychology: Problems and perspectives] (pp. 1–97). Moscow: Izdatel'stvo Nauka.

Zinchenko, V. P. (1991a). Problema psikhologii razvitiya (chitaya O. Mandel'shtama) [The problem of the psychology of development (reading O. Mandel'shtam)]. *Voprosy Psikhologii.* [Problems in psychology], Nos. 4, 5, 6. Pp. 1–142.

Zinchenko, V. P. (1991b). Sistemnyi analyz v psikhologii? (Razvernutyi kommentarii k tezisam A. N. Leont'eva, ili Opyt psikhologicheskoi interpretatsii v nauke [A systems analysis in psychology? An extensive commentary on the theses of A. N. Leont'ev, or an experiment in psychological interpretation in science]. *Psikhologicheskii Zhurnal* [Psychological Journal], No. 4. Pp. 111–182.

Zinchenko, V. P. (1992). Problema psikhologii razvitiya (chitaya O. Mandel'shtama) [The problem of the psychology of development (reading O. Mandel'shtam)]. *Voprosy Psikhologii.* [Problems in psychology], Nos. 3–4, 5–6. Pp. 42–97.

Zinchenko, V. P. (1993). Krizis ili katastrofa (o nedavnem proshlom i nevedomom budushchem psikhologii). [Crisis or catastrophe (the recent past and unknown future in psychology)]. *Voprosy filosofii* [Problems in Philosophy], No. 3. pp. 44–81.

Zinchenko, V. P., & Gordon, V. M. (1978). Strukturno-funktsional'nyi analyz deyatel'nosti [The structural-functional analysis of activity]. *Sistemnye issledovaniya. Ezhegodnik 177.* [Systems research: Yearbook 177]. Moscow: Nauka.

Zinchenko, V. P., & Smirnov, S. K. (1983). *Metodologicheskie voprosy psikhologii* [Methodological problems in psychology]. Moscow: Izdatel'stvo Moskovskogo Universiteta.

2 The need for action in sociocultural research

James V. Wertsch

The goal of sociocultural research is to understand the relationship between human mental functioning, on the one hand, and cultural, historical, and institutional setting, on the other. In a world characterized by rapid political transitions, newly awakened nationalism, and many other forms of potentially positive, but often deadly change, sociocultural research has never been more timely. It represents one of the ways that psychology, anthropology, education, and related disciplines can take a new step in entering into public discourse about today's most compelling issues.

A sampling of issues of concern to sociocultural researchers might include cultural differences in how identity is defined and formed, historical changes in the understanding of human rights, and differences (say, between school and workplace) in how mathematical reasoning practices are carried out. While these examples all involve comparison – a technique that is generally one of the most powerful we have for sociocultural research – it is not the case that, to qualify as sociocultural, a study must employ comparative methods. What *is* essential is that the sociocultural situation of mental functioning be recognized and addressed in some way.

The writing of this chapter was assisted by a grant from the Spencer Foundation. In addition, the author wishes to express his appreciation to the Departamento de Psicología Evolutiva y de la Educación, Basica y Metodologia of the Universidad de Sevilla for its hospitality during his 1992–93 sabbatical visit. The statements made and the views expressed are solely the responsibility of the author.

The fact that sociocultural research is formulated in terms of a *relationship* (i.e., between mental processes and sociocultural setting) raises a set of questions about underlying assumptions. Do mental processes provide the key to understanding sociocultural setting or the other way around? Or is neither (or both) of these formulations appropriate? Such questions, let alone their answers, are seldom made explicit, but that hardly makes them any less important. Indeed, by being left implicit they often have the effect of playing an even greater role than they might otherwise have.

When we go through the process of explicating assumptions about the relationship between mental functioning and sociocultural setting, research agendas often can be seen to fall into two general categories, depending on what is given analytic primacy. In one category are approaches grounded in the assumption that it is appropriate to begin with an account of sociocultural phenomena and then generate analyses of mental functioning. In the other are approaches which assume that the way to understand sociocultural phenomena is to start with psychological or other processes carried out by the individual.

As an illustration of these two basic alternative positions on analytic primacy, consider statements by Aleksandr Luria, one of the founders of the "Vygotsky–Leont'ev–Luria" school of cultural-historical psychology, on the one hand, and by Paul Churchland, a philosopher of cognitive science, on the other. In Luria's view,

> in order to explain the highly complex forms of human consciousness one must go beyond the human organism. One must seek the origins of conscious activity and "categorical" behavior not in the recesses of the human brain or in the depths of the spirit, but in the external conditions of life. Above all, this means that one must seek these origins in the external processes of social life, in the social and historical forms of human existence. (1981, p. 25)

In contrast, Churchland (1988) argues for a reductionist account of human consciousness[1] based on principles of natural science and gives analytic primacy not even to psychological, but to neurological, "connectionist" processes. In response to "cultural embedding objections" to his reductionist program, Churchland notes that such objections are typically based on the observation that humans discriminate and respond to very complex aspects of the environment, including "all of the intricacies that make up a functioning culture" (p. 42). Churchland agrees that complexity must be addressed, but he argues that this is wholly consistent with a reductionist program for understanding the nature of human cognition. What the reductionist must do is explain how a physical system can come to address and manipulate such subtle and culturally configured features. While this is certainly a challenge, it no longer appears to be a problem in principle, for. . . . with suitable teaching, the network generates an internal representation of [features] regardless [of complexity]. This does not mean that the features addressed are magical, or super-physical, or beyond the realm of natural science. It just means that the simplest possible definition or representation of them may well be the entire configuration of the successfully trained network! (p. 42)

These statements by Luria and Churchland are noteworthy for the explicitness of their formulation of underlying assumptions. Even in the absence of such overt formulation, however, I believe that most scholars in the social sciences hold some position on this issue of analytic primacy. In some cases this may simply be a matter of disciplinary orientation. Thus, psychologists may assume that we can explain cultural, historical, or institutional phenomena by appealing to psychological processes, sociologists may assume that we can explain psychological phenomena by appealing to institutional processes, connectionists might try to account for both by reducing them to physical processes, and so forth. One's position on this issue may reflect other factors as well, but a major problem with virtually all such formulations is that there seem to be few bases other than personal preference or disciplinary affiliation for making a selection among the alternatives.

The fact that this debate seems to go on and on with no principled resolution in sight should tell us something – namely, that the academic dispute over whether to give psychological or sociological or cultural processes analytic primacy may reflect a more general debate that is not really resolvable through rational argument. Another way of putting it is that our debates over these issues in academia are embedded in a broader sociocultural setting – something that should come as no surprise to anyone espousing a sociocultural position. My candidate for the relevant sociocultural setting is an ongoing public debate about fundamental ethical and political issues in modern society. In particular, I have in mind a debate grounded in an antinomy between individual and society.

Among the commentators on this antinomy, Elias (1991) has provided an account that is particularly relevant to my argument. According to Elias this antinomy resembles a "curious party game that certain groups in western society are apt to indulge in over and over again" (p. 54). The two opposing groups he has in mind endlessly engage in encounters of the following sort:

One says, "Everything depends on the individual," the other, "Everything depends on society." The first group says: "But it is always particular individuals who decide to do this and not that." The others reply: "But their decisions are socially conditioned." The first group says: "But what you call 'social conditioning' only comes about because others want to do something and do it." The others reply: "But what these others want to do and do is also socially conditioned." (p. 54)

Elias suggests that this "debate" is likely to go on endlessly and fruitlessly because there are no means for rationally resolving it. The reason for this is that at bottom the debate is not grounded in empirical fact or logic, but in "valuations" of individual and society. According to Elias:

In their most popular form, the professions of one side present the "individual" as the means and the "social whole" as the supreme value and purpose, while the other regard "society" as the means and "individuals" as the supreme value and purpose. And in both cases these ideals and goals of political thought and action are often presented as facts. What one side says *should* be is thought and spoken of as if it *is*. For example . . . members of groups in which it is loyal to demand and wish that the claims of individuals *should* have priority over those of the group, often believe they can observe that individuals are the true reality, that which actually exists, while societies are something that comes afterwards, something less real and perhaps even a mere figment of thought, an abstraction. . . . In short, what one understands by "individual" and "society" still depends to a large extent on the form taken by what people wish for and fear. (1991, pp. 83–85)

It is essential for sociocultural research to formulate its position vis-à-vis the individual–society antinomy in some way. If it does not do so, such research is likely to be misunderstood, falsely categorized, and ultimately dismissed as a confused variant of other schools of thought. For example, investigators who presuppose analytic primacy for mental functioning might view sociocultural research as amounting to a form of social learning theory concerned with what Lawrence and Valsiner (1993) term "internalization as cultural transmission." Other investigators who give analytic primacy to mental functioning might be inclined to interpret sociocultural research as amounting to a call for rejecting the study of psychological phenomena altogether in favor of focusing on cultural, historical, and institutional issues.

Many such troubling interpretations are grounded squarely in the individual–society antinomy and the related antinomy between mental functioning and sociocultural setting. The persistence of the interpretations reflects the power these antinomies have in shaping our thought and discussion. Once they are permitted to frame the debate, we are put in the position of having to choose between stark alternatives, a position from which it seems very difficult to extricate ourselves.

As is the case with many antinomies, the key to dealing with this one may be to recognize that the very formulation of issues in either/or alternatives is counterproductive. This is precisely why the term "false" seems to appear so often as a modifier of "antinomy" in general and why I would argue that the individual–society antinomy in particular is at the very least misleading. The major problem in this case is in how the terms put in opposition are understood. They are typically understood as referring to essences or objects (Elias's "true reality") having some kind of independent existence. As long as we give "mental functioning" and "sociocultural setting" or "individual" and "society" this kind of ontological interpretation, sociocultural research is likely to be confused about its agenda and methods.

An alternative that makes it possible to avoid this confusion is to keep in mind that these terms are hypothetical constructs or conceptual tools (tools that may be of only temporary use) in a process of inquiry. In this capacity, they are "inherently necessary for controlled inquiry," as Dewey (1938, p. 263) noted in his account of general propositions, but they are not "linguistic expression[s] of something already known which needs symbols only for the purposes of convenient recall and communication" (p. 263).

In this spirit, I propose that mental functioning and sociocultural setting be understood as dialectically interacting moments, or aspects of a more inclusive unit of analysis – *human action*. As understood here, action is not carried out either by the individual or by society, although there are individual and societal moments to any action. For related reasons an account of action cannot be derived from the study of mental functioning or sociocultural setting in isolation. Instead, action provides a context within which the individual and society (as well as mental functioning and sociocultural context) are understood as interrelated moments.

Action

Adopting human action as the unit of analysis for sociocultural research means that it serves as the fundamental object to be described and interpreted. Such an approach constrasts with describing and interpreting attitudes, concepts, linguistic and knowledge structures, and other such units we often encounter in psychology. As will become apparent, these other units often can be extremely useful in analyzing one or another aspect of action, and employing them is therefore not necessarily antithetical to an analysis of action. However, in an action approach they are viewed as moments, or aspects interacting with others in a more inclusive system. As a result, from the perspective of an analysis of action they tend to be understood in ways that might differ from their interpretation in other conceptual frameworks.

Because analyses concerned with action may be related to analyses based on other units, it is sometimes easy to drift from one to another framework without realizing that this has occurred. Indeed, one of the things that becomes apparent about the category of action is that it seems to be quite "slippery." By this I mean that even those professing a desire to use it as the foundation of their analysis often have a difficult time keeping it squarely in focus. They find themselves drifting into using the categories of some individual–society antinomy or some other set of more familiar constructs. This tends to occur in little-noticed ways that run counter to professed intentions, the process seeming to be much like that outlined by Reddy (1979) in his account of how certain metaphors in English have subtle, yet powerful influences on the conceptualization of models of communication.

The problem of keeping a clear focus on action is certainly not attributable to an absence of sound and, indeed, brilliant efforts to provide theoretical foundations. The kind of foundations I have in mind can be found in the writings of Soviet and Russian writers such as Bakhtin (1986; see Voloshinov, 1973), with his focus on the utterance as a form of action; Vygotsky (1978, 1987), with his emphasis on speech, thinking, and, more generally, "mediated action" (Wertsch, 1985, 1991; Zinchenko, 1985); and Leont'ev (1975, 1981), with his theory of activity. In the West one can find relevant accounts of action in the writings of Bourdieu (1977), with his description of "habitus";

Burke (1962, 1966), with his account of action (including symbolic action) and the motives that shape it; de Certeau (1984), with his focus on practice and resistance; Dewey (1938), with his analysis of "inquiry" as a form of "human conduct"; Habermas (1984), with his studies of "communicative action"; MacIntyre (1984), with his analysis of "intelligible action"; and Mead (1938), with his philosophy of the act.

I believe that all these authors, as well as many others, have something important to say about the notion of action in sociocultural research. My purpose in listing them is to provide some idea of the potential framework involved rather than to explicate how all of them fit into an overall picture. In what follows, I shall limit myself to drawing quite selectively on them to identify some of the basic challenges and claims of the kind of analysis of action I see as necessary in sociocultural research.

A general point of commonality among all these authors is their focus on concrete, dynamic human action existing in real spatiotemporal and social contexts. This contrasts with theorists who have argued for the necessity of abstracting away from the exigencies of contextualized action so as to carry out the kind of inquiry they see as appropriate for scientific study. Thus, instead of grounding inquiry in linguistic abstractions such as *langue* and sentence, Bakhtin (1986) insisted on focusing on the utterance; and instead of grounding inquiry in social structure, Bourdieu (1977) and de Certeau (1984) insisted on focusing on the dynamics of "practice" and "resistance."

The basic difference here is between focusing on one moment of a process abstracted away from others and insisting on the need to focus on multiple dimensions of a process in an integrated conceptual system concerned with contextualized action. In many analyses of the latter sort it may continue to be useful to employ notions about abstract factors such as linguistic and social structure, but these are viewed as contributing to the interpretation of concrete action rather than as the ends of analysis in their own right.

A fundamental issue to be addressed in analyzing action, then, is how several moments of its organization are defined and understood as being involved in a complex dialectic. The general orientation is to view action as being organized or shaped by several analytically distinct but interacting influences. The role of the various influences may vary from one context to another and at various stages of development. However, in every case all influences are recognized as shaping action in some way. Because they are interrelated within a dynamic system, these influences cannot be defined in isolation or in a static way. Their interpretation and role vary depending on how they contribute to shaping the action under consideration.

Obviously, the kind of thinking needed in this formulation must be based on a willingness to deal with multiple, simultaneously acting influences and the dialectics among them. Such issues are not readily interpretable in analytic approaches based on the search for static, unidirectional influences or causes. This is not to deny that it is possible and, on some occasions, even desirable to organize data analyses grounded in these latter assumptions, but such analyses should be viewed as way stations in a more inclusive research strategy rather than final products.

As an example of the kind of dialectic involving moments in action, consider Vygotsky's analysis of "psychological tools," or "mediational means." He made his most extensive and concrete comments on mediation in connection with natural language, but his list of psychological tools also included "various systems for counting; mnemonic techniques; algebraic symbol systems; works of art; writing; schemes, diagrams, maps, and mechanical drawings; all sorts of conventional signs" (1981, p. 137). Fundamental to his understanding of the role of mediational means was the assumption that "by being included in the process of behavior, the psychological tool alters the entire flow and structure of mental functions. It does this by determining the structure of a new instrumental act" (Vygotsky, 1981, p. 137). In such a view the introduction of a psychological tool such as language into the flow of action leads to an important transformation or even a redefinition of that action ("a new instrumental act"). This contrasts with the view in which the inclusion of mediational means would simply facilitate an existing action but leave it qualitatively unchanged.

Vygotsky's line of reasoning is grounded in an analysis of how various influences come into contact and transform action. Specifically, he was arguing that action which had been carried out in the absence of or with a different mediational means is transformed with the incorporation of a new psychological tool. In the "instrumental act," neither the individual nor the mediational means functions in isolation, and if examined in isolation neither can provide adequate foundations for an account of the action carried out. Instead, the analysis of such action must be grounded squarely in the irreducible tension between mediational means and the individual using them.

The kind of action that concerned Vygotsky has been termed "mediated action" (Wertsch, 1991; Wertsch, Tulviste, & Hagstrom, 1993; Zinchenko, 1985). This is action interpreted as involving an irreducible tension between mediational means and the individuals employing these means. One consequence of taking this perspective is that the very notion of agent comes to be redefined. Instead of assuming that individuals, acting alone, are the agents of actions, the appropriate designation of agent is "individual-operating-with-mediational-means." It is only by using this designation that we can hope to provide an adequate response to the underlying question, Who is it who carried out the action or, in the case of speech, who is it who did the talking? (Wertsch, 1991).

Such an expanded notion of agency provides one way of exploring the relationship between mental functioning and the cultural, historical, and institutional settings in which it occurs. Any insights it provides will derive from the fact that the mediational means that shape mental functioning and action more generally are inherent aspects of, and hence serve as indexes of, a sociocultural setting. As Bruner (1990) put it when discussing the closely related notion of symbolic systems that shape human action, they "are already in place, already 'there,' deeply entrenched in the culture and language" (p. 11).

Anything approaching an adequate, detailed account of human action for sociocultural research will emerge only after a great deal more theoretical and empirical inquiry. The basic framework, including the list of basic moments involved, will undoubtedly need to be expanded in many ways, a point to which I shall return in my conclusion. Instead of attempting to map out a general theoretical framework that could deal with all these issues – something that would be quite premature at this point – I shall turn to a couple of illustrations in an effort to provide a more concrete picture of the kind of actions and action analyses I have in mind.

Two illustrations of mediated action

Pole vaulting

The first illustration I shall use may appear to be out of place in a discussion of mental functioning. I employ it, however, for a very specific purpose: Unlike many cases of mediated action, especially those involving language, where the mediational means seem to be ephemeral, the mediational means at issue in this case is very concrete and apparent. The action I have in mind is pole vaulting.

Pole vaulting is a track and field event thought to have originated in an early English practice of vaulting across streams with the aid of a stick. Vaulting for distance became a common sport, and this was succeeded by vaulting for height. The modern event of pole vaulting involves the vaulter racing down a 125-foot runway with a pole in his[2] hands, planting the pole in a vaulting box at the end of the runway, and using the pole and his momentum to lift himself off the ground and over a bar that is held up by two uprights. Pole vaulting has been a part of the modern Olympic Games since their inception in 1896. Records in these games have increased over the years from a height of 10 feet, 10 inches in 1896 to over 20 feet today.

Vaulters first used heavy and inflexible hickory, ash, or spruce poles. Bamboo poles, which were lighter and more flexible, were introduced in the 1900 Olympic Games. The advantages of bamboo poles were quickly recognized, and they were widely adopted. Records set with them lasted until 1957. Cornelius Warmerdam, widely considered to be the greatest vaulter in the history of the sport, used bamboo poles to set six world records. He was the first vaulter to clear 15 feet, and he set a U.S. indoor record of 15 feet 8.5 inches, which lasted from 1943 to 1959.

No one came close to Warmerdam's performance during the era of the bamboo pole, but after World War II vaulters' performances began to improve with the introduction of steel and aluminum alloy poles. The major change that made it possible to eclipse Warmerdam's and all others' records, however, was the introduction of the fiberglass pole in the 1960s. The much greater flexibility and strength of these poles led to a drastic change in vaulting styles. By bending the poles almost to 90 degrees during their takeoff, competitors became capable of vaulting more than 3 feet higher than the records set using bamboo and metal poles. It is fiberglass poles and their descendants that have made it possible for recent vaulters such as Sergei Bubka to reach heights of over 20 feet.

From the perspective of mediated action, pole vaulting is interesting first of all because it provides an excellent illustration of the irreducibility of this unit of analysis. It is clearly futile, if not ridiculous, to try to understand the action of pole vaulting in terms of the mediational means (i.e., the pole) or the individual in isolation. On the one hand, the pole by itself does not magically propel vaulters over a cross bar; it must be used skillfully by the vaulter. On the other hand, a vaulter without a pole or with an inappropriate pole is incapable of participating in the event, or at best can participate at less than an optimal level of performance.

Further insight into the dynamics of this form of mediated action can be obtained by considering how the mediational means and the individuals employing them have changed over the history of the event. This history has been marked by controversy at those points when a new type of pole was introduced. In the early 1960s this controversy emerged with particular force over the introduction of the fiberglass pole. For example, an article about this controversy began as follows:

The astounding resiliency of fiber glass, . . . bending almost double before slinging C. K. Yang of U.C.L.A. higher than pole vaulters are supposed to soar, was the center last week of a crackling controversy. Yang and two other vaulters armed with fiber glass poles had bettered the world's record three times in nine days, and the onslaught was too much for purists objecting to vaulters becoming human projectiles.

The outcry was led by Don Bragg, Olympic champion [who had used an aluminum pole]: "It's ridiculous, and that's why I quit. Why join the circus? There's a trick to the fiber glass style of hanging on and letting the pole do the work." ("How far," 1963)

In the terms employed in this chapter, the controversy reflected in this passage is over whether the introduction of a new mediational means qualitatively transformed one form of mediated action into another. Did the introduction of the fiberglass pole represent an extension of an existing form of mediated action, or did it create a qualitatively new one? In this controversy the specific issue was whether agency had shifted from individual to mediational means to such an extent that the individual should no longer be given credit for carrying out the action.

This issue is apparent at several points in the passage. Note that the pole is credited with "slinging" a vaulter, that vaulters had become "human projectiles," and that the "trick" was one of "hanging on and letting the pole do the work." On the other hand, the passage implicitly recognizes the continuing contribution of the individuals involved when it notes such things as the fact that "they" (albeit "armed" with fiberglass poles) had broken the world record repeatedly.

Bragg specifically complained that "fiberglass takes the human element out of vaulting and makes the vaulter a catapulter" ("A pole," 1962, p. 47). However, other vaulters criticized him, arguing that "[Bragg] tried Fiberglass and couldn't master it. He couldn't make 16 [feet] with either pole. He didn't complain when he used an aluminum pole to break the record Warmerdam set with a bamboo pole" (1962, p. 47). Here again, the two sides of this controversy reflect the two moments of mediated action as outlined earlier.

For my purposes, the major point of interest here is that mediated action can undergo a fundamental transformation with the introduction of new mediational means (in this case, the fiberglass pole). The impact of introducing new means into the action is reflected in this case in the controversy over whether those using the fiberglass poles were even participating in the same event as others. Again, all this is not to say that the mediational means somehow act alone. An individual using the new mediational means had to change as well, since it obviously called for new techniques and skills. In this connection it is worth noting that some athletes vaulted higher with aluminum poles than with fiberglass poles, and for others the opposite was true.

A final point to make about the evolution of pole vaulting is that the impetus for change came from "outside," in the form of a new mediational means. The nature of this change was that an existing form of mediated action was transformed by the introduction of a new mediational means. Another sense in which change came from outside involves the fact that the new mediational means did not originally emerge in the service of the particular form of mediated action at issue. The appearance of the new poles was instead a "spin-off" of other developments in technology that gave rise to fiberglass. It was only after the widespread use of this material in many areas of modern life that it was recognized as having important implications for pole vaulting and came to have the impact it did.

Speaking in sound bites

The second illustration of mediated action that I shall use concerns a common practice in American political discourse: speaking in "sound bites." In recent years many commentators have decried the rise of the "20-second sound bite" in the media and the impact this seems to have had on the forms of speaking and thinking in contemporary U.S. political discourse. It is a problem for which the public blames politicians, politicians blame the media, and the media blame the public.

Studies such as those carried out by Hallin (1992) suggest several dimensions to the issue. Hallin's analysis begins with an empirical study of television news coverage. Specifically, he examined a sample of network evening news broadcasts covering presidential election campaigns from 1968 through 1988 and calculated the average length of the sound bites they included. His results show a steady and striking decrease in the average length of a sound bite from 60 seconds in 1968 to less than 9 seconds in 1988.

In Hallin's view this decrease is part of a larger picture in which television journalists have become more active in structuring the news reports they generate. In contrast to the prevailing practices of the 1960s, for today's television journalist "words, rather than simply being reproduced and transmitted to the audience, are treated as raw material to be taken apart, combined with other sounds and images, and reintegrated into a new narrative" (1992, pp. 9–10). As a result "the modern news story is much more journalist-centered than its predecessor: the journalist, not the candidate or other 'newsmaker' . . . is the primary communicator" (1992, p. 11).

One widely recognized result of such practices is that politicians and other newsmakers have increasingly organized their speech into segments that can fit into the media narratives of television news broadcasts. As Hallin notes, it is ironic that "whoever may have 'started it,' the modern form of TV news encourages exactly the kind of campaigning – based on one-liners and symbolic visuals – that journalists decry" (1992, p. 20). Even though journalists, the public, and newsmakers may find it objectionable, "the truth is that one-liners and symbolic visuals are what get on the air, and it is hardly surprising that the candidates' 'handlers' gravitate toward them" (p. 20).

Hallin argues that several factors seem to underlie the trend toward increasingly shorter sound bites during the two decades between 1968 and 1988. The first is the technical evolution of the television medium. Under this heading Hallin includes not only technology in the narrow sense, such as graphics generators, electronic editing units, and satellites that make it easy to transport video images to a central location for editing. In addition, he is concerned with the evolution of technical culture of television more broadly – "of television 'know-how' and a television aesthetic" (1992, p. 11).

Another factor cited by Hallin for the increasingly mediated nature of television news coverage is "the weakening of political consensus and authority in the years of Vietnam and Watergate, which pushed all of American journalism in the direction of more active conventions of reporting" (1992, pp. 12–13). This encouraged journalists to question and comment on authoritative voices in ways that were relatively rare in the early 1960s. Instead of simply reproducing and transmitting the words of government officials and other major political actors at face value, journalists increasingly felt that it was appropriate, indeed required, to treat these words as raw material to be organized into a critical and questioning narrative line.

Hallin stesses that these first two factors alone, however, cannot account for the striking decrease in the length of sound bites. In addition, he sees a major force to have been economic forces shaping the television industry. In the 1960s, CBS and NBC led the way in expanding their evening news broadcasts from 15 to 30 minutes, and they did so at that point for prestige rather than profit. Indeed, until the early 1970s news was viewed in the television industry as a "loss leader." But during that decade local news began to be a major source of profits for television stations. Not surprisingly, as local television news became more profitable it became more competitive, and with competition came innovation. In this context, as Hallin notes, "consultants were brought in to recommend more effective ways of maintaining audience attention. And their recommendations typically pointed in the direction of a more tightly structured and fast-paced presentation of the news" (1992, p. 16).

These same forces came to have a major impact on network news divisions in the 1970s, and in the 1980s cable and independent stations entered the competition as well. This, along with deregulation, created a novel and challenging context for news organizations that had formerly been largely insulated from ratings pressures. One of the responses was that television news increasingly took on the fast-paced, stacatto look of advertising and popular entertainment, a look characterized by the heavy use of sound bites.

Like pole vaulting, speaking in sound bites is a form of mediated action. To be sure, there are major differences that separate the two cases, perhaps the most important being that the mediational means are less obvious (though no less essential) in the case of sound bites. Instead of taking the form of an object that can be isolated from its use, the mediational means in the case of sound bites takes the form of a pattern of speaking that is often difficult to conceptualize independently of the individuals employing it. Specifically, it is a pattern that constitutes what Bakhtin (1986) termed a "speech genre."

Above and beyond these differences, however, there are parallels that allow us to make a similar set of points about speaking in sound bites and pole vaulting. First, as in pole vaulting, speaking in sound bites can be understood only by taking both the mediational means and the individual using this means into account. The pattern of a speech genre does not do the speaking, on the one hand, but politicians do not feel free to speak without invoking the speech genre, on the other.

Second, as in pole vaulting, the introduction of a new mediational means can be seen to have the effect of transforming mediated action. Hallin used quantitative measures to report his empirical findings, but that by no means precludes the claim that the political discourse he examined underwent a qualitative transformation. As in the case of pole vaulting, this is not to assert that an analysis of the mediational means in isolation can generate an understanding of the mediated action at issue. There are obviously major differences among politicians in the skill with which they appropriate and manipulate the sound bite speech genre.

And finally, as in the case of pole vaulting, much of the impetus for the transformation of this form of mediated action came from "outside." A major part of Hallin's analysis focuses on the institutional forces that gave rise to the sound bite speech genre and in retrospect make its emergence seem almost inevitable. As in the case of fiberglass poles, the new mediational means in this case did not emerge as a part of a reflective process designed to improve the practice at hand. Indeed, most observers would argue that precisely the opposite has resulted.

Action as a unit of analysis for sociocultural research: potential pitfalls and prospects

I have argued that sociocultural research must formulate its position vis-à-vis the individual–society antinomy. The need for doing so derives from the basic formulation of the task of sociocultural research in terms of the relationship between mental functioning and sociocultural setting. I have suggested that the way to avoid the pitfalls of such antinomies is to ground research in a unit of analysis in which the members of the antinomy can be viewed as dialectically interacting moments rather than objects or essences that "actually exist," and I have suggested that a good candidate for such a unit is human action. The particular version of this general candidate that I outlined is mediated action, a version that traces its theoretical roots to figures such as Vygotsky and Bakhtin (Wertsch, 1991).

I am quite certain that some notion of action holds the key to avoiding the pitfalls of false antinomies and dichotomies, as well as many other potential dead ends in sociocultural research (see Wertsch, 1991). Part of my confidence on this point stems from the fact that so many of our most inspiring intellectual progenitors have come to this conclusion. I am less certain that the notion of mediated action I have outlined here will ultimately fill the bill. While I see the ideas of theorists such as Vygotsky and Bakhtin about mediated action as providing many ingenious insights into an account of action, it seems that we must eventually expand the list of moments in the analysis of action beyond the two that have been my primary focus.

How to proceed is one of the major problems for the future of sociocultural research, and instead of trying to invent new wheels, it may be wise to begin by examining some of those left around by others. For these I would turn to figures such as those I listed earlier. As one example of what I have in mind, it seems that some promising ways for elaborating the notion of action can be found in the writings of Burke (1962, 1966). His "pentad" of act, scene, agent, agency (or instrumentality), and purpose was designed to understand action (as opposed to "sheer motion") and the motives that organize it, and several aspects of his formulation seem to have direct implications for sociocultural research.

This is not to say that Burke's framework, any more than Vygotsky's, Bakhtin's, or anyone else's that I know of, can by itself provide sociocultural research with a complete list of moments of action or with a finalized program of inquiry. Furthermore, I do not believe his ideas can simply be grafted onto those of other theorists. For example, agent and agency in Burke's analysis do not correspond neatly with individual and mediational means, respectively, and I therefore do not believe that Burke's analysis should be viewed as a way of simply incorporating and extending the notion of mediated action. It is a commonplace that terms take on different meanings in different theoretical frameworks, and this makes the relationship between Burke's approach and a Vygotskian/ Bakhtinian approach likely to be quite complex.

Nonetheless, there are several obvious implications that Burke's approach has for sociocultural research. For example, it seems to me that an account of mediated action could profitably be extended by addressing issues under the headings of what Burke calls act and scene. More generally, the most important message Burke may have for any account of action we develop in sociocultural research is that it must never lose sight of the notion that action can be understood only in terms of dialectically interacting moments. Other authors from the list I provided earlier have other, equally important contributions to make to the more elaborated notion of action required in sociocultural research.

Of course, sociocultural research is hardly original in drawing on the ideas of Burke (or Dewey, Mead, Bourdieu, or any other of a long list of figures for that matter). Authors such as Gusfield (1989), Hymes (1974), and Kaplan (1983) have turned to Burke for decades. If anything, however, this should be taken to be a promising sign for sociocultural research as it seeks to expand its horizons. Its future depends on engaging with ideas from other figures and traditions while keeping its focus on its basic set of problems. There may be several ways to pursue this future, but as I have argued throughout this chapter, it seems that one of the most promising of these begins by assuming that action provides the framework for interpreting everything else that follows.

Notes

1. Although both Luria and Churchland use the term "consciousness," by no means should one assume that the two authors understand it in the same way. The term fits into quite different theoretical frameworks in the two cases and hence has quite different interpretations.
2. To date, only men participate in this athletic event.

References

A pole is a pole is a . . . *Newsweek, 53*, pp. 47–48, February 19, 1962.

Bakhtin, M. M. (1986). *Speech genres and other late essays* (Caryl Emerson & Michael Holquist, Eds.; V. W. McGee, Trans.). Austin: University of Texas Press.

Bourdieu, P. (1977). *Outline of a theory of practice* (R. Nice, Trans). Cambridge University Press.

Bruner, J. (1990). *Acts of meaning.* Cambridge MA: Harvard University Press.

Burke, K. (1962). *A grammar of motives.* Berkeley: University of California Press.

Burke, K. (1966). *Language as symbolic action: Essays on life, literature, and method.* Berkeley: University of California Press.

Churchland, P. (1988). Reductionism, connectionism, and the plasticity of human consciousness. *Cultural Dynamics, 1*(1), 29–45.

de Certeau, M. (1984). *The practice of everyday life* (Steven F. Rendall, Trans.). Berkeley: University of California Press.

Dewey, J. (1938). *Logic: The theory of inquiry.* New York: Holt, Rinehart, & Winston.

Elias, N. (1991). *The society of individuals* (M. Schroter, Ed.; E. Jephcott, Trans.). Oxford: Blackwell.

Gusfield, J. (1989). *Kenneth Burke on symbols and society.* Chicago: University of Chicago Press.

Habermas, J. (1984). *The theory of communicative action: Vol. 1, Reason and the rationalization of society* (T. McCarthy, Trans.). Boston: Beacon.

Hallin, D. C. (1992). Sound bite news: Television coverage of elections, 1968–1988. *Journal of Communication, 42* (2), 5–24.

How far is a flip with a fiber glass pole? *Life, 54*, p. 36, February 22, 1963.

Hymes, D. (1974). *Foundations in sociolinguistics.* Philadelphia: University of Pennsylvania Press.

Kaplan, B. (1983). Genetic-dramatism: Old wine in new bottles. In S. Wapner and B. Kaplan (Eds.), *Toward a holistic developmental psychology* (pp. 53–74). Hillsdale, NJ: Erlbaum.

Lawrence, J. A., & Valsiner, J. (1993). Conceptual roots of internalization: From transmission to transformation. *Human Development, 36*(3), 150–167.

Leont'ev, A. N. (1975). *Deyatel'nost', soznanie, lichnost'* [Activity, consciousness, personality]. Leningrad: Izdatel'stvo Politicheskoi Literaturi. Published in Eng-

74   James V. Wertsch

lish as *Activity, consciousness, personality.* Englewood Cliffs, NJ: Prentice-Hall, 1978.

Leont'ev, A. N. (1981). The problem of activity in psychology. In J. V. Wertsch (Ed.), *The concept of activity in Soviet psychology* (pp. 37–71). Armonk, NY: Sharpe.

Luria, A. R. (1981). *Language and cognition* (J. V. Wertsch, Ed.) New York: Wiley Intersciences.

MacIntyre, A. (1984). *After virtue: A study in moral theory.* Notre Dame, IN: University of Notre Dame Press.

Mead, G. H. (1934). *Mind, self, and society from the standpoint of a social behaviorist.* Chicago: University of Chicago Press.

Mead, G. H. (1938). *The philosophy of the act.* Chicago: University of Chicago Press.

Reddy, M. J. (1979). The conduit metaphor: A case of frame conflict in our language about language. In A. Ortony (Ed.), *Metaphor and thought* (pp. 284–324). Cambridge University Press.

Voloshinov, V. N. (1973). *Marxism and the philosophy of language* (L. Matejka & I. R. Titunik, Trans.). New York: Seminar Press. (Originally published in 1929)

Vygotsky, L. S. (1978). *Mind in society: The development of higher psychological processes* (M. Cole, V. John-Steiner, S. Scribner, & E. Souberman, Eds.) Cambridge, MA: Harvard University Press.

Vygotsky, L. S. (1981). The instrumental method in psychology. In J. V. Wertsch (Ed.), *The concept of activity in Soviet psychology* (pp. 134–143). Armonk, NY: Sharpe.

Vygotsky, L. S. (1987). *The collected works of L. S. Vygotsky: vol. 1, Problems of general psychology. Including the volume thinking and speech.* (N. Minick, Ed. & Trans.). New York: Plenum.

Wertsch, J. V. (1985). *Vygotsky and the social formation of mind.* Cambridge, MA: Harvard University Press.

Wertsch, J. V. (1991). *Voices of the mind: A sociocultural approach to mediated action.* Cambridge, MA: Harvard University Press.

Wertsch, J. V., Tulviste, P., & Hagstrom, F. (1993). A sociocultural approach to agency. In E. A. Forman, N. Minick, & C. A. Stone (Eds)., *Contexts for learning: Sociocultural dynamics in children's development* (pp. 336–356). New York: Oxford University Press.

Zinchenko, V. P. (1985). Vygotsky's ideas about units of analysis of mind. In J. V. Wertsch (Ed.), *Culture, communication, and cognition: Vygotskian perspectives* (pp. 94–118). Cambridge University Press.

3 Theories of action, speech, natural language, and discourse

Jean-Paul Bronckart

Human action as the main concern of psychology

Reflections on the status of psychology are normally summed up in several commonplace propositions as follows. First, the subject matter of the discipline is *behavior*, or rather observable behavior and the mental phenomena associated with it; radical behaviorism confines itself solely to behavior, and within the framework of this perspective we do not discuss directly the status of animal behavior. Second, behavior is *dynamic;* the human organism behaves (conducts itself), or in other words it interacts actively in its setting or beyond it in the world. Thus, behavior is still *activity*, in the first and general sense of the term, Leont'ev's *Tatigkeit*. Third, active behavior involves a simultaneous transformation of the world and of the organism itself; one form of the organism's transformation is the growth in understanding. Hence, the commonplace yet conclusive formula: *Understanding is derived from activity*. And fourth, the task of psychology is to *interpret* forms of active behavior. It is first of all to explain (or understand) the structure of these forms of behavior, how they function, and how they are constructed. The follow-up task is to explain (or understand) the structure, functioning, and ways in which this understanding produced by the behavior is elaborated.

The quasi-ecumenical nature of these propositions is obviously just a facade; some fundamental differences exist with regard to the actual status of behavior, the foundations of activity, the role of understanding, and, as a result, the actual type of interpretive process to be applied to these objects. The key to these divergences revolves around the status given to human activity, and it is this notion that we propose to examine in terms of five general points.

Leont'ev's interpretation of action and activity

For a wide range of theoretical approaches, undoubtedly a majority, human activity is first and foremost an *externalization of the biological characteristics* of an organism. Not just for Piaget, but also for the radical behaviorists, these are functional characteristics. In contrast, in the neonativist approach dominant today structural characteristics are given priority.

Running against these currents is the perspective which argues that the structuring of human activity is of a *sociocultural* nature. It is within the framework of this option that the term "action" may find itself given a first general meaning. We know from the perspective of Leont'ev (1979) that the notion of activity concerns the most general forms of the functional organization of behavior, through which the members of a species gain access to the world. It is possible to differentiate among activities by looking at the motivations of the species to which they are linked (e.g., activities of feeding, reproduction, avoidance of danger). In the case of socially organized species (and in particular in the case of humankind), activity develops through actions; it breaks down functionally into structures or substructures of behavior oriented toward *goals* and underpinned by the group's *usage of rules.* Thus, actions form the *practical social modalities* through which activities are carried out.

In spite of their global relevance, the concepts introduced by Leont'ev remain inadequate since the problem arises as to the conditions of participation by an individual agent in a socially governed action. What relation is there between the aim of a social action and the representation that the agent has of it? Put another way, what psychological status should be given to the intentions, decisions, and "reasons for acting" that an agent has for participating in an action?

Events and human action

To answer the questions outlined in the preceding section, it is fitting to recall the distinction made by Elizabeth Anscombe (1957) in her volume *Intention*. She distinguished between "events produced in nature" and "human actions." The statement "Two tiles fell off the roof due to the effect of the wind" describes an *event* (the falling of the tiles), and this event may be explained. That is to say, one may attribute a cause, in the classical sense proposed by Hume (an antecedent logically independent of the event and capable of being identified separately). The statement "I arranged for two tiles to fall off the roof to damage my neighbor's car" also describes an event that may be interpreted in a causal manner. But since it also describes a human action, it should moreover be analyzed as referring to an *action*, involving an agent (e.g., human organism endowed with the ability to act, or a capacity for action), a *motive* (or reason for acting), and thus a *purpose* (a plan). Consequently, in addition to a causal (or explanatory) analysis of the objective characteristics of the event, the interpretation of the action requires a comprehensive analysis of the relations that exist between these characteristics and the relevant tools in the repertoire of the agent's capacities for action.

Human action and its context

The analytic framework for actions, as opposed to events, outlined earlier is illuminating, but it fails to address the issue of the *social foundations of human activity* that Leont'ev emphasized, and it should be expanded from the perspective proposed by figures such as Max Weber (1971), Paul Ricoeur (1986), and Jurgen Habermas (1987). Ricoeur makes a point of emphasizing that all human activity is social "not only because it is (generally) the work of several agents so that the role of each one of them cannot be distinguished from those of the others, but also because our acts get away from us and have effects which we had not foreseen" (1986, p. 193). Even if, in the first analysis, an action seems to be the result of the intentional intervention of an agent, the action becomes detached from this and develops its own consequences. In reality the action constitutes an "open work" (in the sense proposed by Umberto Eco). That is to say, it constitutes a phenomenon whose meaning hangs in doubt.

For Ricoeur, the attribution of meaning to action is the result of three categories of factors. First, action is a directed system of behaviors producing effects in the world, and it should be analyzed from this point of view. Second, action simultaneously develops within a social framework producing a set of conventions (values, symbols, rules), and its meaning should consequently also be analyzed as a product of this level of social control. And finally, the way in which agents become integrated into a network of social relations leads agents to "sprinkle" their action with singular characteristics, which are traces of what it "offers" of itself to others. This third aspect of action also merits interpretation.

These three forms of interpreting action have been described by Habermas elsewhere under the headings of "teleological acting," "acting in accordance with norms," and "dramaturgical acting." Habermas completes Ricoeur's analysis by focusing more on the types of "worlds" that support forms of acting. In other words, he focuses on the different "systems of formal coordinates" in relation to which these three aspects of action may be placed and evaluated.

Teleological acting brings into play the coordinates of the "objective world" (the physical world). That is to say, this form of acting focuses on the *unaire* entity put forward by Wittgenstein in the *Tractatus*, "the totality of what the case is." This first form of acting may be evaluated on the criterion of truth (Are the agent's understandings and opinions those that agree with "what the case is"?) and on the criterion of effectiveness (Has the goal been attained?).

Acting in accordance with norms deals with the direction given to actions of a group's members by the values (norms, symbols, etc.) that they share. This second form of acting involves the *social world*, which is the framework defining legitimate forms of interpersonal relations and in which the agents take part insofar as they play a role in these rule-governed interactions. The evaluation of social acting is based only on the criterion of appropriateness (whether action conforms to the norms recognized as legitimate).

Finally, dramaturgical acting refers to the fact that "the participants in an interaction form a kind of reciprocal audience for themselves to which each one of them plays" (Habermas, 1987, p. 101). Each agent has privileged access to the intimate sphere of his or her thoughts, wishes, feelings, and so forth and can control the interaction by ruling (or controlling) the access of the audience to his or her own subjectivity. According to Habermas, dramaturgical acting involves a *subjective world*, or a world of the agent's "actual experiences," to which the agent has privileged access. In our view, however, this third world comes largely (or totally) from the internalization of the social world. This third form of acting may be evaluated according to the criterion of sincerity: To what extent may the light that agents shed on themselves through their style of action be considered sincere or truthful?

In postulating these three forms of acting, Habermas is in fact defending a central hypothesis according to which all human action, as it unfolds, exhibits three forms of *claims to validity*. It presupposes a common understanding of an objective world, on the basis of which claims to truth can be assessed; it presupposes the sharing (acceptance) of relevant rules from the social world, through which the claims of appropriateness can be evaluated. And finally, it presupposes the recognition of the subjective world of every agent, through which claims of sincerity can be evaluated. And it is these abstract presuppositions (that is to say, independent of predetermined content) that make up the *context* of human action or meaningful action.

Communicative action, the foundation of meaningful action

The context of an action may thus be defined as being composed of the three worlds put forward by Habermas. But these worlds are formal, they are made up of understandings (of representations), and the latter are necessarily the product of a construction.

According to Piaget's theory, the elaboration of understanding comes primarily from the progressive differentiation of modalities of interaction between the organism and the objective world, then from the abstraction and internalization of the logical properties of this interaction. For Piaget, it is these *bio-logical* structures alone that make possible the construction of an objective world at the same time as a subjective world (moving from the state of initial indifference or egocentrism to a state of decentration) and that then allow for the construction of the social world (later processes of socialization).

For Habermas, on the other hand, the construction of the three worlds comes from the "rationalization" of a subject's "actual world," which is a result of the *communicative action* characteristic of all of human society. The production of meaningful actions in effect requires the establishment of an "understanding" (an agreement) between interactants on what the situation of action (the context) is in the sense defined earlier. And it is communicative action (or *signifying activity*, or, simpler still, *human language*) that constitutes the medium for (and in) which this necessary intercomprehension occurs. Signifying activity thus constitutes the fundamental process that enables the members of a group to establish a minimum level of agreement on the basis of which the event is transformed into a meaningful action.

In animal species, if individuals working together on the realization of a certain task have the capacity for representation, they are conscious of the world that makes up the context, and this consciousness of the situation includes the representation of other actants. The animal is furthermore capable of dealing appropriately with the communicative signals emitted by other interactants. But the communicative episodes of the animal world have a clear "releasing" character; the correspondence between the behavioral signal and the response is direct. It is not the object of any procedure of negotiation (and thus reply), as is borne out by the apparent absence of all dialogue. This implies that the only context prepared by the animal in the framework of its participation in an action is that of its nonnegotiated representations of the world, which comes back to saying that the animal only manages the actions within the framework of its own "actual world."

In the human species, communicative action introduces an intermediate term between the signal (or phonetic production) and the response. This is a socially negotiable (and contestable) proposition relating to the forms of connecting the signal to the world. Viewed another way, communicative action consists of the elaboration of *interpretants* (as understood by Peirce, 1931) or of *values* (as understood by Saussure, 1960) that lie at the heart of every semiotic system. In Vygotskian terms, it is in the construction of these negotiated values that the fusion of the processes of representation and communication occurs, which constitutes the human. In Habermas's terminology, it is in this very social production that the formal coordinates of the objective, social, and subjective worlds are drawn up with respect to internal frameworks in which human *rationalization* may spread.

Characteristics of communicative action

From the preceding discussion, it follows that communicative action (or human language) has first and foremost an *illocutionary function;* it basically consists of action in which validity claims relative to the three worlds are sent out by the interactants. To the extent that the rational worlds are built and permanently transformed by this action, language should be considered as the "author of the world," and this is the first meaning that one can give to the concept of mediation.

But the formal relations that are established between phonetic productions and representations of the world tend to become crystallized over time, and it is these crystallizations that make up *signs*. We are coming back here to Saussure, for whom signs are the formal means of correspondence between phonetic representations and representations of the world. But according to this author's theory, these correspondences are relative to a system, or to a *natural language*. They are dependent on sociocultural context and develop over time. The two faces of the sign (the signifier and the signified, or meaning) are thus no more than momentarily stable, as a result of their fundamentally sociocultural nature. Language activity is thus endowed with a second function, a *locutionary* or declarative nature: Broad layers of represented worlds are found recodified in the particular signs and systems that organize them. The subject internalizes this verbal knowledge, and this itself makes up, as such, a filter for the subject's access to the world. This is the second meaning that may be attributed to the concept of mediation.

As human activities mediated by language develop and change, the language also tends to become channeled into different forms of organization or *discourses*. Discourses are the modalities for structuring language activity through which illocutionary and locutionary aspects are integrated; they "tell" the world while acting within it. Generalizing the Aristotelian notion of mimesis, one can interpret the elaboration of all discursive structure as a step attempting to go beyond the state of disagreement characteristic of the actual (or nonrationalized) world. In other words, it is like an attempt to understand the world by proposing a refiguration or schematization.

For example, narration may put forward a fictional world in which agents, motives, intentions, circumstances, and so forth are "staged" in such a way that they form a concordant structure. The individual events and incidents to which they are linked turn into a meaningful configurational structure or "story." So just as is the case with meaningful action, the discourses formed have the status of open works – works on whose foundation subjects build their understanding of the world. This is the third meaning that one can give to the concept of mediation.

If one accepts the points outlined in the five preceding sections, one should consider that meaningful action is formed in and by speech, a particular activity of the human species that generates the rational worlds that define context. But one should also agree that speech appears in the form of diverse natural languages, which relate to the story and forms of organization of a social group and that the unities (or signs) of this language are fundamentally sociocultural. And finally, we should consider that each natural language occurs in diverse discourses, and these forms of discourse are adapted to, as well as help redirect, situations of action. In other words, discourses give situations of action a meaning. In this sense, individual discourse constitutes the most objective outline of the actual activity and interpretation of human action.

As stated earlier, action is first and foremost the object of the social sciences (e.g., sociology, anthropology, history). If, as proposed at the beginning of this chapter, it is also psychology's primary concern, then the question is, How should we go about taking this step? This question leads us to the second part of the chapter, which concerns the elements of a program for a sociocultural psychology.

Elements of a program of sociocultural psychology

Given its present state of development, psychology should outline two different projects. The first concerns the interpretation of human activity, particularly the way in which agents take part in the signification of action. The second concerns the knowledge that is built and transformed in the action. The first project relates to practical reason, the second to pure reason.

A psychology of practical reason (or of action): some parameters

I begin by noting that all human action also constitutes an event occurring in nature, a sequence of observable behaviors comprised of an initial state, some transformations, and a final state. This can form the object of a first step of interpretation on an explanatory level (the construction of systemic or cybernetic models). This is the path that has been taken by various contemporary research approaches, most notably by Piaget and certain cognitivists. It should nevertheless be understood that the contributions of this first step in interpretation are, by definition, confined to the general characteristics of the architecture of action. This step cannot contribute anything more than some interpretive elements of the teleological aspects of action; they concern the objective world alone. Insofar as the objective world is one world, this kind of cognitive psychology is necessarily universalizing and, as a result, biologizing.

But my interest in meaningful action stems from the fact that it constitutes an intervention in the context of the three rational worlds produced by communicative action. On this level, meaningful action brings an *agent* into play – in other words, a "particular base" that, alone or with other bases, intervenes in releasing the event's initial stage and in partially controlling the transformations and the final stage.

Consequently, from a psychological point of view, the *purpose of action* is that dimension of the action's global meaning that can be attributed to the agent. Depending on the context in which action is incorporated, agents find themselves endowed with multiple forms of *agentivity* about which they are aware. They know that they can act on the objective world; they know that they are in a network of social norms; and they know that they give an impression of themselves in each interaction. Purpose thus constitutes the whole of *proactive representations* connected with the three worlds that agents construct as a result of their agentivity at the moment of intervention. This is evidently the product of a complex dialectic between the representation of the agents themselves and the representation of determinations that make up the formal worlds.

From the same psychological point of view, the *motive* or *reason for acting* is the part of the "causality" of the event-action that can be attributed to the agent. It is made up of the entirety of the *retroactive representations* of the three formal worlds that the agent requests at the moment of intervention. Insofar as a reason for acting (like the purpose) is always "a reason for carrying out a specific, unique action," the relationship between the action and its motive is not registered in the form of the logical independence of an antecedent and consequent that characterizes so-called causality. The motive has a relationship of involvement with the action, which explains why, in the area of cognitive psychology, it can only be understood through the "grasp of consciousness" that Piaget has rightly underscored as being secondary, partial, and ultimately not very informative.

> *A psychology of practical reason (or of action):*
> *what methods?*

How should we go about developing an interpretive approach to these parameters and the role that they exercise on the actual characteristics of action? As we know, psychology is struggling to develop a truly scientific approach in this area. Radical behaviorism puts forward two basic concepts – the history of reinforcements and the contingencies of reinforcement – that could constitute an outline for the study of determinations that intervene in the decisions of every agent. However, the conception of the setting that this approach puts forward is confined to the objective world (to what is observable in physical space-time). Furthermore, the methodology that it has developed does not allow for taking into account the representational nature of the treatment of these determinations.

In contrast, classical phenomenology centers directly on the actual world of agents (preconsciousness and representational consciousness) and advocates a reflexive (or introspective) method by which the subjects, in an inward-looking act, could "regain" in a clear and intelligible manner all the parameters of their intervention in the world. This step of "pure comprehension" leads to some philosophical dead ends, which have been analyzed in detail by Ricoeur (1986). Using a different route,

Piaget (1965) demonstrated its clearly nonscientific nature. Finally, the currents of research grouped together in the cognitivist "haze" shy away from the problem of action, hiding in that of the architecture of human knowledge.

For my part, I am attempting to develop a psychological approach to "human action as practice" within the framework of two different methodological approaches. The first is centered on the analysis of a typical form of meaningful action – *educational action* (but a similar approach could be developed with regard to other types of action such as therapeutic interventions). The second methodological approach is centered on the analysis of *discourses,* insofar as they constitute reconfigurations of human action.

Educational action as meaningful action

Educational action develops on three levels. It has its source in what is called the *educational system* – in other words, in the whole of discourses through which a society expresses its expectations (or aims) in matters related to education. The contents of these discourses concern the objective world as well as the social and subjective worlds and constitute a *prefiguration* of the actions that should be managed so that (ideally, of course) the little person becomes a full member of the society concerned.

This system produces a variety of *teaching systems* – in other words, institutions that differ according to the age of the pupils, their supposed cognitive level, their socioeconomic status, and so on. These institutions have a fixed material organization (e.g., number of pupils per class), and they produce discourses relating to the goals to be reached – the formulation and the programming of the teaching contents – as well as to the methodological steps to be taken. These discourses shape the educative action that is actually carried out within the framework of *didactic systems.* The didactic systems are structures composed of the teacher, the pupils, and the contents that are the object of their transaction.

The work that Bernard Schneuwly (1988) and several other members of our team (e.g., Dolz, Rosat, and Schneuwly, 1991a) are carrying out in this field is centered around the two categories of agents involved in didactic systems: the educator and the pupil. In the case of the former, it is first a question of analyzing the content of the discourses coming from educational systems and then of studying the effects that these discourses have on the teacher. The research of this group centers, on the one hand, on the representations that teachers build through their action, which requires the use of the comprehensive methods developed by the social sciences (controlled interviews, questionnaires, etc.). On the other hand, this research centers on the didactic action itself and involves controlled observation of work practices in class.

The first step sheds light on the construction of purposes and on the teachers' reasons for acting, which derive from the internalization of discourses coming from systems on which they depend. The second step provides access to the actual structure of the educational event, within the multiple constraints of a situation of action. Comparisons of the two types of data make possible an evaluation of how the purposes and motives of the teacher-agent influence the realization of educational action.

With regard to the second category of agent in this process – the pupil – additional studies have been carried out. Having planned with the teachers diverse forms of educational action (taking the form of "didactic sequences"), the issue here is one of analyzing the optimum conditions for reaching the goals established by the teaching systems. I cannot go into this approach in detail here, but it has been examined at some length elsewhere (see esp. Schneuwly, 1988).

The analysis of discourses

The discourse analysis to which we now turn has been presented at length in *Le fonctionnement des discours* (Bronkart, Bain, Schneuwly, Davaud, & Pasquier, 1985), some aspects of which I will now summarize. Our research in this area consists of four major phases.

The first phase has led to the compilation of a vast body of *authentic texts* (oral and written) that were produced in the framework of diverse activities. This collection of texts is accompanied by the most complete body of information possible on the different parameters that make up the *production situation:* the type of social interaction in which the discourse occurs, roles developed by the agent and their receivers, the goal pursued, the space-time of the activity, and so forth. The extra-linguistic parameters of the speech thus collected form the empirical base on which inferences are made relating to the characteristics of the worlds represented, worlds that constitute the context of the verbal production.

The second phase of this research consists of an in-depth study into the characteristics of linguistic units that appear in each text. We applied various techniques of statistical analysis to carry this out. In particular, we focused on the distribution of each unit and its discriminative power (by comparison with texts from other groups). This second phase allows the identification of subgroups of texts characterized by the emergence of relatively specific subsets of units, and on this basis it allows the establishment of a table of sets of units that ideally define a *type of discourse.* This then makes it possible to measure the degree of dependence between the types thus identified and the situations within whose framework they were produced.

The third phase of this research has led to the identification of *values* that make it possible to identify units in the organization of texts and/ or discourses. This central stage of our approach involves creating a model of *language operations,* or of different procedures for treating worlds where linguistic units form the objective tracks. The "base of concepts" that we have put forward in *Le fonctionnement des discours* is organized on three levels (about which I shall not go into detail here).

The fourth phase of our approach concerns the *validation* of the model by returning to the empirical data. Given the present state of our research, this phase, which is basically explanatory in nature, seems rather premature. This is because the conceptual base elaborated to date cannot be considered a formalizable model. In the absence of a global model, the formulation of "local models" is foreseeable, however. These relate to the operations that underpin the functioning of previously delimited subsets of linguistic units. In the case of "units of a temporal character," for example, we are attempting to formulate an exhaustive model of underlying operations (cf. Bronckart, 1990, 1993), and we have undertaken various experimental, comparative, and developmental projects aimed at testing validity (see Dolz, 1990; Dolz, Rosat, & Schneuwly, 1991b).

One of the long-term goals of this project is to distinguish, through the formulation of treatment procedures (or speech operations), between what belongs to the "eventual" status of the discursive action and what belongs to the status of meaningful action. In relation to the nature of an event, the issue is, on the one hand, what constraints bear on the production of all speech or all discourse (that is the only real question that possible "universals of speech" pose). On the other hand, the issue is the constraints imposed by particular lexical and morpho-syntactic organizations that may be found in natural languages. These constraints of speech and language in fact delimit the whole range of possibilities open to agents of verbal productions as they make their decisions, and these decisions are what make up the identifiable operations in relation to the meaningful action. This basically involves, first of all, examining inferences related to the probable variables that constitute the context and referent of a text. And second, on the basis of an internal analysis of operations that support the units of discourse, it involves inferences about the representations that these operations request and effectively transform. Taking these two steps allows us to establish a valid rule for the parameters of meaningful action that the agent carries out and codifies verbally in discourse.

A psychology of pure reason (or of consciousness)

If, as everyone seems to admit, consciousness comes from action and if action presents the characteristics outlined earlier, one may, on a hypothetical and programmatical level, form a schema of the ontogenesis of consciousness organized in four stages.

The first stage concerns the sensorimotor stage defined by Piaget. In this period, the child builds elements of representation of the objective world for which the Piagetian description is still valid. But as Bruner (1987), in particular, has demonstrated, this period is above all characterized by intense social interaction (which Piaget neglected in his explanation of development, even though he did in fact address it in the same work), and it is within the framework of this interaction that other understandings are built, those of *meaning linked to action*, purpose, common attention to a referent, rules of exchange, and so forth.

To describe these *illocutionary competences*, one may, following Bickerton (1981, 1990), invoke a "protospeech" and recognize that because it is an essential part of sensorimotor capacities, it is common to the child and to higher animals. But it should also be recognized that these representations really belong only to the "actual world" (I prefer this term to that of "popular psychology" that Bruner proposes in *Acts of Meaning;* 1990), in the sense that they have not yet become the object of social negotiations that will develop with the emergence of the so-called symbolic function. To explain how, in the human species, this protospeech turns into speech, I do not think it is necessary to invoke some "innate theory of the spirit." I am instead of the opinion that it will be essential to study the modalities through which adult humans, themselves endowed with a rational understanding of contexts of action, guide and orient children during communicative action. And using comparative studies it will be possible to determine the part that sociocultural variables play in this first stage of development.

The second stage in the ontogenesis of consciousness concentrates on the acquisition of signs and their organization – that is to say, the *locutionary* aspects of communicative action. It is through the mastery of these units of recodification of actual representations that the rational representations of contexts of action (in other words, objective, social, and subjective worlds) are elaborated. Vygotsky's developmental hypothesis finds its real meaning here. On the one hand, human rationality is a product of the locutionary function of speech, and on the other hand, insofar as this function only occurs within the framework of particular natural languages, the basis of its rationality is of a sociocultural nature. The initial representations of worlds are constructed by the appropriation of values by a group, since these have been codified in the natural language that the group uses. Having focused too exclusively on the syntactic aspects of the development of language, it seems to me that psychology has neglected the central feature of this stage of language acquisition, a feature concerning an essentially semantic question: How are the actual meanings of a language rebuilt?

The third stage in the ontogenesis of consciousness is characterized by the *internalization* of signs, which provides the ingredients from which "thinking operations" will develop. In this process of constructing so-called understanding, one cannot fail to be struck by the thinness of descriptions put forward by cognitive psychology for the long period in ontogenesis lasting from the emergence of the symbolic function to the construction of concrete operations. So it seems to me reasonable to put forward the hypothesis that during this stage some processes of *abstraction* and *generalization* of meanings in a particular language are at work. These meanings are organized in diverse discursive structures and are dependent on the context. They are processes bordering ultimately on the construction of cognitive concepts of universal validity. Such a hypothesis has two implications: (a) Consciousness is first and foremost sociocultural, and only subsequently and under certain circumstances logical-cognitive; and (b) logical-mathematical operations do not come directly from the logic of the action at work in a sensorimotor stage, but from the logic that underlies human action as well as its recodification in discursive structures.

The fourth stage in the ontogenesis of consciousness is characterized by the *appropriation of discursive structures* themselves. A difficult and long process of appropriation occurs during which humans learn to reshape their action and give a status to the purposes and reasons of others. This carries on well beyond the period of formal operations, as many studies have shown. By carrying out this appropriation, humans come to understand themselves and the role that they play in the actions in which they participate.

References

Anscombe, G. E. M. (1957). *Intention.* London: Basil Blackwell.

Bickerton, D. (1981). *Roots of language.* Ann Arbor, MI: Karoma.

Buckerton, D. (1990). *Language and species.* Chicago: University of Chicago Press.

Bronckart, J-P. (1987). Interactions, discours, significations. *Langue Française, 74,* 29–50.

Bronckart, J-P. (1990). Some determinants of the production of temporal markers. In D. E. Blackman & H. L. Lejeune (Eds.), *Behavior analysis in theory and practice: Contributions and controversies* (pp. 183–198). New York: Basil Blackwell.

Bronckart, J-P. (1992). El discurso como acción: Por un nuevo paradigma psicolinguistico, *Anuario de Pscicologia, 54,* 3–48.

Bronckart, J-P. (1993). Temps et discours: Etudes de psychologie du langage, *Langue Francasie, 93,* 1–128.

Bronckart, J-P., Bain, D., Schneuwly, B., Davaud, C., & Pasquier, A. (1985). *Le fonctionnement des discours: Un modèle psychologique et une méthode d'analyse.* Paris: Delachaux & Niestlé.

Bruner, J. S. (1987). *Comment les enfants apprennent à parler.* Paris: Retz.

Bruner, J. S. (1990). *Acts of meaning.* Cambridge, MA: Harvard University Press.

Dolz, J. (1990). *Catégorie verbale et action langagière: Le fonctionnement des temps du verbe dans les textes écrits des enfants catalans.* Unpublished doctoral thesis, University of Geneva.

Dolz, J., Rosat, M-C., & Schneuwly, B. (1991a). Elaboration et évaluation de deux séquences didactiques relatives à trois types de textes. *Le Française Aujour-d'hui, 93,* 32–59.

Dolz, J., Rosat, M-C., & Schneuwly, B. (1991b). Tense alteration: A textual competence in construction. *European Journal of Psychology of Education, 6,* 175–185.

Eco, U. (1965). *L'oeuvre ouverte.* Paris: Seuil.

Fodor, J. A. (1983). *The modularity of mind.* Cambridge, MA: MIT Press.

Habermas, J. (1987). *Théorie de l'agir communicationnel.* Paris: Fayard.

Leont'ev, A. N. (1979). The problem of activity in psychology. In J. V. Wertsch (Ed.), *The concept of activity in Soviet psychology* (pp. 37–71). Armonk, NY: Sharpe.

Peirce, C. S. (1931). *Collected papers.* Cambridge, MA: Harvard University Press.

Piaget, J. (1936). *La naissance de l'intelligence chez l'enfant.* Neuchatel: Delachaux & Niestlé.

Piaget, J. (1937). *La construction du réel chez l'enfant.* Neuchatel: Delachaux & Niestlé.

Piaget, J. (1946). *La formation du symbole chez l'enfant.* Neuchatel: Delachaux & Niestlé.

Piaget, J. (1965). *Sagesse et illusions de la philosophie.* Paris: PUF.

Piaget, J. (1967). *Biologie et connaissance.* Paris: Gallimard.

Piaget, J. (1970). *Epistémologie des sciences de l'homme.* Paris: Gallimard.

Ricoeur, P. (1983). *Temps et récit,* Vol. 1. Paris: Seuil.

Ricoeur, P. (1986). *Du texte a l'action: Essais d'herméneutique II.* Paris: Seuil.

Saussure, F. de. (1960). Cours de linguistique générale, cinquième édition. Paris: Payot. (1st edition, 1916).

Schneuwly, B. (1988). *Le langage écrit chez l'enfant: La production des textes informatifs et argumentatifs.* Paris: Delachaux & Niestlé.

Skinner, B. F. (1979). *Pour une science du comportement: Le behaviorisme.* Neuchatel: Delachaux & Niestlé.

Vygotsky, L. S. (1934). *Myshchlenie i rech'.* Translated into French by F. Seve, *Le langage et la pensée.* Paris: Édition Sociales, 1985.

Wittgenstein, L. (1961). *Tractatus logico-philosophique.* Paris: Gallimard.

Weber, M. (1971). *Economie et société.* Paris: Plon.

Wertsch, J. V. (Ed.) (1981). *The concept of activity in Soviet psychology.* Armonk, NY: Sharpe.

Wertsch, J. V. (1985). *Vygotsky and the social formation of mind.* Cambridge, MA: Harvard University Press.

von Wright, G. H. (1971). *Explanation and understanding.* London: Routledge & Kegan Paul.

Part II

Mediation in action

4 Writing and the mind

David R. Olson

I take it as fundamental to the cultural psychology envisioned by Vygotsky and others that cultural, historical activities shaped and continue to shape perception, action, and, indeed, consciousness. Some would go so far as to suggest that mind is a cultural artifact, not in the sense that it does not exist, but rather that it exists in the way that laws and debts exist – namely, as cultural inventions used for managing social action and interaction. Others take mind to be real, a kind of mental organ, for which cultures provide various forms of expression. However it is to be ultimately explained, a central preoccupation of a cultural psychology is with the ways that the culture gives shape to mind – to perception, thought, and action.

And I take it as equally fundamental to that cultural psychology that the intellectual development of children be seen, at least in part, as the acquisition of symbolic and representational systems of the culture. Learning a language is the primary means of acquiring the folkways of the culture. Further, learning the various notational systems of the culture – that is, the cultural means of storing and communicating information in a variety of written and ritualized forms – plays a secondary, but nonetheless significant role.

Yet it is an embarrassing fact that despite a half century of research and discussion of these assumptions, we have not yet succeeded in making our case to the world that (a) the cognitive processes and cognitive structures of individuals are transformed in a conspicuous way by the acquisition of a natural language or (b) that the cognitive processes and structures are transformed significantly by the acquisition of our best recognized cultural (and intellectual) tool, namely, writing.

In regard to the first, Whorf's (1956) celebrated claim that we carve up the world along lines laid down by our native language is taken as true by many cultural psychologists in spite of the fact that little or no evidence is available to sustain it (Schlesinger, 1991). In regard to the second, although Vygotsky serves as a founding father for cultural psychology, his view provides more of an orientation than a falsifiable theory about the role of cultural symbols in cognitive functioning. Both Vygotsky (1962, p. 99; 1978, chap. 7) and Luria (1946; cited by Downing, 1987, p. 36) suggested that writing not only allowed one to do new things, but, more importantly, turned speech and language into objects of reflection and analysis. The beginning reader, Luria suggested,

is still not able to make the word and verbal relations an object of his consciousness. In this period a word may be used but not noticed by the child, and it frequently seems like a glass window through which the child looks at the surrounding world without making the word itself an object of his consciousness and without suspecting that it has its own existence, its own structural features. (1946; cited by Downing, 1987, p. 61)

Although this is an extremely important claim and one that I shall pursue, it should be noted that it is not obvious why a secondary activity makes the primary activity conscious – that is, why writing makes speech into an object of consciousness. Speech itself is usually considered to be a "problem space" in its own right (Karmiloff-Smith, 1979). Nor does Vygotsky indicate what particular features of language become such objects of thought, nor whether writing itself is essential or merely useful for this new consciousness. Indeed, Scribner and Cole (1981) concluded that writing had no general effects on cognition. Hence, cultural psychology provides no defense against the more common cynical view "How could writing something down change our mental representation of it?" (Carruthers, 1990). The fact of the matter is that a satisfactory answer to that challenge has not been forthcoming. If mind is in some way a reflection of the culture, it should follow that cultural representations such as writing play a determinable role in the cognitive economy. Yet that role remains largely obscure.

For Piaget, as I understand him, children's mastery of the symbolic world – the world of representations – was not basically different from their mastery of the natural world. Language did not create a representational or symbolic function; rather the representational function that was based on the ability to hold objects in mind in their absence made language learning possible. Similarly, learning to read was seen as an exercise in the use of existing cognitive resources rather than the creation of new resources for thinking. Writing, on this view, is an interesting system or object to be known and children's knowledge of that object has been shown to undergo important reorganization with development (Ferreiro & Teberosky, 1979/1982). Yet from the Piagetian perspective, the acquisition of knowledge of writing was not expected to affect cognition in any more general way.

This is the assumption I wish to challenge. I want to argue that writing adds a new type of structure to the world and in coming to use that structure, that is, in reading and writing, learners learn something that we have by and large overlooked. Of course, they have learned to read and write—that goes without saying. But what the inventors of writing systems learned and what children in learning to read and write them continue to learn, in addition, was something vastly more important. What they had learned, I shall argue, was a model for thinking about speech and language. What follows, then, is an account of how forms of writing could have altered, and indeed continue to alter, cognition and consciousness.

The relation between speech and writing

Making marks that can serve mnemonic and communicative purposes is as old as human culture itself. What such marks may be taken as representing by those who make and those who read them is the critical question. A glimpse at our own alphabetic writing systems suggest that what a writing system "represents" is what is said – an ideal writing system is a fully explicit representation of oral language.

Indeed, this is the classical assumption expressed by Aristotle and seconded in this century by such linguists as Saussure and Bloomfield. Aristotle (b. 384 B.C.) wrote in *De interpretatione* (1.4–6): "Words spoken are symbols or signs of affections or impressions of the soul; written words are the signs of words spoken (1938, p. 115). Bloomfield identified speech with language and saw writing as "a way of recording language" (1933, p. 21). Mattingly (1972) expressed the same view, namely, that writing is "a simple cipher" on speech.

That assumption is pervasive. It underlies both early and recent theories of the evolution of writing systems – from pictorial, to logographic, to syllabic, to alphabetic scripts; it underlies contemporary theories of reading that treat learning to read as a matter of learning how to "sound out" words; and more importantly, it underlies our traditional assumption that writing is of limited cognitive significance, that is, merely a transcription – a mnemonic and communicative convenience.

However, the assumption that writing is transcription of speech suffers from what I take to be a fatal flaw. It assumes what it needs to explain. Historically, it assumes that the inventors of writing systems already knew what they needed to know about language and its structure – that it is composed of words, phonemes, sentences, and the like and that inventing an optimal script was a matter of finding suitable marks for representing that knowledge. Developmentally, it assumes that prereaders already know the structure of their language and that what is required is to learn how that structure is represented by a script. Neither assumption is warranted. Rather, it may be argued that the relation between speech and writing is just the reverse. Rather than writing providing a cipher on speech, writing serves as a model for speech. My central claim is that we come to think about our speech, indeed to hear our speech, in terms of the categories laid down by our scripts. Reversing the assumption about speech and writing will allow us to rethink both the history of writing and the processes of learning to read. In addition it will allow us to see the cognitive and conceptual implications of literacy in a new light. To this project we now turn.

The history of writing

The Aristotelian assumption regarding writing, that it is mere transcription, has been largely responsible for the bold evolutionary theories of writing advanced by such historians of writing as Diringer (1968) and Gelb (1963). These theories tended to regard the history of writing as the series of failed attempts at and faltering steps toward the representation of the elementary constituents of speech, namely, phonemes. That story tended to place the alphabet at the evolutionary pinnacle.

In fact, the evolutionary theory does nicely account for the successive emergence of script types beginning with pictures and ending with the alphabet. Gelb (1963) distinguished four stages in this evolution beginning with picture writing that expressed ideas directly, followed by word-based writing systems, then by sound-based syllabic writing systems including unvocalized syllabaries or consonantal systems, and terminating with the Greek invention of the alphabet. And Diringer (1968) saw in the evolution of the alphabet the "history of mankind." As Havelock (1982, p. 11) put it, "At a stroke the Greeks provided a table of elements of linguistic sound not only manageable because of economy, but for the first time in the history of *homo sapiens,* also accurate." Thus, the achievement is seen as one of a series of successes in representing more fundamental aspects of the linguistic system, ultimately phonemes, to make a system that is both economical (employs a small number of signs) and complete (capable of representing anything that can be said). The history of writing, on this view, is the record of attempts to represent the sound patterns of speech.

As Harris (1986) points out, such descriptions are misleading in that they take a characterization of the current state (or at least a part of that state) as if it were the goal toward which writing was evolving; that is, as if all attempts at writing, always and everywhere, were crude attempts at the transcription of the sound patterns of speech. On the contrary it may be argued, as Harris (1986) and Gaur (1984/1987) have done, that writing systems were created not to represent speech, but to communicate information. The relation to speech is at best indirect and secondary.

The evolutionary story is misleading in two other ways. First, if it is assumed that writing systems represent different levels of structure of language – ideas, words, syllables, phonemes – it follows that writing systems can be classified as to their type. This is the typical portrayal of writing systems and their history (Gelb, 1963; Sampson, 1985). However, if writing systems are communicational systems in their own right that are then taken as models of speech – inadequate models at that – it follows that these classifications are at best rough descriptions and not clearly different types. DeFrancis (1989) has recently made this point, emphasizing the essential oneness of writing systems.

Second, the traditional assumption that the history of writing is the progressive evolution that culminates in the alphabet is misleading in the ethnocentrism implicit in such a view (Coulmas, 1989; DeFrancis, 1989). The limitation of the evolutionary theory is that it leads to an underestimation of the optimality of alternative writing systems, such as the *logographic script* employed in China and the mixed logographic and syllabic script employed in Japan. At the end of World War II, Douglas MacArthur, commander of the Allied forces, was urged by a panel of Western educationists to completely revise the educational system of Japan and abolish "Chinese derived ideograms" if he wanted to help Japan develop technological parity with the West (Gaur, 1994). They needn't have worried. Furthermore, an authority on Chinese science, J. Needham (1954–59, 1969), has concluded that the Chinese script was neither a significant inhibitory factor in the development of modern science in China nor an impediment to scientists in contemporary China.

The view I shall elaborate is that writing systems provide the concepts and categories for thinking about the structure of spoken language, rather than the reverse. Awareness of linguistic structure is a product of a writing system, not a precondition for its development. If true, this will not explain the evolution of writing as the attempt to represent linguistic structures such as sentences, words, or phonemes for the simple reason that prewriters had no such concepts. The explanation for evolutionary changes in the writing systems of the world will have to be found elsewhere.

The hypotheses I shall examine then are, first, that writing systems are developed for mnemonic and communicative purposes, but because they are "read" they provide a model for language and thought. We introspect on language and mind in terms of the categories prescribed by our writing systems. And second, the evolutionary development of scripts, including the alphabet, is the simple consequence of attempting to use a graphic system invented to be "read" in one language, for which it is thereby reasonably suited, to convey messages to be "read" in another language, for which it is not well suited. In each case the development of a functional way of communicating with visible marks was, simultaneously, a discovery of the representable structures of speech. This, I believe, is the sense in which some radical writers have talked about writing being prior to speech (Derrida, 1976; Householder, 1971).

Let us examine these hypotheses in light of the available evidence on the history of writing. It is, of course, impossible to know with certainty what the earliest graphic representations represented. The Neolithic revolution beginning some 10 thousand years ago was marked by the beginning of pottery making, food preparation, and domestic agriculture, as well as the psychological developments involved in the ornamentation and burial of the dead. Those developments were more or less contemporaneous with the beginning of drawing and the use of tallies (Goody, 1987, p. 10; Schmandt-Besserat, 1986, 1987). Our question is how such representational systems developed and how they were "read"; for how they were read will determine how they came to serve as models of speaking. My account is based largely on the analyses provided by Gelb (1963), Diringer (1968), and the more recent writings of Goody (1987), Gaur (1984/1987), Sampson (1985), Schmandt-Besserat (1986), and Harris (1986). My hypothesis linking speech and writing borrows heavily from Harris (1986).

Although both tallies and drawings are graphic representations and may serve similar functions, historically those functions and structures have tended to diverge, drawings remaining iconic and tallies becoming arbitrary and conventional. But attempts to account for or correctly describe that divergence have remained a major theoretical puzzle. It is an anachronism to try to explain the evolution of graphic signs as the attempt to express ideas via *ideographs*, for there is no reason to believe that early writers had any clear notion of ideas prior to the invention of writing either (Havelock, 1982; Snell, 1960).

The earliest writing systems, as well as many contemporary ones, exhibit these diverse properties and functions. Geometric signs were used to indicate ownership in Mesopotamia 4 millennia ago in ways analogous to the trademarks, crests, and cattle brands used to this day; tally sticks were used in ancient China to keep records of debts or other data, and tallies were used in Britain by the Royal Treasury until 1826; knotted cords were used for keeping records in ancient China and elsewhere and reached an extremely high level of complexity in the *quipu* of precolonial Peru; and *emblems* – that is, seals, totem poles, coats of arms, hallmarks, banners, and religious signs – made up a part of graphic codes in ancient times just as they do today (Gaur, 1984/1987, pp. 18–25).

Some of these graphic devices not only symbolized objects or events, but also represented a sequence of events that could be narrated, that is, told rather than just named. Best known is the so-called picture writing of the type developed by the aboriginal peoples of North America. The Ojibwa employed a series of depictions inscribed on birchbark scrolls to represent the rituals of the culture including the creation of the world and of the Ojibwa people. Such scrolls could be interpreted only by the shaman and could be described in quite different ways depending on the narrator's purpose. Similar representational systems were employed in ancient southern Mexico (Smith, 1973; but see also Coe, 1992, for evidence that the Mayan writing system is a syllabary) and are employed to this day by storytellers in India (Gaur, 1984/1987, p. 55) and in Ethiopia (Goody, 1987, p. 9). Such visual graphic systems served as mnemonics by means of which a suitably trained expert could recover important cultural information. To describe the use of such systems as "reading" perhaps stretches the modern meaning of that term unduly; certainly, in such cases no clear distinction is made between *reading a text* and *describing a picture*. Such graphic systems do bring the cultural meanings or interpretations of symbols into memory and consciousness, but they do little to contribute to such notions as language, word, or phoneme. Specifically, while a graphic device would be taken as saying "the same thing" on each occasion of reading, it would not bring such linguistic notions as a "word" or "the same words" into consciousness, for there is nothing in the graphic form that can be taken as a model for such linguistic constituents; a picture of a dog is simultaneously a picture of a domesticated quadruped, a collie, a pet, man's best friend, and so on. There is no one-to-one mapping between linguistic element and visible sign.

We may note that emblematic forms of "writing," such as that involved in the use of visual signs to indicate one's totem or one's tribe, do not create a distinction between the name and the thing; the emblem simultaneously stands for the totem and the name of the totem. Similarly, one may have a concept of a name without having the concept of a word; a word is a linguistic unit, a name is a property of an object. Emblems, like names, represent things not words. Harris has suggested that the failure to distinguish words from names produces a form of emblematic symbolism that may extend to various gods and spirits and

is often bound up in various ways with word magic and practices of name-giving. It reflects, fundamentally, a mentality for which reality is still not clearly divisible into language and non-language, anymore than it is divisible into the physical and the metaphysical, or into the moral and the practical. (1986, pp. 131–132)

Of course, a little of that word magic exists in all of us; if not a crime, it is at least a sin to desecrate a prayer book.

But the puzzle remains as to how such tokens and emblems that represent things ever turn into signs that represent words and consequently how their recognition could ever turn into reading as we know it. Historical evidence may help to provide the needed clue.

One extremely important graphic form from which most Western writing systems may have evolved is the token system developed for accounting purposes in Mesopotamia beginning in the ninth millennium B.C. The system – developed by the ancient Sumerians living in what is now southern Iraq, about the time that hunter-gatherer societies were giving way to an agricultural way of life – consisted of a set of clay tokens of distinctive shapes and markings, used to keep records of sheep, cattle, and other animals, as well as goods such as oil and grain.

About the fourth millennium B.C. roughly at the time of the growth of cities, the variety of tokens increased greatly, presumably because of the increasing number of types of items to be inventoried, and the tokens began to be pierced in such a way that they could be strung together. Shortly thereafter, they were placed in envelopes or *bullae*, which, like the string, could mark off a single transaction. Schmandt-Besserat (1986, 1987) has suggested that the markings on these bullae constitute the first true writing. The connection between the tokens and the writing comes from the fact that the contents of the bullae were indicated on the surface of the bullae itself by impressing the token in the soft clay before baking it. But once the contents are marked on the envelope, there is no need for enclosing the actual tokens. The envelope has become a writing surface, and the shapes of the tokens when inscribed onto the surface become the earliest written texts. The tokens that represented units of goods are the origin of the Sumerian signs representing unit of goods. All of the 18 signs denoting commodities such as grain, animals, and oil that appear on the earliest tablets derive from tokens. But were such tokens taken as representing words or things? Have we here taken the critical step toward what we now consider writing to be? Harris (1986) has argued that the decisive step from tokens to scripts occurs when symbols shift from token-iterative to emblem-slotting systems, or what I prefer to think of as acquiring a syntax. A system that represents three sheep by three symbols for a sheep (i.e., sheep, sheep, sheep) is categorically different, he suggests, from one that represents the same three sheep by two tokens, one representing sheep, the other the number. Just as syntax is what makes a language a language, it is the syntax that makes a graphic system "generative," for it permits the combination and recombination of symbols to express a broad range of meanings.

An example of such a script is that from Ur, dated some 2900 B.C. and now filed as 10496 in the British Museum, which inventories the contents of a storehouse. The tablet is squared off into cells each of which lists a product and an amount. The symbol for a jar resting on a pointed base stands for beer, while the round impressions stand for quantities. Quantity is represented by two shapes, one produced by the end of a round stylus, perhaps representing 10, and the other produced by the edge of the stylus, perhaps representing units. Although much uncertainty surrounds just what various marks indicate, the cell in question could presumably be read as "23 vats of beer." Thus, this elementary script has a syntax and could be taken as a precise model for an oral utterance.

But there is no reason for believing that such graphic signs yet represented a particular word or words in a natural language. The tablet described could be read out in any language much as the Arabic numeral 4 can be read out as "four" or "quatre."

It is not essential to claim, as do most theorists, that syntactical scripts now represent speech; it is equally true that such a script *is* now a language. That is to say, we need not assume that these early writers were conscious of or had a model of language as consisting of words ordered by a syntax that they tried to get their script to represent. Rather we can explain the relation between language and script by saying that a script with a syntax provides, for the first time, a suitable model for speech.

Two developments suggest that syntactic scripts were then taken as a model for speech. The first is that the signs now come to be seen as representing words rather than things. Paleographers (Gaur, 1984/ 1987; Nissen, 1986) note that by the third millennium (2900 B.C.), the earliest literary texts written in cuneiform appeared, and such scripts clearly indicated the linguistic knowledge of the writer. That is, the script allows the reader to infer the language of the writer; early tablets, as we have seen, do not. But what, exactly, is involved in this achievement?

The first is the introduction of word signs. The sign for *beer* in the cuneiform tablet mentioned earlier represents beer not the word "beer." Nor does the sign for a bee necessarily represent the word "bee"; it may just represent the object, a bee. But if the sign is now appropriated to represent the verb "be," the sign has become a word sign, a *logograph*. The principle involved in this case is that of the *rebus*, the use of a sign that normally represents one thing to represent a linguistic entity that sounds the same; this entity is a word. What must be emphasized is that the rebus principle does not merely play upon preexisting word knowledge; the substitution of the signs on the basis of their sound is what brings words into consciousness. A script that can be taken as representing both syntax and the words combined by the syntax produces a canonical writing system, one that is capable in principle of representing everything that can be said.

Such scripts provide a model for a language that may now be seen as independent of the things the language is about. But a new understanding of language as consisting of words also has conceptual implications. It spells the death of "word" magic or, more precisely, "name" magic. Words are no longer emblems; they are now distinguished from both things and from names of things; words as linguistic entities come into consciousness. It becomes feasible to think of the meanings of words independently of the things they designate simply because the written form provides a model, the concept, or categories for thinking about the constituents of spoken form. To elaborate, when the word is thought of as representing a thing rather than as an intrinsic property of the thing, word magic loses its power. An action on the name, as in a hex, does not affect the named because the word, unlike the name, is not a part of the thing; it is, as we say, just a word.

Such a writing system, independent of whether it was an alphabet, could have been instrumental in assisting the ancient Greeks bring a new and important set of concepts into consciousness. Havelock (1982) and Snell (1960) noted that notions like idea, mind, and word first developed and became the subject of analysis and reflection in classical Greek culture. Whereas for the Homeric Greeks notions like justice and courage were exemplified in the deeds of gods and heroes, for the literate Greeks they became philosophical concepts. The writing system, Havelock argued, was partly responsible. My suggestion is that the graphic system may play such a role by providing a model for language in a way that emblematic symbols never could. Rather than attempting to capture the existing knowledge of syntax, writing provided a model for speech, thereby making the language available for analysis into syntactic constituents, the primary ones being words, which then became subjects of philosophical reflection as well as objects of definition. Words became things.

Once a writing system has a syntax, the emblems or tokens can now be seen as words rather than emblems, and the construction can be seen as a sentence rather than a list. The structures present in the *script* now provide some of the categories needed for introspecting on the implicit structures of language. Such scripts are logographic in that the tokens now represent the major grammatic constituents of the language, namely, words. But, to repeat, it does not follow that the inventors of such a script already knew about words and then sought to represent them in the script. The opposite may be true. The scribal inventions dictated a kind of reading that *allowed language to be seen as composed of words related by means of a syntax.* Writing thereby provides the model for the production of speech (in reading) and for the introspective awareness of speech as composed of grammatic constituents, namely, words.

The possibility that graphic systems with a syntax can be read as expressions in a natural language is what makes the written form a model for the spoken. Of course, graphic schemes can always be verbalized or discussed; but only when it becomes possible to differentiate the activity of describing what a picture shows from reading what a text says can the graphic structure be seen as a model for the syntactic properties of language.

Not all graphic features need be verbalized, and not all verbalized differences need appear in the script. The decisive factor in the elaboration of the script will not be the verbal models (for as we have noted, such models are not available prior to writing), but rather the attempt at a functional, unambiguous representation (Gaur, 1984/1987; Harris, 1986). In English script, a word beginning with a capital letter is not read any differently than one beginning with a lowercase letter; the convention facilitates interpretation not pronunciation; it does not follow a verbal model. Conversely, English script does not employ different graphic signs for long and short vowels; both long and short /a/ are written "a." Hence, a script is not initially or primarily an attempt at a complete linguistic representation.

A further indication that writing, rather than being an attempt to represent speech, provides a model for that speech, comes from the work of Larsen (1989), who pointed out that Sumerian texts fail to represent many morphological elements, and the script offered information that could not be lexicalized. There was no attempt to record verbal statements but rather to fill administrative needs. When literary texts were written, beginning about 2600 B.C., they were written in that "administrative script" and were, therefore, not complete renderings of a text but rather "an aid for someone who was to give an oral performance" (p. 130).

Is every script with a syntax a writing system? In terms of the history of writing it seems necessary to conclude that when signs acquired a syntax, they were writing systems. On that basis we would say that the set of signs for Arabic numerals and operators is a writing system. But is it a logographic script as usually claimed? Not really, for as mentioned, the signs do not represent words in any particular language. Such a script can be verbalized in more than one way: $3 \times 4 = 12$ can be read as three fours make twelve and so on, and they can be lexicalized in any oral language. The way out of our dilemma is to recall that scripts are not primarily attempts to represent "what is said," but to represent events, and some of those representations can be taken as a model of speech. Numerical notations provide one kind of model, logographic scripts another, and so on.

To conclude this discussion, we may say that the evidence examined here tends to sustain our first hypothesis – namely, that writing, far from transcribing speech, tends to provide a model for that speech. To invent a writing system is, in part, to discover something about speech; the history of writing is essentially the theoretical modeling of verbal form. The script provides the model, however distorted, of one's speech.

The history of the alphabet

Next, let us turn to the hypothesis regarding the historical changes in scripts that led eventually to the alphabet. General purpose logographic scripts can represent anything that can be said. But the device of one token for each expressible semantic difference (essentially one sign for one word or morpheme) requires an extremely large set of tokens. Indeed, modern dictionaries of Chinese, the best exemplar of a so-called logographic script (but see Unger & deFrancis, 1994, for a critique of this classification) lists some 50,000 characters. Three principles of character or graphic formation appear to have been involved. First, ease of recognition is increased by employing iconic representations of objects – the sun being represented by a circle or waves by a wavy line. Second, economy is improved by borrowing the sign for an object to represent another word or part of a word with a similar sound, the so-called acrophonic or phonographic principle employed in the rebus. Third, ambiguity is decreased by distinguishing homophones (words that sound the same but mean different things) by an unverbalized *determinative* that indicates the semantic class to which the word belongs. A logographic script such as Chinese, while cumbersome to Western eyes, is no longer thought of as primitive or limited, as it was even two decades ago (Unger & deFrancis, 1994). Why then did some logographic scripts give way to the syllabaries and alphabets? Before we attempt to answer that question, it is worth noting the clear shift in that direction in the evolution of scripts.

The ancient Sumerian script remained primarily logographic and rarely resorted to phonographic, that is, sound-based, signs. When adopted by the Akkadians in the third millennium B.C. to represent a somewhat different language, the phonographic properties of the script were greatly expanded, giving rise to the Babylonian and Canaanite cuneiform, the best known of such scripts.

Egyptian hieroglyphic script, which developed around 3100 B.C., employed a system similar to that of cuneiform, although there is no evidence that the script was borrowed from the Babylonians. Simple signs were logographs, the drawing of a leg representing the word "leg," two legs meaning "to go," and so on. Complex signs were made by combining simple signs, each of which represented a sound drawn from a simple sign, along with an indicator specifying the domain to which the word belonged. Thus, the sign for "sun" may be borrowed to represent "son" on the basis of their similar sound, the latter being turned into a complex sign by the addition of an indicator sign or determinative, say, that of a man (Gaur, 1984/1987, p. 63).

The Egyptian hieroglyphic inscriptions on the Rosetta stone that allowed the decipherment of the hieroglyphic code early in the nineteenth century provide a clear illustration of how such a script works. Many of the signs were found to represent semantic values such as the cartouche or oval around such royal names as Ptolemy and Cleopatra. Other signs represent sound values corresponding to syllables and to the letters of an alphabet. The first sign in the name Ptolemy is identical to the fifth sign in the name Cleopatra and must, therefore, represent a sound similar to that represented by our letter "p." The bird sign in the sixth and ninth positions in Cleopatra represent the sound similar to that represented by our letter "a." The two symbols after the final bird sign are "determinatives" indicating that this is a feminine name.

Subsequent developments that gave rise, eventually, to the alphabet may be traced in large part to the consequences of borrowing. A shift in what a script "represents" is a consequence of adapting a script to a language other than that for which it was originally developed, an activity that led logographs to be taken as representations of syllables and later for syllables to be taken as representations of phonemes. Let us explore this hypothesis in detail.

The first syllabary was the result of using Sumerian logographs to represent a Semitic language, Akkadian (Larsen, 1989, p. 131). To represent an Akkadian word such as *a-wi-lu-um*, 'man,' with Sumerian logographs, the Akkadians simply took the Sumerian graphs that could be read as *a, wi, lu,* and *um,* ignoring the fact that in Sumerian each graph represented a separate word: *a* would mean 'water,' *wi* would mean something else, and so on. Reading Akkadian would then be a matter of pronouncing this series, and the graphs would now be taken to represent syllables of Akkadian rather than words, as they had done in Sumerian. Logographs had become syllabics. Note that the argument is not that this use was the product of the application of the acrophonic principle of using signs to represent syllables, but rather that the new use of old graphs for a new language produced a script in which the constituents *could be seen* as representing syllables. The syllable is as much a product of the graphic system as a prerequisite for it. To state this point as neutrally as I can, for it remains an open question, the old script is fitted to the new language as a model is fitted to data; the data are then seen in terms of that model. In this case, the model is that of audible constituents, and the flow of speech is heard, perhaps for the first time, as a string of separable, itemizable syllables.

The first writing system based exclusively on such principles was Linear B, a Mycenaean Greek script developed around 1600 B.C. and deciphered only in modern times by an English architect, Michael Ventris, in 1952. The script is strictly syllabic, each syllable employing a distinctive graph. The script was apparently abandoned because the Greek language has complex syllable structures (e.g., C–V–C) in addition to those simple syllables (C–V) represented by the script; consequently, the script is thought to have been seriously deficient, that is, it allowed an unacceptable level of ambiguity.

The immediate ancestor of the Greek alphabet has been viewed by some as a simplified form of syllabary (Havelock, 1982) and by others as an abstraction from a syllabary (Gelb, 1963). The script was invented by speakers of some Semitic language, possibly Phoenician, who lived in the northern part of the Fertile Crescent, that area of arable land connecting Babylonian and Egyptian civilizations. Modern versions of Semitic script include the Hebrew script and the Arabic script.

Semitic languages, however, have the interesting property of carrying the lexical identities of the language in what we think of as consonants; what we think of as vowels were used only for inflections. To illustrate, the string of sounds /k/, /t/, /b/ vocalized in somewhat different ways all convey the basic lexeme "write" with vocalic differences marking grammatical subject, tense, and aspect: *katab* 'he wrote,' *katabi* 'I wrote,' *katebu* 'they wrote,' *ketob* 'write,' *koteb* 'writing,' *katub* 'being written.' All can be written simply *ktb*.

Because the vowels provide only grammatical rather than lexical or morphemic information, some Semitic writing systems never developed any device for representing them. This is not necessarily a flaw in the script, because inserting vowels would make morpheme and word identification more difficult. Obviously, some semantic distinctions are not marked in the script and must be inferred from context. Some scripts, such as Hebrew, add *matres lectionis*, literally, mothers of reading, a pointing system to distinguish vocalic sounds, especially for sacred texts in which proper articulation is important as well as in books written to be read by children. Whether such additions in fact facilitate reading remains an open question.

The major achievement of such scripts, from an evolutionary perspective, is the representation of a group of syllables such as the English "pa," "pe," "pi," "po," "pu," by a single graphic sign, say, "p." If the discovery of the common property of such different syllables is the product of abstraction, it is a remarkable intellectual achievement; that, in fact, is the traditional view. But if it is simply the failure to discriminate them – treating the vocalic variants as of little or no significance and hence disregarding them – then it is the simple product of borrowing, that is, of applying a script devised for a language for which it was important to mark vocalic differences (different vowels make different syllables) to a language for which it was not important to mark such differences. In fact, both Gelb (1963) and Havelock (1982) deny that such a script represents consonants; rather, they claim, it constitutes an unvocalized syllabary, one that simply does not distinguish vocalic differences. Others such as Sampson (1985) refer to it as a consonantal writing system. In my view, the script is a simplification, a discarding of characters thought to be redundant just as "going to" gets attenuated to "gonna" to form "I'm gonna go home" in vernacular speech. But once so attenuated, the graphic system *can be seen as* a representation of consonants, particularly when, as we shall see, it was borrowed by the Greeks to represent yet another quite different language.

Regardless of how it was arrived at, the Phoenician's new set of 22 graphic signs with a memorized order beginning *aleph, bet, gemel* was adequate for representing a full range of meanings, and the graphs can be seen as representing not only syllables but the consonantal sounds of the language.

The "final" transition from consonantal to *alphabetic* writing occurred, uniquely in history, when the Semitic script was adapted to a non-Semitic language, Greek. The application, bypassing Linear B, occurred about 750 B.C. Scholars have traditionally considered the Greek invention to be the stroke of genius. While not minimizing the significance of the Greek achievement, it is now recognized that the development of the alphabet, like that of the syllabary, was a rather straightforward consequence of applying a script that was suitable for one language to a second language for which it was not designed, namely, of applying a script for a Semitic language in which vocalic differences were relatively insignificant to the Greek language in which they were highly significant (Harris, 1986; Sampson, 1985).

Many of the syllable signs from the Semitic alphabet fitted and could be utilized directly for representing Greek; these came to be the consonants. But unlike a Semitic language, Greek, like English, is an Indo-European language in which vowel differences make lexical contrasts – "bad" is different from "bed." Moreover, words may consist simply of vowels, words may begin with vowels, and words with pairs of vowels are not uncommon. To fill the gap, six Semitic characters that represented sounds unknown in Greek, were borrowed to represent these isolated vowel sounds. But equipped with such signs representing vowel sounds, the Greeks were in a position to "hear," perhaps for the first time, that those sounds also occurred within the syllables represented by the Semitic consonant signs. In this way syllables were dissolved into consonant–vowel pairings and the alphabet was born.

Again, the point to note is that such a theory does not require the assumption that the Greeks attempted to represent phonemes; it does not assume the availability to consciousness of the phonological structure of language. Rather, the script can be seen as a model for that structure. That is, phonological categories such as consonants and vowels need not exist in consciousness to be captured by writing. Rather, writing provides a model for speech; all that is required is that speech be seen – more precisely, heard – in terms of that model.

Such a roundabout explanation of the relation between script and awareness of language is required, as well, to explain the fact, first pointed out by Harris (1986), that the Greeks, the inventors of the alphabet, never developed an adequate theory of phonology. The sound patterns they described were a direct reflection of the Greek alphabet; "Consequently, the Greeks were led to ignore phonetic differences which were not reflected in Greek orthography" (p. 86). In this the Greek linguists were not different from children who are exposed to the alphabet, as we shall see in the examination of children learning to read. Ehri (1985) has shown that children think there are more "sounds" in the word "pitch" than in the word "rich," even if phonologists inform us that they are equivalent. Obviously, children, like the classical Greeks, introspect their language in terms of their alphabet.

Learning to read

While no one these days literally believes that ontogeny recapitulates phylogeny, the difficulties children have in learning to read indicate quite clearly that learning to read is not so much a matter of seeing how speech (what they know) is represented in writing (what they don't know) but of coming to hear their speech in terms of the forms and categories offered by the script. Thus, their problem is identical to that we have discussed in the history of writing. When prereading children "read" logos such as "Coke" or take the inescapable golden arches as "McDonald's," it is unlikely that they take the emblem as a representation of a word rather than as an emblem of the thing. Consequently, there is no reason to suppose that recognizing such logos contributes to children's understanding of what a word is or to their reading skills more generally (Masonheimer, Drum, & Ehri, 1984). Note, too, that this is not a claim about understanding the arbitrariness of names, an understanding that has been examined in children by Sinclair (1978) and Berthoud-Papandropoulou (1978). Rather, the distinction attributable to literacy, I propose, is that between names and words.

In learning to read and write, children learn to make just such a distinction. If nonreading preschool children are given a pencil and asked to write "cat," they may write a short string of letter-like forms. If then asked to write "three cats," they repeat the same initial string three times (Ferreiro, 1985). Conversely, if such prereading children are shown a text that reads "Three little pigs" and the text is then read to them while the words are pointed out, they tend to take each of the words as a representation, an emblem, of a pig. Consequently, if the final word is erased and children are asked, "Now what does it say?" they may reply, "Two little pigs." Alternatively, if each of the three words is pointed to in turn and children are asked what each says, they reply, "One little pig; another little pig; and another little pig" (Serra, 1992). That is, signs are seen as emblems rather than as words by prereading children (Berthoud-Papandropoulou, 1978; Ferreiro, 1985,

1991; Ferreiro & Teberosky, 1979/1982). Furthermore, children's first concept of word is a unit of print rather than a unit of speech (Francis, 1987; Reid, 1966).

Not only do children have to learn that language consists of an "item-izable" set of constituents called "words," but they must also learn to hear speech as composed of submorphemic constituents, namely, sylla-bles and phonemes. Consider, first, children's recognition of syllables. Sensitivity to some syllabic constituents, especially those relevant to rhyme and alliteration, preexist literacy. On the basis of their compre-hensive review, Goswami and Bryant (1990) concluded that although young children are not aware of phonemes, they are sensitive to the ini-tial and final sounds of words and phrases, what they refer to as "onsets" and "rimes," and this sensitivity may be relevant to early word recogni-tion (see also Treiman, 1991). Consequently, early readers may take even alphabetic signs as if they are representations of syllables and read them as such.

Second, syllabic scripts are easily acquired. Scribner and Cole (1981) noted that the Vai learned to read their syllabaries in a matter of weeks, and Berry and Bennett (1994) noted that Cree syllabics could be ac-quired in a few days. McCarthy (1994) noted that the whole Cree nation became literate in a mere 10-year span in the 1840s. She goes on to suggest that the ease with which such learning takes place sug-gests that not much has in fact been learned about the structure of language in this case; the mapping from script to syllable is relatively straightforward.

But it does not follow that awareness of language as a string of syllables is completely independent of knowledge of a script. Scribner and Cole (1981) found that Vai literates, familiar with a syllabic script, were much more skilled in integrating separate syllables into phrases and decomposing phrases into such syllables than were nonliterates. This suggests that the learning of a syllabary is a matter of coming to hear one's continuous speech *as if* it were composed of segmentable constituents. Yet it is a surprisingly easy task for even quite young children (Fox & Routh, 1975; Karpova, 1977).

The same process of discovery is involved in an even more conspic-uous way in children's learning of subsyllable constituents, phonemes; a useful diagnostic for children with reading difficulties is the ability to delete consonants from a spoken word. Given /fish/ and asked to delete /f/, such children have enormous difficulty in producing /ish/. It is tempting to infer that this is a developmental effect – involving undue complexity – rather than a consequence of literacy. Not so. That the alphabet serves as a model for speech, rather than as a representation of preexisting knowledge, is shown by the elegant studies on phonological awareness in adult speakers who are not readers. The studies of segmental or phonological awareness, in particular those conducted with nonliterate adults, have established that familiarity with an alphabetic writing system is critical to one's awareness of the segmental structure of language. People who are exposed to the alphabet *hear* words as composed of the sounds represented by the letters of the alphabet; those not so exposed do not. Morais, Bertelson, Cary, and Alegria (1986) and Morais, Alegria, and Content (1987) found that Portuguese fishermen who lived in a remote area and had received even minimal reading instruction some 40 years earlier (though had done little or no reading since) were still able to carry out such segmentation tasks, while those who had never been to school could not. Similar findings have been reported for Brazilian nonliterate adults by Bertelson, de Gelder, Tfouni, and Morais (1989). Scholes and Willis (1991) found that nonreaders in rural parts of the American Southeast had grave difficulties with a large variety of such metalinguistic tasks. Even more impressive is the finding by Read, Zhang, Nie, and Ding (1986), who found that Chinese readers of traditional character scripts could not detect phonemic segments, whereas those who could read Pinyin, an alphabetic script representing the same language, could do so. To learn to read any script is to find or detect aspects of one's own implicit linguistic structure that can map onto or be represented by that script.

The discovery of levels of structure – words, syllables, phonemes – in learning to read is nicely exploited in Frith's (1985) three-stage model. Frith suggests that early readers treat an alphabet as if it were a logograph, each letter string as a whole representing a word. As they begin to attempt to spell words, they decompose those logographs into alphabetic constituents, each representing a phoneme. At a third stage they begin to see relations between letters and therefore detect morphemes, seeing the "boy" in "cowboy," for example.

I have been suggesting that the invention of a writing system does two things at once. It provides a graphic means of communication, but, because it is then verbalized (i.e., read), it comes to be seen as a model of that verbalization. As scripts became more elaborate, they provided increasingly precise models of speech, of "what was said." Thus, cultures developed a more precise criterion for deciding whether two utterances were "the same words." There is considerable evidence that members of traditional cultures treat alternative expressions of the same meaning as being the same words; members of literate cultures tend to use the stricter criterion of verbatim repetition (Finnegan, 1977; Goody, 1987).

This shift in criterion in judging the same words can also be seen in children as they become more literate (Hedelin & Hjelmquist, 1988). In our recent work on children's understanding of the fixity of text (Torrance, Lee, & Olson, 1992), we examined the ability of children ranging in age from 3 to 10 years to distinguish between verbatim repetitions and paraphrases of an utterance. A series of stories were presented in which a puppet was to produce either an exact repetition of what a character in a story had said or a paraphrase of what the person in the story wanted. Needless to say, the experimenter "spoke" for the puppet, while the children judged the adequacy of the response. Whereas they could readily reject incorrect paraphrases, children under 6 years found it impossible to reject a paraphrase when they were asked to accept only "exactly what was said." We inferred that they could not systematically distinguish between a verbatim repetition and a paraphrase of that utterance. This is just what one would expect on the basis of the theory that writing is an important factor in "fixing a text." Indeed, if the analysis I have proposed is correct, these distinctions are products of learning certain graphic conventions.

The relation between a script and one's model of speech is relevant to current discussions of dyslexia and learning to read; those who assume that reading is decoding assume, erroneously, that the phonology is available to consciousness; those who assume that reading is meaning detection assume, erroneously, that sound–symbol mapping is either irrelevant or impossible. The way between these extremes is to note that scripts provide a model for speech; learning to read is precisely learning that model. Ironically, learning to read is largely a matter of learning to hear speech in a new way.

Cognitive implications of reading

The argument to this point is that writing affects consciousness and cognition through providing a model for speech – a theory for thinking about what is said. It is this new consciousness of language that is central to the conceptual implications of writing. Once a script is taken as a model for speech, it becomes possible to increase the mapping between the two, to allow a relatively close transcription of speech. As scripts became more elaborate, their lexicalization or "reading" becomes more constrained. In fact, no script ever succeeds in completely determining the reading – any actor can read a simple statement in many different ways. The script merely determines which variants will be treated as equivalent, as "the same words." It seems clear that any phonographically based text, whether syllabary or alphabet, determines in large measure the lexical and grammatic properties of a reading. It is less certain for a logographic script such as Chinese, which is designed to be read in quite different dialects and may, I am told, allow some variability in lexical and grammatic rendering even within a single community of readers.

How scripts control the reading is nicely illustrated by Boorman (1986) in his discussion of the history of musical scores. In the sixteenth century, composers began to add notations to their scores to restrict performers' autonomy in realizing a musical composition. As a consequence the language of music became more complex. The trend was part of a general reaction against the ambiguity of scribal and early printed forms. Thus, parallel developments occurred in the development of conventions for the punctuation of texts in the same period (Morrison, 1987).

Once a script is taken as a model for the formal properties of language, the formation of explicit analysis of those properties by means of logics, grammars, and dictionaries becomes possible (Goody, 1987). Alphabetic scripts are also taken, somewhat mistakenly, as models of phonology (Harris, 1986). In all cases, the script becomes a useful model for the language, turning some structural aspects of speech into objects of reflection, planning, and analysis.

But the fact that alphabetic scripts can be lexicalized in only one way creates a blind spot that we have only recently come to recognize. Because an alphabetic script can transcribe anything that can be said, it is tempting to take it as a complete representation of a speaker's utterance. Just as the readers of a logographic script or a syllabic script may be unaware of what their script does not represent – namely, the phonological properties of their language – so we, alphabetics, may be unaware of what our writing system does not explicitly represent. In fact, our writing system also represents only part of the meaning; it is a simple illusion that it is a full model of what is said. An utterance spoken with an ironic tone is represented in writing the same way as the same utterance spoken with a serious tone. Again, a skilled actor can read the same text in many different ways. So the graphic form does not completely determine the reading.

The blind spot that our alphabetic script continues to impart leads us into two kinds of errors. First, it invites the inference that any meaning we personally see in a text is actually there and is completely determined by the wording – the problem of literalism. Conversely, any other "reading" of that text is seen as the product of ignorance or "hardness of heart." How to cope with this interpretive problem attracted the best minds of Europe for a millennium, giving rise ultimately to the new way of reading we associate with the Reformation. Second, it leads literate people to an oversimplified notion of what "to read" means. Does "read" mean to lexicalize or "decode" a text, or does it mean to construct a meaning? Is it decoding or interpretation? Battles over the verb "read" are usually nonproductive; what is critical is understanding what a script represents and what it fails to represent.

So what aspects of speech are not represented in a writing system? This, too, has many classical answers. Plato thought that writing represented the words, but not the author. Rousseau (1754–91/1966) thought it represented the words, but not the voice. Some say that it represents the form, but not the meaning. I suggest that while writing provides a reasonable model for what the speaker said, it does not provide much of a model for what the speaker meant by it or, more precisely, how the speaker or writer intended the utterance to be taken. It does not well represent what is technically known as illocutionary force. Writing systems, by representing the former, have left us more or less blind to the latter.

I have tried to establish four points. First, writing is not the transcription of speech, but rather provides a conceptual model for that speech. It is for this reason that typologies of scripts – as logographic, syllabic, and alphabetic – are at best rough descriptions rather than types; there never was an attempt to represent such structural features of language. Second, the history of scripts is not, contrary to the common view, the history of failed attempts and partial successes toward the invention of the alphabet, but rather the by-product of attempts to use a script for a language for which it is ill suited. Third, the models of language provided by our scripts are both what is acquired in the process of learning to read and write and what is employed in thinking about language; writing is in principle metalinguistics (Olson, 1991). Thus, our intellectual debt to our scripts for those aspects of linguistic structure for which they provide a model, and about which they permit us to think, is enormous. And finally, the models provided by our script tend to blind us toward other features of language that are equally important to human communication.

Writing systems, then, do represent speech, but not in the way that is conventionally held. Far from transcribing speech, writing systems create the categories in terms of which we become conscious of speech. We arrive at Vygotsky's conclusion about the opacity of writing, but via a quite different route. To paraphrase Whorf (1956), we introspect our language along lines laid down by our scripts. It is the introspectibility of speech that contributes to a new understanding of mind.

References

Aristotle. (1938). *De interpretatione* (H. P. Cook, Trans.). London: Loeb Classical Library.

Berry, J. W., & Bennett, J. A. (1994). Syllabic literacy and cognitive performance among the Cree and Ojibwe people of northern Canada. In I. Taylor & D. R. Olson (Eds.), *Scripts and literacy: Reading and learning to read alphabets, syllabaries, and characters* (pp. 341–357). Dordrecht: Kluwer.

Bertelson, P., de Gelder, B., Tfouni, L. V., & Morais, J. (1989). The metaphonological abilities of adult illiterates: New evidence of heterogeneity. *European Journal of Cognitive Psychology, 1,* 239–250.

Berthoud-Papandropoulou, I. (1978). An experimental study of children's ideas about language. In A. Sinclair, J. Jarvella, & W. Levelt (Eds.), *The child's conception of language* (pp. 55–64). New York: Springer-Verlag.

Bloomfield, L. (1933). *Language.* New York: Holt, Rinehart, & Winston.

Boorman, S. (1986). Early music printing: Working for a specialized market. In G. Tyson & S. Wagonheim (Eds.), *Print and culture in the Renaissance: Essays on the advent of printing in Europe* (pp. 222–245). Newark: University of Delaware Press.

Carruthers, M. J. (1990). *The book of memory: A study of memory in medieval culture.* Cambridge University Press.

Coe, J. D. (1992). *Breaking the Maya code.* New York: Thames & Hudson.

Coulmas, F. (1989). *The writing systems of the world.* Oxford: Blackwell.

DeFrancis, J. (1989). *Visible speech: The diverse oneness of writing systems.* Honolulu: University of Hawaii Press.

Derrida, J. (1976). *Of grammatology* (G. Spivak, Trans.). Baltimore, MD: Johns Hopkins University Press.

Diringer, D. (1968). *The alphabet: A key to the history of mankind* (3rd ed.). New York: Funk & Wagnalls.

Downing, J. (1987). Comparative perspectives on world literacy. In D. Wagner (Ed.), *The future of literacy in a changing world* (pp. 25–47). Oxford: Pergamon Press.

Ehri, L. C. (1985). Effects of printed language acquisition on speech. In D. R. Olson, N. Torrance, & A. Hildyard (Eds.), *Literacy, language, and learning: The nature and consequences of reading and writing* (pp. 333–367). Cambridge University Press.

Ferreiro, E. (1985). Literacy development: A psychogenetic perspective. In D. R. Olson, N. Torrance, & A. Hildyard (Eds.), *Literacy, language, and learning: The nature and consequences of reading and writing* (pp. 217–228). Cambridge University Press.

Ferreiro, E. (1991). Psychological and epistemological problems on written representation of language. In M. Carretero, M. Pope, R-J. Simons, & J. Pozo (Eds.), *Learning and instruction: European research in an international context* (Vol. 3, pp. 157–173). Oxford: Pergamon Press.

Ferreiro, E., & Teberosky, A. (1982). *Literacy before schooling (Los sistemas de escritura en el desarrollo del niño).* Exeter, NH: Heinemann (English translation)/Mexico DF: Siglo Veintiuno Editors. (Original work published 1979)

Finnegan, R. (1977). *Oral poetry: Its nature, significance, and social context.* Cambridge University Press.

Fox, B., & Routh, D. (1975). Analyzing spoken language into words, syllables, and phonemes: A developmental study. *Journal of Psycholinguistic Research, 4,* 331–342.

Francis, H. (1987). Cognitive implications of learning to read. *Interchange, 18*(1–2), 97–108.

Frith, U. (1985). Beneath the surface of developmental dyslexia. In K. E. Patterson, J. C. Marshall, & M. Coltheart (Eds.), *Surface dyslexia: Neuropsychological and cognitive studies of phonological reading* (pp. 301–330). London: Erlbaum.

Gaur, A. (1987). *A history of writing.* London: British Library. (Original work published 1984)

Gaur, A. (1994). The history of writing systems. In I. Taylor & D. R. Olson (Eds.), *Scripts and literacy: Reading and learning to read alphabets, syllabaries, and characters* (pp. 19–30). Dordrecht: Kluwer.

Gelb, I. J. (1963). *A study of writing* (2nd ed.). Chicago: University of Chicago Press.

Goody, J. (1987). *The interface between the oral and the written.* Cambridge University Press.

Goswami, U., & Bryant, P. (1990). *Phonological skills and learning to read.* Hove: Erlbaum.

Harris, R. (1986). *The origin of writing.* London: Duckworth.

Havelock, E. (1982). *The literate revolution in Greece and its cultural consequences.* Princeton, NJ: Princeton University Press.

Hedelin, L., & Hjelmquist, E. (1988). Preschool children's mastery of the form/content distinction in spoken language. In K. Ekberg & P. E. Mjaavatn (Eds.), *Growing into the modern world* (pp. 639–645). Trondheim: Norwegian Centre for Child Research, University of Trondheim.

Householder, F. (1971). *Linguistic speculations.* Cambridge University Press.

Karmiloff-Smith, A. (1979). Micro- and macrodevelopmental changes in language acquisition and other representational systems. *Cognitive Science, 3,* 91–118.

Karpova, S. N. (1977). *The realization of verbal composition of speech by preschool children.* The Hague: Mouton.

Larsen, M. T. (1989). What they wrote on clay. In K. Schousboe & M. T. Larsen (Eds.), *Literacy and society* (pp. 121–148). Copenhagen: Centre for Research in the Humanities, Copenhagen University.

Masonheimer, P., Drum, P., & Ehri, L. (1984). Does environment print identification lead children into word reading? *Journal of Reading Behavior, 16,* 257–271.

Mattingly, I. G. (1972). Reading, the linguistic process, and linguistic awareness. In J. Kavanagh & I. Mattingly (Eds.), *Language by eye and by ear.* Cambridge, MA: MIT Press.

McCarthy, S. (1994). The Cree syllabary and the writing system riddle: A paradigm in crisis. In I. Taylor & D. R. Olson (Eds.), *Scripts and literacy: Reading and learning to read alphabets, syllabaries, and characters* (pp. 59–75). Dordrecht: Kluwer.

Morais, J., Alegria, J., & Content, A. (1987). The relationships between segmental analysis and alphabetic literacy: An interactive view. *Cahiers de Psychologie Cognitive, 7,* 415–438.

Morais, J., Bertelson, P., Cary, L., & Alegria, J. (1986). Literacy training and speech segmentation. *Cognition, 24,* 45–64.

Morrison, K. F. (1987). Stabilizing the text: The institutionalization of knowledge in historical and philosophical forms of argument. *Canadian Journal of Sociology, 12,* 242–274.

Needham, J. (1954–59). *Science and civilization in China.* Cambridge University Press.

Needham, J. (1969). *The grand titration: Science and society in East and West.* Toronto: University of Toronto Press.

Nissen, H. J. (1986). The archaic texts from Uruk. *World Archeology, 17*(3), 318–334.

Olson, D. R. (1991). Literacy as metalinguistic activity. In D. R. Olson & N. Torrance (Eds.), *Literacy and orality* (pp. 251–270). Cambridge University Press.

Read, C. A., Zhang, Y., Nie, H., & Ding, B. (1986). The ability to manipulate speech sounds depends on knowing alphabetic reading. *Cognition, 24,* 31–44.

122   David R. Olson

Reid, J. F. (1966). Learning to think about reading. *Educational Research, 9,* 56–62.

Rousseau, J-J. (1966). Essay on the origin of languages. In J. H. Moran & A. Gode (Eds.), *On the origin of language: Two essays by Jean-Jacques Rousseau and Johann Gottfried Herder* (pp. 5–74). New York: Ungar. (Original work published 1754–91)

Sampson, G. (1985). *Writing systems.* Stanford, CA: Stanford University Press.

Schlesinger, I. M. (1991). The wax and wane of Whorfian views. In R. L. Cooper & B. Spolsky (Eds.), *The influence of language on culture and thought: Essays in honor of Joshua A. Fishman's 65th birthday* (pp. 7–44). Berlin: Mouton de Gruyter.

Schmandt-Bessarat, D. (1986). Tokens: Facts and interpretations. *Visible Language, 20*(3), 250–272.

Schmandt-Bessarat, D. (1987). *Oneness, twoness, threeness: How ancient accountants invented numbers.* New York: New York Academy of Sciences.

Scholes, R. J., & Willis, B. J. (1991). Linguists, literacy, and the intensionality of Marshall McLuhan's Western man. In D. R. Olson & N. Torrance (Eds.), *Literacy and orality* (pp. 215–235). Cambridge University Press.

Scribner, S., & Cole, M. (1981). *The psychology of literacy.* Cambridge, MA: Harvard University Press.

Serra, E. (1992). *Children's understanding of how writing affects speech.* Unpublished paper, Centre for Applied Cognitive Science, Ontario Institute for Studies in Education, Toronto.

Sinclair, H. (1978). Conceptualization and awareness in Piaget's theory and its relevance to the child's conception of language. In A. Sinclair, J. Jarvella, & W. Levelt (Eds.), *The child's conception of language* (pp. 191–200). New York: Springer-Verlag.

Smith, M. E. (1973). *Picture writing from ancient southern Mexico.* Norman: University of Oklahoma Press.

Snell, B. (1960). *The discovery of the mind: The Greek origins of European thought* (T. G. Rosenmeyer, Trans.). New York: Harper & Row.

Torrance, N., Lee, E., & Olson, D. (1992, April). *The development of the distinction between paraphrase and exact wording in the recognition of utterances.* Paper presented at the meeting of the American Educational Research Association, San Francisco.

Treiman, R. (1991). The role of intrasyllabic units in learning to read. In L. Rieben & C. Perfetti (Eds.), *Learning to read: Basic research and its implications* (pp. 149–160). Hillsdale, NJ: Erlbaum.

Unger, J. M., & deFrancis, J. (1994). Logographic and semasiographic writing systems: A critique of Sampson's classification. In I. Taylor & D. R. Olson (Eds.), *Scripts and literacy: Reading and learning to read alphabets, syllabaries, and characters* (pp. 45–58). Dordrecht: Kluwer.

Vygotsky, L. (1962). *Thought and language.* Cambridge, MA: MIT Press.

Vygotsky, L. (1978). *Mind in society: The development of higher psychological processes.*

M. Cole, V. John-Steiner, S. Scribner, & E. Souberman (Eds.), Cambridge, MA: Harvard University Press.

Whorf, B. L. (1956). Science and linguistics. In J. B. Carroll (Ed.), *Language, thought, and reality: Selected writings of Benjamin Lee Whorf* (pp. 207–219). Cambridge, MA: MIT Press.

5 An approach to an integrated sensorimotor system in the human central brain and a subconscious computer

Tadanobu Tsunoda

A method of detecting higher-order auditory laterality in normal humans

A prevalent method of determining functional differences between human cerebral hemispheres has been the medical examination and clinical psychiatric observation of brain-injured patients, which is believed to provide sufficient data for assuming the lateralization of specific cerebral functions. But this clinical approach is clearly limited in its capacity to measure the functions of normal brains, and it is important to note that even a small injury can affect the mechanism of the whole brain.

In recent years, several techniques of investigating laterality in normal human subjects free of brain injury have been developed, among which the sensory approach to brain laterality has opened up new possibilities previously unexplored by clinical researchers. The dichotic-listening test developed by D. Kimura (1961) is the best known and most widely employed method.

In this test, the subject is required to listen simultaneously to two different melodies delivered to the respective ears and then identify the melodies from a pool of sample melodies. It is generally found that the subject recalls the melody heard from the left ear more accurately. If verbal or arithmetic problems are delivered to both ears, information heard in the right ear more than that heard in the left ear helps the subject correctly solve these problems.

124

When inputs from each ear are placed in a mutually competing situation, the ipsilateral nerve routes are suppressed and the contralateral nerve routes are activated, causing the ear on the contralateral side of the verbal hemisphere to function dominantly when the subject solves verbal and arithmetic problems. The opposite ear is dominant when the subject solves melody problems. Apparently, therefore, the verbal and music processing regions of the brain are separated between the right and left hemispheres.

During the 1960s, the author developed his Tsunoda test (Tsunoda, 1966, 1968, 1969, 1971, 1973) in an effort to measure cerebral laterality as accurately as possible. This test is designed to determine the function of a subcortical "automatic switching mechanism" by applying a sensorimotor feedback method involving the finger-tapping motions and an auditory feedback of the tapping. Unlike most psychological tests, the Tsunoda test requires the subject to be strictly controlled and master a correct tapping technique. Consequently, other researchers have found it difficult to repeat the Tsunoda test.

Today, advanced technologies such as auditory evoked potential (AEP) analysis, AEP topography, and positron computed tomography are expected to cast greater light on cerebral laterality. However, the Tsunoda test based on a sensorimotor feedback has proved extremely effective in the measurement of laterality in the subconscious central brain, which lies below the conscious region of the brain.

The measurement of auditory laterality by the Tsunoda test

The most important purpose of the auditory function in humans is to communicate with spoken language. Traditionally, auditory studies have been limited to listening to a sound input, while studies of speech have been confined to making a speech output. Thus, the auditory and speech studies have been considered as two independent research fields.

But it is evident from our everyday conversation that our speech and auditory activities are inseparable. In particular, it is essential that we listen to our own speech sounds. Each person has a feedback circuit of speaking, listening to him- or herself, and monitoring that speech. The Tsunoda test applies the principle of this feedback circuit to the measurement of cerebral laterality in the auditory function of the normal brain.

During the 1950s, B. S. Lee (1950) in the United States discovered a delayed auditory feedback effect, whereby the subject, during a normal conversation, begins to stutter and is unable to maintain normal speech performance when the feedback of his or her own speech is delayed by about 0.2 second. Similarly, it was found that subjects performing a finger tapping task begin to fail to tap a certain rhythm when the feedback of the tapping sounds is delayed.

The Tsunoda test has adopted this delayed auditory feedback effect in tapping tasks (Tsunoda, 1975). Under the Tsunoda test, the normal subject is trained to tap a quick, consistent rhythm with a finger. The subject's tapping of an electronic switch triggers an identical rhythm of sounds from a tape recorder or an oscillator. These rhythmic sounds, each of 0.01 to 0.07 second in duration, are transmitted to one ear of the subject as a synchronous feedback of his or her tapping rhythm. The subject is instructed to listen only to this feedback. A moment later, however, the same feedback sound, except with a delay, is transmitted to the other ear. The subject must try to maintain the correct tapping by listening only to the synchronous feedback while ignoring the delayed feedback.

The correct tapping is eventually disturbed as the intensity (in decibels) of the delayed feedback is gradually raised. The threshold intensity of the delayed feedback sound at which the correct tapping is interfered is measured by a recording device. The difference between this threshold and the intensity of the synchronous feedback is recorded as the "resistance value" for the ear that has received the synchronous feedback.

The same procedure is repeated, this time transmitting the synchronous and delayed feedbacks to the opposite ears. The resistance value is measured and compared with the first resistance value. The ear that has scored a greater resistance value is considered dominant over the opposite ear, and in the case of cerebral hemispheres the side contralateral to the dominant ear is considered dominant due to the activation of the contralateral nerve pathway. Thus, the Tsunoda test measures cerebral dominance in terms of decibels.

The Tsunoda test allows the use of a variety of verbal and nonverbal sounds as a feedback. When a verbal sound is used, the right ear, which is contralateral to the verbal hemisphere, shows a greater resistance to the delayed feedback. When a nonverbal sound is used, however, the left ear shows a greater resistance. The large majority of subjects who have mastered the tapping skill have shown a right-ear, or left-hemisphere, dominance for verbal sounds and a left-ear, or right-hemisphere, dominance for nonverbal sounds, each with a resistance value of 40 dB or more.

Characteristics of cerebral laterality

Employing the Tsunoda test, the author examined a variety of sounds existing in everyday life, using only Japanese subjects in the first 6 years of study and then including foreign subjects thereafter (Tsunoda, 1978, 1979). The test sounds ranged from verbalizations (the five Japanese vowel sounds /ta/, /pa/, /ga/, etc.), human emotional sounds (sob, snore, moan, exclamation), sounds in nature (insect chirping, animal crying, or from streams, waves, raindrops, wind), the sounds of Western musical instruments (piano, violin, flute, recorder), and the sounds of Japanese musical instruments (*shakuhachi,* flute; *shamisen,* guitar; *biwa,* lute; *nokan,* flute; *shinobue,* flute; *sho,* flute; *hichiriki,* flageolet) to mechanical sounds (pure tone, white noise, pulse wave, square wave, FM sound, AM sound, band noise, composites of band noises).

All of these sounds were broken up into short segments of 10–70 milliseconds. It was impossible, therefore, for the subjects to identify the sources of the feedback sounds they were listening to.

The results of Tsunoda tests were first revealed in 1974, finding different hemisphere dominance patterns between the Japanese and Westerners, as shown in Figure 5.1. Subsequent tests have indicated similar results.

Table 5.1 shows the results of a Tsunoda test of Japanese subjects exposed to feedback sounds. A verbal hemisphere dominance was induced by (a) a sound containing two or more inharmonic formants or (b) a sound whose formants are harmonic and contain FM sounds. On the other hand, a nonverbal hemisphere dominance was aroused by (c) a composite sound in which the frequencies of its constituent sounds are harmonic, (d) a white noise that has no particular acoustic characteristics, and (e) a composite sound having a large number of constituent sounds. Notably, (a) and (b) resemble human vowel sounds in acoustic structure.

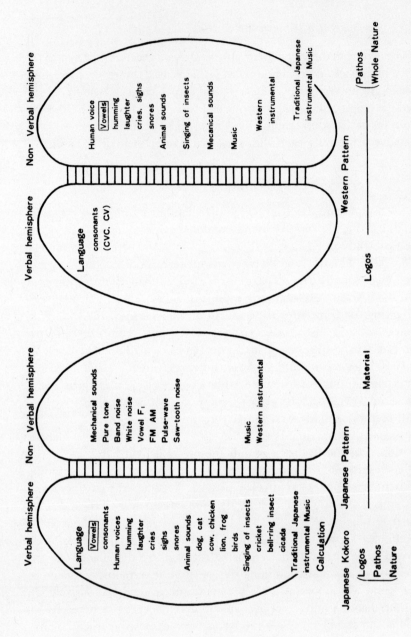

Figure 5.1. Difference of cerebral dominance of verbal sounds and natural sounds between Japanese and Westerners, and their culture patterns.

	Left hemisphere (R ear) dominance	Right hemisphere (L ear) dominance
Sound patterns	Speech sounds CV, VCV, CVC, VV vowels vowels (F1 + F2) whispering Composite of two or more sounds of which one has 1.5 % or more FM or two have 0.1 % or more FM (characteristics of vowels) Composite of two or more sounds in noninteger ratio	Pure tone, Band noise all frequencies exept 40, 60 and annual ring system Mechancal sounds Fm, Am, Pulse wave Square wave tone Saw tooth noise etc Composite of two or more noises in integer ratio
Sound from surroundings	Language and human voices Emotional sounds sobbing, laughter, sighs, snores, cries, humming etc Natural sounds animal & insect sounds sound of streams, wind rain and surf Japanese instrumental music	Part of singing voice Human voice with higher harmonic distortion Mechanical noise Western instrumental music
Characheristics	Language, Calculation Emotion Nature, Organic Inharmonic	 Matter Inorganic Harmonic

Table 5.1. Auditory cerebral dominance obtained by key-tapping method (Japanese subjects).

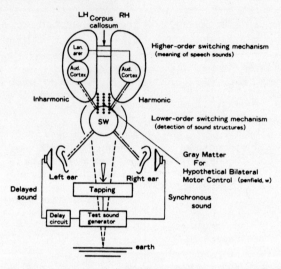

Figure 5.2. Automatic switching mechanism and Penfield's centrencephalic automatic sensorimotor mechanism.

Significantly, these results indicated that even though feedback sounds do not have linguistic meaning and have been broken up into unidentifiable short sounds, the switching mechanism still sorts them into a group having a basic verbal sound structure and one having no such structure. Thus, it is concluded that auditory stimuli from the ears are distributed to the right or left hemisphere automatically at the subconscious level in the Tsunoda test, without the influence of the conscious cortical brain.

The subcortical automatic switching mechanism

In view of the preceding findings, the author in 1976 proposed the concept of an "automatic switching mechanism" (Tsunoda, 1985), most likely existing in the brain stem area (see Figure 5.2). Tests on non-Japanese nationals, second- and third-generation Japanese who were born and raised abroad, foreign nationals raised in a Japanese-speaking environment, and Japanese children who have lived abroad for a number of years with their families have indicated that the hemisphere dominance patterns are not genetically determined but are formed by one's linguistic environment from the age of 6–9 years. People raised with the Japanese language during this critical period have the Japanese dominance pattern, and those raised with other languages during the same period have a non-Japanese pattern. The linguistic environment ceases its influence after 9 years of age.

The pattern of Japanese brain dominance features the preferential processing by the verbal hemisphere of all sounds having a basic vowel-like structure. The non-Japanese dominance pattern is marked by the preferential processing by the verbal hemisphere of syllabic sounds consisting of consonants and a vowel and excluding steady-state vowel and other sounds having a vowel-like acoustic structure.

The automatic switching mechanism, therefore, is believed to distinguish verbal from nonverbal information at the subcortical level on the basis of the physical acoustic structures of auditory stimuli. Although this switching mechanism is found in the brain in both Japanese and non-Japanese subjects, the switching mechanism for Japanese differs from that for non-Japanese subjects in that the former also selects steady-state vowels and vowel-like nonverbal sounds, in addition to syllables, as verbal sounds, while the latter screens only syllables as verbal sounds.

The difference has been attributed to the abundance of vowel-only and vowel-heavy meaningful words in the Japanese language. Polynesian people, whose language is also rich in vowel-only and vowel-heavy meaningful words, have been found to show the same dominance pattern as do Japanese.

The findings obtained from the Tsunoda test have been confirmed by the EEG study of brain evoked potentials by Y. Kikuchi (1983, 1988; Kikuchi & Tsunoda, 1985, 1986) at my university laboratory.

Concepts of the Tsunoda test and Penfield's centrencephalic automatic sensorimotor mechanism

Although we commonly distinguish the conscious from the unconscious level in cognitive processes, I doubt we can so clearly draw a border between the two realities. Taking our everyday verbal communication as an example, we quite consciously select our subject matter and start our conversation, but once it is started, it becomes a quite automatic process; we do not think of the phrasing of the next sentence, let alone how the mouth and tongue should be coordinated to articulate the words.

The process of articulation involving the integrated functions of the inhalation muscles, vocal cords, exhalation muscles, tongue, palate, lips, and chin has been studied in detail by phoneticians. Articulation, like chewing, is mostly an automatic process enabled by the integrated sensorimotor system, which has both genetic and learned abilities. Similarly, most of our "conscious" actions and activities are supported by subconscious, routine functions to make our life simple and smooth.

W. Penfield (1975; Penfield & Roberts, 1966), examining the verbal responses, flash backs, and memories of many clinical epileptic patients under electric stimulation of their cortical brains, hypothesized that the highest brain mechanism exists in the higher part of the brain stem. Penfield reported that when an epileptic patient loses consciousness, a "computer" or the centrencephalic sensorimotor mechanism is automatically activated by a switch, so that the patient can still walk around or even play a melody on the piano.

Since the death of Penfield, the concept of an integral sensorimotor mechanism in the central brain has remained unpopular, but there is great value in his long-term observation of the behavior and brain condition of persons during consciousness.

Applying Penfield's concepts, I believe that the Tsunoda test directly activates the integrated sensorimotor computer system of the central brain by linking the rhythmic motion of the finger and the auditory function with a feedback mechanism. While Penfield arrived at the computer through clinical observations, I have reached it through the activation of the peripheral auditory nervous system.

Figure 5.2 compares the sensorimotor computer proposed by Penfield and my hypothesized automatic switching mechanism. Both are believed to exist in the central, subconscious part of the brain. Both concepts lay special importance on sensorimotor integration.

The Tsunoda test combines the auditory and motor functions by converting the finger tapping performance into an auditory feedback. The involvement of the motor system may give the impression that the accuracy of the Tsunoda test may be lower than those of conventional auditory tests, but it is essential to note that the process of our everyday conversation involves the subconscious motions of the articulating organs. Once the subject masters the skill of concentrating his or her attention to the auditory feedback and making the finger tapping an automatic, subconscious activity, the switching mechanism reveals its function with a surprisingly high level of accuracy.

Directions and limitation of human brain studies

At present it is possible to measure the laterality of the human brain cortex in relation to verbal and nonverbal sounds by applying the computerized image processing of auditory evoked potentials and auditory evoked neuromagnetic fields, but these advanced technologies still have difficulty determining the computer-like functions of the switching mechanism in the central brain, which lies below the cortex. In contrast, the Tsunoda test accesses the automatic switching mechanism in the central brain as a result of the application of a sensorimotor feedback arrangement that precludes the conscious activities of the cortical brain.

The automatic switching mechanism, as measured by the Tsunoda test, is an extremely precise computer that shows additional functions, the integration of time and space information, the integration of different sensory functions, and the response to direct current magnetic fields. Magnetic resonance imagery, considered the most precise technique for examining the human brain, requires intense magnetic force on the order of tens of thousands of gauss; however, the automatic switching mechanism of the human brain responds to a weak magnetism of as low as 0.5 gauss.

Conclusion

I believe that the Tsunoda test has helped shed light on the subconscious world and bridged natural science and human science by acknowledging the influence of the linguistic environment on brain laterality. All human beings, regardless of nationality, have an innate switching mechanism organized to efficiently process one's native language learned from 6–9 years of age.

The switching mechanism apparently has two capabilities – one related to the vowel-abundant Japanese and Polynesian languages, the other to consonant-heavy Indo-European and other languages. Because of the switching mechanism, the Japanese and Polynesians process human emotional sounds and sounds existing in nature as verbal sounds. On the other hand, people who speak consonant-heavy languages process these sounds as nonverbal sounds.

The switching mechanism of the brain is an extremely precise system functioning at the subcortical level and is capable of detecting the slightest difference in input sounds, whether verbal or nonverbal. Auditory input is selected unconsciously according to the characteristics of the switching mechanism formed while learning one's native language.

To avoid any misunderstanding, I must emphasize that the different functional pattern found for Japanese and Polynesians stems from their specific linguistic environments and therefore is not an innate trait.

References

Kikuchi, Y. (1983). Hemispheric differences of the auditory evoked potentials in normal Japanese. *Audiology, Japan, 26,* 699–710.

Kikuchi, Y. (1988). Sound structure and auditory laterality. *Audiology, Japan, 31,* 219–239.

Kikuchi, Y., & Tsunoda, T. (1985). A comparative study on human cerebral dominance by the Tsunoda Method and Auditory Evoked Potential (AEP)-Method as a cerebral dominance test. *Audiology, Japan, 28,* 725–738.

Kikuchi, Y. & Tsunoda, T. (1986). Physical characteristics of sounds and hemispheric AEP asymmetry. *Audiology, Japan, 29,* 35–42.

Kimura, D. (1961). Cerebral dominance and the perception of verbal stimuli. *Canadian Journal of Psychology, 15,* 166–171.

Lee, B. S. (1950). Some effects of side-tone delay. *Journal of Acoustic Society of America, 22,* pp. 103–127.

Penfield, W. (1975). *The mystery of the mind: A critical study of consciousness and human brain.* Princeton: Princeton University Press.

Penfield, W. & Roberts, L. (1966). *Speech and brain mechanism.* Princeton, NJ: Princeton University Press/New York: Atheneum.

Tsunoda, T. (1966). Tsunoda's method: A new objective testing method available for the orientation of the dominant cerebral hemisphere toward various sounds and its clinical use. *Indian Journal of Otolaryngology, 18,* 78–88.

Tsunoda, T. (1968). An audilological approach to speech disorders due to cortical lesion. *Practica Otologica Kyoto, 66* (Suppl.) 1296–1313.

Tsunoda, T. (1969). Contralateral shift of cerebral dominance for nonverbal sounds during speech perception. *Journal of Auditory Research, 9,* 221–229.

Tsunoda, T. (1971). The difference of the cerebral dominance of vowel sounds among different languages. *Journal of Auditory Research, 11,* 305–314.

Tsunoda, T. (1973). The characteristic pattern of the cerebral dominance for vowel sound found in Japanese second-generations. *Proceedings of the Japan Academy, 49,* 643–647.

Tsunoda, T. (1975). Functional differences between right and left cerebral hemispheres detected by the key tapping method. *Brain and Language, 2,* 152–170.

Tsunoda, T. (1977). Asymmetry of olfaction, emotion and autonomic system in human brain. *Shinkei Kenkyu no Shimpo, 21,* 1217–1228.

Tsunoda, T. (1978). Logos and pathos: Difference in the mechanism of vowel sound and natural sound perception in Japanese and Westerners, and in regard to mental structure. Colloquium on body language in dentistry. *Journal of Dental Health, 2,* 35–43.

Tsunoda, T. (1979) Difference in the mechanism of emotion in Japanese and Westerner. *Psychotherapy and Psychosomatics, 31,* 367–372.

Tsunoda, T. (1985). *The Japanese brain: Uniqueness and universality.* (Translated by Yoshinori Diwa). Tokyo: Taishukan.

Part III

Sociocultural setting, intersubjectivity, and the formation of the individual

6 Observing sociocultural activity on three planes: participatory appropriation, guided participation, and apprenticeship

Barbara Rogoff

This chapter proposes a sociocultural approach that involves observation of development in three planes of analysis corresponding to personal, interpersonal, and community processes. I refer to developmental processes corresponding with these three planes of analysis as apprenticeship, guided participation, and participatory appropriation, in turn. These are inseparable, mutually constituting planes comprising activities that can become the focus of analysis at different times, but with the others necessarily remaining in the background of the analysis. I argue that children take part in the activities of their community, engaging with other children and with adults in routine and tacit as well as explicit collaboration (both in each others' presence and in otherwise socially structured activities) and in the process of participation become prepared for later participation in related events.

Developmental research has commonly limited attention to either the individual or the environment – for example, examining how adults teach children or how children construct reality, with an emphasis on either separate individuals or independent environmental elements as the basic units of analysis. Even when both the individual and the environment are considered, they are often regarded as separate entities

I am grateful for the comments of Mary Gauvain, Denise Goldsmith, Jonathan Tudge, and Cynthia DuVal and for discussions with Pilar Lacasa, Jackie Baker-Sennett, Christine Mosier, Eugene Matusov, Pablo Chavajay, Nancy Bell, Batya Elbaum, Barbara Radziszewska, Paul Klaczynski, Kurt Fischer, and Rob Wozniak that helped me to think about the issues presented in this paper. The research presented was supported by the Spencer Foundation.

rather than being mutually defined and interdependent in ways that preclude their separation as units or elements (Dewey & Bentley, 1949; Pepper, 1942; Rogoff, 1982, 1992).

Vygotsky's emphasis on the interrelated roles of the individual and the social world in microgenetic, ontogenetic, sociocultural, and phylogenetic development (Scribner, 1985; Wertsch, 1985) includes the individual and the environment together in successively broader time frames. Likewise, Vygotsky's interest in the mutuality of the individual and the sociocultural environment is apparent in his concern with finding a unit of analysis that preserves the essence of the events of interest rather than separating an event into elements that no longer function as does the whole (e.g., studying water molecules rather than hydrogen and oxygen to understand the behavior of water; Cole, 1985; Leont'ev, 1981; Wertsch, 1985; Zinchenko, 1985).

The use of "activity" or "event" as the unit of analysis – with active and dynamic contributions from individuals, their social partners, and historical traditions and materials and their transformations – allows a reformulation of the relation between the individual and the social and cultural environments in which each is inherently involved in the others' definition. None exists separately.

Nonetheless, the parts making up a whole activity or event can be considered separately as foreground without losing track of their inherent interdependence in the whole. Their structure can be described without assuming that the structure of each is independent of that of the others. Foregrounding one plane of focus still involves the participation of the backgrounded planes of focus.

By analogy, the organs in an organism work together with an inherent interdependence, but if we are interested in foregrounding the functioning of the heart or the skin, we can describe their structure and functioning, remembering that by themselves the organs would not have such structure or functioning. (See Rogoff, 1992, for further discussion of this issue.) Similarly, we may consider a single person thinking or the functioning of a whole community in the foreground without assuming that they are actually separate elements. "The study of mind, of culture, and of language (in all its diversity) are internally related: that is, it will be *impossible* to render any one of these domains intelligible without essential reference to the others" (Bakhurst, 1988, p. 39, discussing Ilyenkov and activity theory).

Vygotsky's and Dewey's theories focus on children participating with other people in a social order with a seamless involvement of individuals in sociocultural activity. For Vygotsky (1978, 1987), children's cognitive development had to be understood as taking place through their interaction with other members of the society who are more conversant with the society's intellectual practices and tools (especially language) for mediating intellectual activity. Dewey (1916) provided a similar account:

Every individual has grown up, and always must grow up, in a social medium. His responses grow intelligent, or gain meaning, simply because he lives and acts in a medium of accepted meanings and values. (p. 344)

The social environment . . . is truly educative in its effects in the degree in which an individual shares or participates in some conjoint activity. By doing his share in the associated activity, the individual appropriates the purpose which actuates it, becomes familiar with its methods and subject matters, acquires needed skill, and is saturated with its emotional spirit. (p. 26)

Without an understanding of such mutually constituting processes, a sociocultural approach is at times assimilated to other approaches that examine only part of the package. For example, it is incomplete to focus only on the relationship of individual development and social interaction without concern for the cultural activity in which personal and interpersonal actions take place. And it is incomplete to assume that development occurs in one plane and not in others (e.g., that children develop but that their partners or their cultural communities do not) or that influence can be ascribed in one direction or another or that relative contributions can be counted (e.g., parent to child, child to parent, culture to individual).

In this chapter I discuss apprenticeship, guided participation, and participatory appropriation (Rogoff, 1990, 1993), which I regard as inseparable concepts reflecting different planes of focus in sociocultural activity – community/institutional, interpersonal, and personal. I conceive of planes of focus not as separate or as hierarchical, but as simply involving different grains of focus with the whole sociocultural activity. To understand each requires the involvement of the others. Distinguishing them serves the function of clarifying the plane of focus that may be chosen for one or another discussion of processes in the whole activity, holding the other planes of focus in the background but not separated.

The metaphor of *apprenticeship* provides a model in the plane of community activity, involving active individuals participating with others in culturally organized activity that has as part of its purpose the development of mature participation in the activity by the less experienced people. This metaphor extends the idea of craft apprenticeship to include participation in any other culturally organized activity, such as other kinds of work, schooling, and family relations.[1] The idea of apprenticeship necessarily focuses attention on the specific nature of the activity involved, as well as on its relation to practices and institutions of the community in which it occurs – economic, political, spiritual, and material.

The concept of *guided participation* refers to the processes and systems of involvement between people as they communicate and coordinate efforts while participating in culturally valued activity. This includes not only the face-to-face interaction, which has been the subject of much research, but also the side-by-side joint participation that is frequent in everyday life and the more distal arrangements of people's activities that do not require copresence (e.g., choices of where and with whom and with what materials and activities a person is involved). The "guidance" referred to in guided participation involves the direction offered by cultural and social values, as well as social partners;[2] the "participation" in guided participation refers to observation, as well as hands-on involvement in an activity.

The concept of *participatory appropriation* refers to how individuals change through their involvement in one or another activity, in the process becoming prepared for subsequent involvement in related activities. With guided participation as the interpersonal process through which people are involved in sociocultural activity, participatory appropriation is the personal process by which, through engagement in an activity, individuals change and handle a later situation in ways prepared by their own participation in the previous situation. This is a process of becoming, rather than acquisition, as I argue later.

The remainder of this chapter explores the concepts of apprenticeship, guided participation, and especially, participatory appropriation in greater detail. I illustrate them with observations of the processes involved in planning routes, keeping track of sales and deliveries, and calculating charges as Girl Scouts of America sell and deliver Girl Scout cookies. This activity was chosen for investigation because it allows us as researchers to examine personal, interpersonal, and community processes that we ourselves have not devised.

Apprenticeship

A metaphor that has appealed to many scholars who focus on the mutual embeddedness of the individual and the sociocultural world is that of apprenticeship. In apprenticeship, newcomers to a community of practice advance their skill and understanding through participation with others in culturally organized activities (Bruner, 1983; Dewey, 1916; Goody, 1989; John-Steiner, 1985; Lave & Wenger, 1991; Rogoff, 1990). The metaphor focuses attention on the active roles of newcomers and others in arranging activities and support for developing participation, as well as on the cultural/institutional practices and goals of the activities to which they contribute.

The apprenticeship metaphor has at times been used to focus on expert–novice dyads; however, apprenticeship involves more than dyads. Apprenticeship relates a small group in a community with specialization of roles oriented toward the accomplishment of goals that relate the group to others outside the group. The small group may involve peers who serve as resources and challenges for each other in exploring an activity, along with experts (who, like peers, are still developing skill and understanding in the process of engaging in activities with others of varying experience). Apprenticeship as a concept goes far beyond expert–novice dyads; it focuses on a system of interpersonal involvements and arrangements in which people engage in culturally organized activity in which apprentices become more responsible participants.

Research that focuses on the community plane using the metaphor of apprenticeship examines the institutional structure and cultural technologies of intellectual activity (say, in school or work). For example, it encourages the recognition that endeavors involve purposes (defined in community or institutional terms), cultural constraints, resources, values relating to what means are appropriate for reaching goals (such as improvisation versus planning all moves before beginning to act), and cultural tools such as maps, pencils, and linguistic and mathematical systems.

I describe Girl Scout cookie sales and delivery in the three sections of this chapter dealing with apprenticeship, guided participation, and participatory appropriation to highlight the point that these different planes of analysis are mutually constituting and cannot stand alone in the analysis of the activity. In this section, description of this activity as apprenticeship – focusing on the community and institutional aspects of the activity – would be impossible without reference to the personal and interpersonal aspects of the endeavor. Likewise, to understand the personal or interpersonal processes that become the focus of later sections, it is essential to understand the historical/institutional contexts of this activity, which define the practices in which scouts and their companions engage and at the same time are transformed by successive generations of scouts. Individual scouts are active in learning and managing the activity, along with their companions, as they participate in and extend community, institutional practices that began more than 7 decades before.

For readers who are familiar with the activity of Girl Scout cookie sales and delivery, information in this plane of analysis may be so taken for granted that it seems unnecessary to state. However, that is in the nature of cultural understanding: It is essential, yet so taken for granted that special efforts are needed to draw attention to important features of the obvious (Smedslund, 1984).

Our team (Rogoff, Lacasa, Baker-Sennett, & Goldsmith, in preparation) chose to study cookie sales because we wanted to go outside the usual institutions of research such as those of schooling and laboratories, which of course also involve interpersonal and institutional contexts, but which are more difficult to study because researchers are more likely to take them for granted. Systems in which one is completely immersed are difficult even to detect. Analysis of the sociocultural nature of social and individual activity is difficult for researchers embedded in educational situations or research traditions that are often seen as the way things must be rather than just one way that things happen to be.

Comparisons across cultures are often useful in drawing the attention of insiders of a community to unnoticed assumptions and practices. Fortunately, the readership of this chapter – an international community of scholars – requires making the cultural/institutional plane explicit, for the practices involved in Girl Scout cookie sales are local to the United States. Historical changes in the practices of this activity provide another tool for becoming more aware of the cultural/community plane of analysis as present generations of scouts and cookie companies continue to contribute to the ongoing, developing cultural process constituting the practices of the apprenticeship. So, what follows in this section is an account of the institutional/cultural plane of the activity, which I am viewing as apprenticeship.

Cookie sales are a major annual fund-raising effort of the Girl Scouts of America, a voluntary organization dedicated to girls' moral education, the development of home, academic, and outdoor skills, and career preparation. The scouts meet on a weekly basis in units called troops, which involve about a dozen scouts and one or two women as leaders. The funds from cookie sales are used to support the troops' activities, regional administration, and girls' participation in day camps and summer camps run by the organization.

The scouts compose the sales force, trained and supervised by the organization, that goes door to door selling to family and friends (or getting their parents to sell cookies at work). Most scouts participate in the sales and take their economic role very seriously; their parents must sign a form agreeing to be responsible for the large sums of money involved. Originally, the cookies were both baked and sold by the scout troops; now the scouts sell cookies provided by large baking companies. Many scouts have older sisters or mothers who themselves sold Girl Scout cookies when they were scouts; older customers are often eager to buy cookies as they remember their own efforts to sell Girl Scout cookies.

Our study involved working with two troops of 10- and 11-year-old scouts in Salt Lake City, Utah. In one troop, we became "cookie chairs" and underwent the training to serve as the troop's organizers of the sale (a role usually filled by a mother of a girl in the troop, which one of us was). In the other troop, we observed the process. The girls became our collaborators and suggested that we give them tape recorders to carry around to record their sales and deliveries, which we did.[3]

The collective activity of planning cookie sales and delivery occurs with the constraints and resources provided by traditions and practices of the Girl Scout organization and associated baking companies, which set deadlines and provide organizational supports to the girls in their efforts to keep track of sales, cookies, and money, as well as to manage their time and resources. The scouts (currently) take orders on a glossy order form provided by the cookie company and deliver cookies a month later, according to dates set by the regional administration. The cookie order form is color coded in a way that facilitates keeping track of the different kinds of cookie. (For example, customers order Thin Mints by indicating the number of boxes desired in the green column; the number of Trefoils is indicated in the yellow column. The boxes and cases of cookies and other materials maintain this color coding.) The order form is laid out to facilitate calculation of amounts of money, presentation of information to customers, and keeping track of deliveries.

To illustrate focusing on the apprenticeship or community plane of analysis, this section has described Girl Scout cookie sales in terms of institutional organization and evolution of community practices. These, of course, could not be described without reference to the contributions and development of individual girls and their companions in the shared endeavor. Understanding the processes that become the focus at each plane of analysis – individual, interpersonal, and community/institutional – relies on understanding the processes in the background as well as those in the foreground of analysis.

Guided participation

"Guided participation" is the term that I have applied to the interpersonal plane of sociocultural analysis. It stresses the mutual involvement of individuals and their social partners, communicating and coordinating their involvement as they participate in socioculturally structured collective activity (Rogoff, 1990; Rogoff & Gardner, 1984).

The concept of guided participation is not an operational definition that one might use to identify some and not other interactions or arrangements. Rather, it is meant to focus attention on the system of interpersonal engagements and arrangements that are involved in participation in activities (by promoting some sorts of involvement and restricting others), which is managed collaboratively by individuals and their social partners in face-to-face or other interaction, as well as in the adjustment of arrangements for each others' and their own activities.

The concept does not define when a particular situation is or is not guided participation, but rather provides a *perspective* on how to look at interpersonal engagements and arrangements as they fit in sociocultural processes, to understand learning and development. Variations and similarities in the *nature* of guidance and of participation may be investigated (such as in adults' and children's responsibilities in different cultural communities, Rogoff, Mistry, Göncü, & Mosier, 1993), but the concept of guided participation itself is offered as a way of looking at all interpersonal interactions and arrangements.

The interpersonal plane of analysis represented by guided participation is made up of the events of everyday life as individuals engage with others and with materials and arrangements collaboratively managed by themselves and others. It includes direct interaction with others as well as engaging in or avoiding activities assigned, made possible, or constrained by others, whether or not they are in each other's presence or even know of each other's existence. Guided participation may be tacit or explicit, face-to-face or distal, involved in shared endeavors with specific familiar people or distant unknown individuals or groups – peers as well as experts, neighbors as well as distant heroes, siblings as well as ancestors. It includes deliberate attempts to instruct and incidental comments or actions that are overheard or seen as well as involvement with particular materials and experiences that are available, which indicate the direction in which people are encouraged to go or discouraged from going.

Participation requires engagement in some aspect of the meaning of shared endeavors, but not necessarily in symmetrical or even joint action. A person who is actively observing and following the decisions made by another is participating whether or not he or she contributes directly to the decisions as they are made. A child who is working alone on a report is participating in a cultural activity with guidance involving interactions with the teacher, classmates, family members, librarian and authors, and the publishing industry, which help the child set the assignment and determine the materials and approach to be used.

Guided participation is thus an interpersonal process in which people manage their own and others' roles, and structure situations (whether by facilitating or limiting access) in which they observe and participate in cultural activities. These collective endeavors in turn constitute and transform cultural practices with each successive generation.

Processes of communication and coordination of efforts are central to the notion of guided participation. New members of a community are active in their attempts to make sense of activities and may be primarily responsible for putting themselves in a position to participate. Communication and coordination with other members of the community stretches the understanding of all participants, as they seek a common ground of understanding in order to proceed with the activities at hand. The search for a common ground as well as to extend it involves adjustments and the growth of understanding. As Dewey (1916) put it, people "live in a community in virtue of the things which they have in common; and communication is the way in which they come to possess things in common" (p. 5).

Communication and coordination occur in the course of participation in shared endeavors, as people attempt to accomplish something. Their activity is directed, not random or without purpose; understanding the purposes involved in shared endeavors is an essential aspect of the analysis of guided participation. As people direct their activity toward implicit, explicit, or emerging goals, they may not be able to articulate their goals. Their goals may not be particularly task oriented (e.g., their aim may be to pass time enjoyably or to avoid an unpleasant task) or held entirely in common with others (e.g., some may resist the direction of others). However, people's involvements are motivated by some purpose (though it may often be sketchy), and their actions are deliberate (not accidental or reflexive), often in an opportunistic, improvisational fashion (see Baker-Sennett, Matusov, & Rogoff, 1992, in press).

The perspective of guided participation, which builds on basic notions of Vygotsky's theory, emphasizes routine, tacit communication and arrangements between children and their companions. However, the concept of guided participation is intended to encompass scenarios of cognitive development that are less central in the Vygotskian account – especially the arrangements and interactions of children in cultural communities that do not aim for school-based discourse and concepts (Rogoff et al., 1993) and the arrangements and interactions of middle-class children in their routine involvement in everyday cognitive activities at home and in their neighborhoods. It also draws attention to the active nature of children's own efforts to participate and observe the skilled activities of their community.

In the study of Girl Scouts selling and delivering cookies, analysis of guided participation involves attention to the arrangements between people, including the availability of particular resources and constraints (e.g., order forms, transportation, deadlines, children's and customers' daily schedules), as well as their close and complex interpersonal involvements. The cookies are usually sold and delivered with a partner – another scout, a sibling, or a parent. Child partners were more common during the sales phase (and some girls noted that younger partners were better because "cute" makes for more sales). Adult partners were common during the delivery phase, when money needed to be collected and bulky merchandise delivered. Usually the management of the money was handled by a parent in collaboration with the scout; often the scouts recruited parents to drive them around with the cookies to make their deliveries, but they sometimes worked with siblings who helped carry boxes or loaned a toy wagon. The balance of responsibility between adults and children in keeping track of money and deliveries often changed over the course of the weeks of delivery.

The means of handling the problems of sales and delivery involved using various strategies developed in the process as well as those borrowed from others and from long-standing cultural traditions. In organizing the individual orders, the girls often bundled the boxes for each order together using a technique that in some cases we could track as being borrowed from scouts with more experience or from mothers (e.g., putting a rubber band around the boxes and labeling the bundle with a Post-it adhesive note with the customer's address and the amount due). In calculating amounts due, the girls had available to them many sources of support: the number system used in their community and school, the calculation box on the order form provided by the organization, discussions with their mothers as they performed calculations for many customers, and talk-aloud calculations by customers at the time of the sale (when they filled out the order form) that demonstrated how calculations on a unit price of $2.50 could be handled – for example, by thinking of a box costing a fourth of $10, rather than by multiplying out each digit.

Guided participation included some arrangements and interactions that were meant to instruct (e.g., training organized by the national organization), and some that were simply available (e.g., in the format of the order form) or did not have the intent of instruction or assistance (e.g., in the conversations with customers or arguments among partners regarding how to proceed). The girls as well as their social partners were active in borrowing and developing one or another approach and making use of the resources available, as well as in negotiating a balance of responsibility for shared efforts. Their efforts were purposeful, with the general goals of selling cookies, delivering them as promised, not losing any money, and earning incentives (prizes and reduced rates for summer camp) offered by the organization for high sales.

An account of the Girl Scouts' activity illustrates the interpersonal plane of shared involvement and arrangements within cultural activity and at the same time requires reference to the other two planes of analysis. Understanding guided participation in Girl Scout cookie sales and delivery requires understanding the cultural/institutional plane and the individual plane of analysis. The girls and their companions participated in and contributed to intellectual and economic institutions and traditions of their nation and the scout organization (such as numerical systems, accounting, exchange of money and goods), with associated cultural values (such as efficiency, persuasion of others within societal bounds of propriety, competition for achievement, and responsible completion of agreed-upon tasks). The next section focuses on the individual plane of analysis of sociocultural activity, using the concept of participatory appropriation, to examine how individuals change through their participation in cultural activities.

Participatory appropriation

I use the term "participatory appropriation" (or simply "appropriation") to refer to the process by which individuals transform their understanding of and responsibility for activities through their own participation. This notion is a companion concept to those of apprenticeship and guided participation. The basic idea of appropriation is that, through participation, people change and in the process become prepared to engage in subsequent similar activities. By engaging in an activity, participating in its meaning, people necessarily make ongoing contributions (whether in concrete actions or in stretching to understand the actions and ideas of others). Hence, participation is itself the process of appropriation.

I have used the terms "appropriation" and "participatory appropriation"[4] to contrast to the term "internalization" in discussing how children gain from their involvement in sociocultural activity (Rogoff, 1990, in press). Rather than viewing the process as one of internalization in which something static is taken across a boundary from the external to the internal, I see children's active participation itself as being the process by which they gain facility in an activity. As Wertsch and Stone (1979, p. 21) put it, "The process *is* the product." Or in Dewey's words:

The living creature is a part of the world, sharing its vicissitudes and fortunes, and making itself secure in its precarious dependence only as it intellectually identifies itself with the changes about it, and, forecasting the future consequences of what is going on, shapes its own activities accordingly. If the living, experiencing being is an intimate participant in the activities of the world to which it belongs, then knowledge is a mode of participation, valuable in the degree in which it is effective. It cannot be the idle view of an unconcerned spectator. (1916, p. 393)

The participatory appropriation view of how development and learning occur involves a perspective in which children and their social partners are interdependent, their roles are active and dynamically changing, and the specific processes by which they communicate and share in decision making are the substance of cognitive development.

My contrast with the term "internalization" concerns the usage that it often receives in information processing and learning accounts, where it implies a separation between the person and the social context, as well as assumptions of static entities involved in the "acquisition" of concepts, memories, knowledge, skills, and so on. The dynamic approach of participatory appropriation does not define cognition as a collection of stored possessions (such as thoughts, representations, memories, plans), but rather treats thinking, re-presenting, remembering, and planning as active processes that cannot be reduced to the possession of stored objects (see Baker-Sennett, Matusov, & Rogoff, 1992; Gibson, 1979; Leont'ev, 1981; Rogoff, 1990.) Instead of studying individuals' possession or acquisition of a capacity or a bit of knowledge, the focus is on the active changes involved in an unfolding event or activity in which people participate. Events and activities are inherently dynamic, rather than being static conditions to which time is added as a separate element. Change and development, rather than static characteristics or elements, are assumed to be basic (see Pepper, 1942).

Some scholars use the term "internalization" in ways resembling how I use the term "participatory appropriation." Translations of Vygotsky often refer to internalization, but his concept may be similar to my notion of appropriation, at least in emphasizing the inherent transformation involved in the process.[5] Berger and Luckmann (1966) also provide a related account using the term "internalization." Forman (1989) summarized their approach:

Berger and Luckmann argued that there are three components to the social construction of reality: externalization, objectivation, and internalization. All three components are necessary to their theory and together they explain how social institutions, technologies and knowledge are created, maintained, legitimated, and transmitted through social interaction. They proposed that knowledge begins as a natural by-product of the externalization of human activity. As people try to interact over time with each other, an implicit mutual understanding develops between them. Soon, however, this tacit knowledge becomes objectified in explicit concepts and rules to which language and other sign systems can refer. The final step in the process occurs when this knowledge needs to be internalized by people who were not part of its creation. (p. 57)

I first noticed the word "appropriation" in Bakhtin's (1981) writing, as I was searching for a way to express the difference between my views and the version of internalization involving importing objects across boundaries from external to internal. Bakhtin argued that the words people use belong partially to others, as they appropriate words from others and adapt them to their own purposes.

However, it is important to clarify some ambiguities in the use of the term "appropriation." It seems to have three uses: One use is simply the same as internalization – something external is imported. The second use goes beyond this but in my view is still a version of the concept of internalization – something external is imported and transformed to fit the purposes of the new "owner." An example of this use is Harre's (1983) explicit reference to appropriation as a process that precedes transformation. Newman, Griffin, and Cole (1989) also seem to refer to the internalization of something external in referring to the appropriation of cultural resources and tools (such as systems of language) through involvement in culturally organized activities in which the tool plays a role.

The third use of the term "appropriation" is my concept of participatory appropriation, in which the boundary itself is questioned, since a person who is participating in an activity is a part of that activity, not separate from it. The idea that the social world is external to the individual becomes misleading from this approach. Rather, a person participating in an activity is involved in appropriation through his or her own participation. Appropriation occurs in the process of participation, as the individual changes through involvement in the situation at hand, and this participation contributes both to the direction of the evolving event and to the individual's preparation for involvement in other similar events. In my view, appropriation *is* a process of transformation, not a precondition for transformation. Thus, I use the term "appropriation" to refer to the change resulting from a person's *own participation* in an activity, not to his or her internalization of some external event or technique.

Participation involves creative efforts to understand and contribute to social activity, which by its very nature involves bridging between several ways of understanding a situation. Communication and shared efforts always involve adjustments between participants (with varying degrees of asymmetry) to stretch their common understanding to fit with new perspectives in the shared endeavor. Such stretching to fit several views and to accomplish something together *is* development and occurs in the process of participation. Participants' individual changes in role and understanding extend to their efforts and involvements on similar occasions in the future.

The purpose of my emphasis on participatory appropriation rather than internalization is to distinguish between two theoretical perspectives: The appropriation perspective views development as a dynamic, active, mutual process involved in peoples' participation in cultural activities; the internalization perspective views development in terms of a static, bounded "acquisition" or "transmission" of pieces of knowledge (either by internal construction or by the internalization of external pieces of knowledge; see Figure 6.1). These are, I believe, quite different theoretical views.

An important difference between the participatory appropriation and the internalization perspectives concerns assumptions about time. In the internalization perspective, time is segmented into past, present, and future. These are treated as separate and yield problems of how

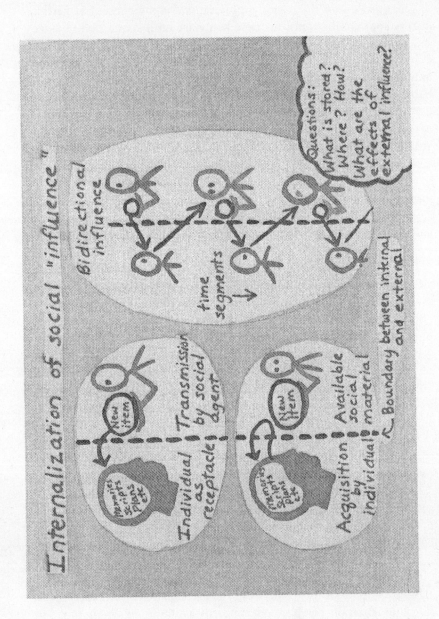

Figure 6.1.

to account for relations across time that are often handled by assuming that the individual stores memories of the past that are somehow retrieved and used in the present, and that the individual makes plans in the present and (if they are stored effectively) executes them in the future. The links between these separate time segments are bridged in mysterious ways to bring information or skills stored at one point in time to use in another. It involves a storage model of mind, with static elements held in the brain, and needs a homunculus or difficult-to-specify executive process to bring the elements stored at one epoch to implement in a later epoch (see Baker-Sennett, Matusov, & Rogoff, 1992). This is the same mysterious executive process that is required in the internalization perspective to acquire, accumulate, and store external pieces of knowledge or skill in the brain.

In the participatory appropriation perspective, time is an inherent aspect of events and is not divided into separate units of past, present, and future.[6] Any event in the present is an extension of previous events and is directed toward goals that have not yet been accomplished. As such, the present extends through the past and future and cannot be separated from them. Pepper gave a supporting example: The meaning of a word in a sentence (i.e., the present) brings with it the previous meanings of that word in other sentences and of other words already expressed in that sentence (the past in the present) and is also directed toward the overall idea to which the word contributes that is not yet fully expressed (the future in the present).

When a person acts on the basis of previous experience, his or her past is present. It is not merely a stored memory called up in the present; the person's previous participation contributes to the event at hand by having prepared it. The present event is different from what it would have been if previous events had not occurred; this does not require a storage model of past events.

Analogies can be drawn from physical and organizational change. The size, shape, and strength of a child's leg is a function of the growth and use that is continually occurring; the child's leg changes, but we do not need to refer to the leg accumulating units of growth or of exercise. The past is not *stored* in the leg; the leg has developed to be as it is currently. Likewise, the current situation of a company is a function of previous activities, but we do not need to account for changes in company direction or policy in terms of accumulated units of some kind. It is more useful simply to talk about the activities involved in the changes over time.

In this view, there is no need to segment past, present, or future or to conceive of development in terms of the acquisition or transmission of stored units. Development is a dynamic process, with change throughout rather than accumulation of new items or transformation of existing items.

In this view, participatory appropriation is an aspect of ongoing events. A person who participates in events changes in ways that make a difference in subsequent events. Participatory appropriation is ongoing development as people participate in events and thus handle subsequent events in ways based on their involvement in previous events. This contrasts with the internalization perspective in which one would look for exposure to external knowledge or skill, followed by internalization with or without transformation by the individual, followed by evidence of such internalization as the person retrieves the acquired knowledge or skill independently (see Rogoff, Radziszewska, & Masiello, in press).

In some efforts to understand internalization of social events time is used as a tool, but still with the assumptions of a separation between internal and external, of time as independent of events, of boundaries between past, present, and future, and of development as acquisition of static pieces of information or skill. Sequential analyses of social interaction, for instance, may examine change over time by breaking an event into smaller units (of either time or moves made by one person or the other) but often define the contribution of each partner separately in order to look at the impact of one upon the other. For example, a study may examine maternal assistance and child learning by choosing categories of maternal behavior (questions, directives, praise) and categories of child behavior (errors, correct response, off-task behavior) and examining the contingencies between them. Such a sequential strategy is consistent with the internalization perspective, in which time is separate from events, the external and internal events are arbitrarily separated, and development is seen as accumulation (see Figure 6.1).

The participatory appropriation perspective focuses instead on events as dynamically changing, with people participating with others in coherent events (where one could examine each person's contributions as they relate to each other, but not define them separately), and development is seen as transformation. Inherent to the participatory appropriation view is the mutual constitution of personal, interpersonal, and cultural processes, with development involving all planes of focus in sociocultural activity (see Figure 6.2).

The internalization view is based on an assumption that the individual is the primary unit of analysis, with static interpersonal and cultural influences added onto "basic" individual processes. In the internalization model, the individual is either a passive recipient of external social or cultural influence – a receptacle for the accumulation of knowledge and skill – or an active seeker of passive external social and cultural knowledge and skill. In the participatory appropriation perspective, personal, interpersonal, and cultural processes all constitute each other as they transform sociocultural activity.

The transformations involved in participatory appropriation are developmental in the sense that they are changes in particular directions. The direction of development varies locally (in accord with cultural values, interpersonal needs, and specific circumstances); it does not require the specification of universal or ideal end points of development.

The questions to investigate are different if we move from internalization approaches and instead view cognitive development as participatory appropriation through guided participation in a system of apprenticeship. Questions of where memories are stored or how information is taken from external events or how children accumulate knowledge or implement plans all become less relevant ways to study development from this sociocultural approach.[7]

Instead, we begin to examine in closer focus the actual processes by which children participate with other people in cultural activity and the ways they transform their participation. The investigation of people's actual involvement in activities becomes the basis of our understanding of development rather than simply the surface details that we try to get past. The central question becomes how people participate in sociocultural activity and how their participation changes from being relatively peripheral (see Lave & Wenger, 1991), observing and carrying out secondary roles, to sometimes being responsible for managing such activities.

Viewing development as participatory appropriation recasts the clas-

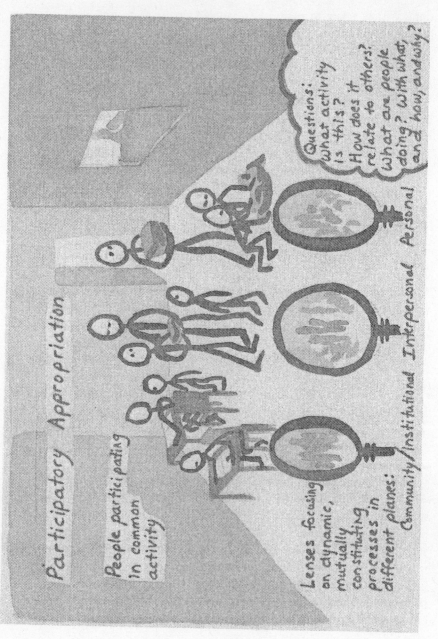

Figure 6.2.

sic question concerning the transfer of knowledge. How an individual approaches two situations has to do with how he or she construes the relations between their purposes or meanings. Hence, the process is inherently creative, with people actively seeking meaning and relating situations to each other.

This creative process, of course, is itself a sociocultural activity. People, by themselves and with companions, puzzle out how to manage a new situation on the basis of their own and their shared history, to reach their own and their shared goals, through subtle and explicit communication indicating the "kind" of a situation in which they are involved. All such communication is at one and the same time particular and general, as reference is made to the here and now in ways that draw on concepts one has met before (Dewey, 1916). For example, to refer to an object with a label (e.g., "This is a chapter") links the present object with a general class of objects of sociocultural import. The ways that objects and events are classified in language and in action are sociocultural generalizations within which we all function and that we extend when we figure out how to handle a thing or event that is somewhat novel to us.

From my perspective, orienting our inquiry by focusing on how people participate in sociocultural activity and how they change their participation demystifies the processes of learning and development. Rather than searching for the nature of internalization as a conduit from external bits of knowledge or skill to an internal repository, we look directly at the efforts of individuals, their companions, and the institutions they constitute and build upon to see development as grounded in the specifics and commonalities of those efforts, opportunities, constraints, and changes.

In the study of Girl Scout cookie sales and delivery, we were able to observe changes in how the girls participated in a number of aspects of the activity.[8] In the calculation of charges to customers, we could track in many cases how the girls took on greater responsibility over the course of the delivery, with their mothers often initially managing the calculations and supervising the girls in keeping track of customers who had paid; in the course of participating in a system that was often set up by the mothers, the girls took on greater responsibility for handling these complicated and important aspects of the activity.

We could also track how the girls, over the course of the activity, became more familiar with the layout of the routes connecting their customers and often managed their parents' driving as the parents helped the girls deliver. We observed (actually, eavesdropped on) the girls learning to manage the complex planning involved in developing spatial routes with sufficient flexibility to be efficient within the interpersonal and material resources and constraints of the situation.

We could observe how the girls sometimes participated with customers, following the structure provided by the scout organization in the format of the order sheet, which provided the girls with talk-aloud calculations that revealed arithmetic strategies. We followed the process by which the girls made use of and extended cultural tools (writing, calculating, using Post-it notes to remember, developing a common language to refer to places to be visited) that tied their efforts in this activity to practices in other institutions of their culture.

These observations all revealed cognitive developmental processes that occurred as the girls participated in this sociocultural activity. Through the girls' participation, they developed in ways that we could see leading to changed later participation. Their participatory appropriation was an ongoing feature of their guided participation in the apprenticeship system through which we can view the personal, interpersonal, and cultural processes of this activity.

Although it is beyond the scope of this chapter to discuss methodological considerations, the sociocultural approach that I have presented involves shifting such considerations associated with the changes in the conceptual base. The approach does not prescribe the use of specific methodological tools but does emphasize the relation of particular tools to the theoretical purposes to which they are put. An analysis of shifts in the interpretation of data given such a sociocultural approach is available in Rogoff, Radziszewska, and Masiello (in press). The tools that I have used for studying patterns of sociocultural activities emphasize close analysis of events through ethnographic methods, abstraction of generalities based on this analysis, extensive use of graphing of information and application of quantitative methods to check and communicate the patterns discerned through the ethnographic and graphic analyses (see Rogoff et al., 1993, for discussion and examples of these methods).

In sum, I have presented a sociocultural approach that is based on consideration of personal, interpersonal, and community planes of focus in the analysis of developmental process involved in the participation of individuals with others in cultural practices. The approach emphasizes seeking patterns in the organization of sociocultural activities, focusing variously on personal, interpersonal, or community aspects of the activities, with the other aspects in the background but taken into account. Research resulting from this approach emphasizes observing both similarities and differences across varying sociocultural activities, as well as tracking the relations among aspects of events viewed in different planes of analysis. Such a sociocultural analysis requires considering how individuals, groups, and communities transform as they together constitute and are constituted by sociocultural activity.

Notes

1. The metaphor appears to me to be equally applicable to culturally organized activities that can be regarded as desirable or undesirable. Although my own research focuses on learning to participate in activities valued in the communities studied, I think that the conceptual framework can be well applied to learning to participate in activities censured in the communities studied (such as interpersonal violence and addictive behavior, which raise concern).
2. Such direction/guidance does not simply include facilitation of involvement in certain activities; it also includes restriction or very indirect channeling of the activities in which people participate, for example, the exclusion of children from some adult activities or the message that they are allowed to participate only in certain ways. Guidance is thus direct or indirect structuring of people's possibilities for participation that promotes some particular direction of development.
3. They also suggested that we disguise ourselves as bushes and follow them around, which we did not.
4. These two terms mean the same thing in my account. I add the word "participatory" to emphasize that in my use of the term, appropriation is necessarily through a person's *own* involvement, not an incorporation of something external. This is a point of difference with others who also use the term "appropriation," as I discuss in this section.
5. However, Vygotsky's characterization of internalization as proceeding from the interpersonal to the intrapersonal involves a separation in time of social and individual aspects of the activity, which is at odds with my idea of participatory appropriation, in which a person's participation is at one and the same time a social and an individual process.
6. My discussion of time is greatly influenced by Gibson's theory and Pepper's account of a contextual world hypothesis. I am endebted to Beth Shapiro and Christine Mosier for discussion of these issues.
7. The metaphor of stored mental representation and the characterization of plans,

memories, concepts, etc. as objects of inquiry may still be useful in some scholarly endeavors. I am not arguing for necessarily dropping the metaphor but for recognizing it *as a metaphor*, perhaps useful for communication between scholars, but not to be automatically assumed to characterize the functioning of the people whom we study. It seems more parsimonious to drop it for some research.

8. We focus here on the development of the girls through their participation in this activity; similar analyses could be done of the development of the troop leaders, family members, customers, and researchers through their participation in the activity.

References

Baker-Sennett, J., Matusov, E., & Rogoff, B. (1992). Sociocultural processes of creative planning in children's playcrafting. In P. Light & G. Butterworth (Eds.), *Context and cognition: Ways of learning and knowing* (pp. 93–114). Hertfordshire, UK: Harvester-Wheatsheaf.

Baker-Sennett, J., Matusov, E., & Rogoff, B. (1992). Planning as developmental process. In H. Reese (Ed.), *Advances in child development* (Vol. 24, pp. 253–281). San Diego: Academic.

Bakhtin, M. M. (1981). *The dialogical imagination* (M. Holquist, Ed.). Austin: University of Texas Press.

Bakhurst, D. (1988). Activity, consciousness and communication. *Newsletter of the Laboratory for Comparative Human Cognition, 10,* 31–39.

Berger, P. L., & Luckmann, T. (1966). *The social construction of reality.* New York: Doubleday.

Bruner, J. S. (1983). *Child's talk: Learning to use language.* New York: Norton.

Cole, M. (1985). The zone of proximal development: Where culture and cognition create each other. In J. V. Wertsch (Ed.), *Culture, communication, and cognition: Vygotskian perspectives* (pp. 146–161). Cambridge University Press.

Dewey, J. (1916). *Democracy and education: An introduction to the philosophy of education.* New York: Macmillan.

Dewey, J., & Bentley, A. F. (1949). *Knowing and the known.* Boston: Beacon.

Forman, E. A. (1989). The role of peer interaction in the social construction of mathematical knowledge. *International Journal of Educational Research, 13,* 55–70.

Gibson, J. J. (1979). *The ecological approach to visual perception.* Boston: Houghton Mifflin.

Goody, E. N. (1989). Learning, apprenticeship and the division of labor. In M. W. Coy (Ed.), *Apprenticeship: From theory to method and back again* (pp. 233–256). Albany: State University of New York Press.

Harre, R. (1983). *Personal being.* Oxford: Basil Blackwell.

John-Steiner, V. (1985). *Notebooks of the mind: Explorations of thinking.* Albuquerque: University of New Mexico Press.

Lave, J., & Wenger, E. (1991). *Situated learning: Legitimate peripheral participation.* Cambridge University Press.

Leont'ev, A. N. (1981). The problem of activity in psychology. In J. V. Wertsch (Ed.), *The concept of activity in Soviet psychology* (pp. 37–71). Armonk, NY: Sharpe.

Newman, D., Griffin, P., & Cole, M. (1989). *The construction zone: Working for cognitive change in school.* Cambridge University Press.

Pepper, S. C. (1942). *World hypotheses: A study in evidence.* Berkeley: University of California Press.

Rogoff, B. (1982). Integrating context and cognitive development. In M. E. Lamb & A. L. Brown (Eds.), *Advances in developmental psychology* (Vol. 2, pp. 125–170). Hillsdale, NJ: Erlbaum.

Rogoff, B. (1990). *Apprenticeship in thinking: Cognitive development in social context.* New York: Oxford University Press.

Rogoff, B. (1992). Three ways to relate person and culture: Thoughts sparked by Valsiner's review of *Apprenticeship in Thinking. Human Development. 35,* 316–320.

Rogoff, B. (1993). Children's guided participation and participatory appropriation in sociocultural activity. In R. Wozniak & K. Fischer (Eds.), *Development in context: Acting and thinking in specific environments* (pp. 121–153). Hillsdale, NJ: Erlbaum.

Rogoff, B., Baker-Sennett, J., Lacasa, P., & Goldsmith, D. (in press). Development through participation in sociocultural activity. In J. Goodnow, P. Miller, & F. Kessel (Eds.), in everyday planning. *Cultural practices as contexts for development.* San Francisco: Jossey-Bass.

Rogoff, B., & Gardner, W. P. (1984). Adult guidance of cognitive development. In B. Rogoff & J. Lave (Eds.), *Everyday cognition: Its development in social context* (pp. 95–116). Cambridge, MA: Harvard University Press.

Rogoff, B., Mistry, J. J., Göncü, A., & Mosier, C. (1993). Guided participation in cultural activity by toddlers and caregivers. *Monographs of the Society for Research in Child Development, 58* (7, Serial No. 236).

Rogoff, B., Radziszewska, B., & Masiello, T. (in press). The analysis of developmental processes in sociocultural activity. In L. Martin, K. Nelson, & E. Tobach (Eds.), *Cultural psychology and activity theory.* Cambridge University Press.

Scribner, S. (1985). Vygotsky's uses of history. In J. V. Wertsch (Ed.), *Culture, communication, and cognition: Vygotskian perspectives* (pp. 119–145). Cambridge University Press.

Smedslund, J. (1984). The invisible obvious: Culture in psychology. In K. M. J. Lagerspetz & P. Niemi (Eds.), *Psychology in the 1990's* (pp. 443–452). Amsterdam: Elsevier.

Vygotsky, L. S. (1978). *Mind in society: The development of higher psychological processes.* Cambridge, MA: Harvard University Press.

Vygotsky, L. S. (1987). *Thinking and speech.* In R. W. Rieber & A. S. Carton (Eds.), *The collected works of L. S. Vygotsky* (N. Minick, Trans.) (pp. 37–285). New York: Plenum.

Wertsch, J. V. (1985). *Vygotsky and the social formation of mind.* Cambridge, MA: Harvard University Press.

Wertsch, J. V., & Stone, C. A. (1979, February). A social interactional analysis of learning disabilities remediation. Paper presented at the International Conference of the Association for Children with Learning Disabilities, San Francisco.

Zinchenko, V. P. (1985). Vygotsky's ideas about units for the analysis of mind. In J. V. Wertsch (Ed.), *Culture, communication, and cognition: Vygotskian perspectives* (pp. 94–118). Cambridge University Press.

7   The constitution of the
subject: a persistent question

Ana Luiza B. Smolka, Maria Cecília R. De Goes, and Angel Pino

One of the persistent questions debated within developmental, social, and cognitive psychology concerns the formation of individual consciousness or the constitution of the individual subject. The purpose of this chapter is to contribute to the discussion of this issue, reviewing selected topics and arguments raised by authors representative of the historical-cultural approach. In looking at a number of current tendencies and past contributions, we debate some of the conceptual aspects that concern us in relation to empirical investigative work and that seem to have relevant consequences at the theoretical-methodological level.

Although the role of social reality in the formation of the individual subject is a widely accepted (and obvious) idea, controversies and ambiguities arise when the nature of this role and the genesis of the individual processes are conceptualized. The approaches to this problem involve theoretical elaborations that tend to privilege either intra- or interindividual functioning. In the first case, we conceptualize individual functioning according to sociogenetic principles; in the second, we find contributions in studies relying on the concept of intersubjectivity. We will initially focus on these two tendencies.

Sociogenesis and individual processes

Within the discussions of sociogenetic approaches, we highlight the contributions of Valsiner (1987, 1994) in his attempts to develop a

This ongoing research work has been sponsored by grants from FAPESP – Fundaçao de Amparo à Pesquisa do Estado de São Paulo.

consistent explanatory model for understanding the formation of the individual.

In examining interpretations of the relationships between the individual and social reality, Valsiner (1992) points to three models of sociogenesis, which are based on the notions of harmonious learning, fusion, and contagion. In the first of these interpretations, society provides what is to be learned through mechanisms that transfer knowledge, and thus the developing individual is shaped to be a participant of that society. As a learner of available forms of action and knowledge, the developing person is "socialized," coming to be harmoniously inserted in the social world. The second interpretation, based on the idea of fusion, emphasizes the unification of personal and social aspects, dispensing with the need to configure structural peculiarities of the personal and the social worlds. As to the third type of interpretation, the notion of social contagion implies the metaphor of infectious diseases, allowing for a conception of sociogenesis as a process by which social interaction affects (infects) the subject through semiotic mechanisms (viruses). And, what is more important, it differs from the other models in the sense that it also allows for the idea that the subject can neutralize or resist the infection through forms of immunity that can impede contagion.

Valsiner (1994) argues that explanations of sociogenesis must account for instances of "maximum social relatedness," as well as instances of "seemingly total independence" of the subject in relation to the social world. These diverse possibilities can only be encompassed by a bidirectional model of cultural transmission, since unidirectional models assume a fixedness of what is to be transmitted and a passivity of the recipient of the transmission. Such a bidirectional model should also emphasize the active role of the developing person, whose functioning is based on transformational mechanisms (also discussed elsewhere by that author; e.g., Lawrence & Valsiner, 1993; Valsiner, 1987).

In attempting to meet such requirements, he proposes the notion of coconstruction, relating the child and social others, as the theoretical nucleus. The irregularities of behavior patterns and oppositions in social relationships are admitted as part of development, while genetic formations are described as movements from dedifferentiation to differentiation, or from chaotic/fluid to clear forms.

The problem that is privileged in this discussion of sociogenesis is the explanation of the novel forms of action in development and, consequently, that of the contribution of the individual as an epistemic and psychological subject. The emergence of features in development that are not part of the "social input" – the fact that the child acts in ways that do not follow the goals set by his or her socializers (Valsiner, 1988) – is accounted for by the idea of an inclusive separation of individual and social worlds. This leads to the assumption of a collective and a personal culture, made possible by sociogenetic mechanisms that create both social and personal phenomena *in parallel*. "Inclusive separation" allows for the subject to be constituted by the social world ontogenetically, but to be a separate entity (with an individual psychological world) ontologically. Yet, assuming a semiotic nature of self-constraining and other-constraining mechanisms, Valsiner emphasizes the active role of the subject in the process of handling dialogicality, the multiplicity of voices in inter- and intrapersonal functioning.

When delineating his coconstructionist model, Valsiner (1994) adheres to the contagion metaphor. The child faces social suggestions, organized with high redundancy in everyday experiences. The cultural environment, though heterogeneous, organizes these suggestions in a similar direction, making inevitable the child's encounter with them. However, the child can resist social prescriptions when developing knowledge and forms of action. The contribution of the subject is seen as the creation and activation of antibodies present in the personal culture, which allow him or her to resist the viruses in some way.

Some problems arise in these arguments when we look for clues concerning the issue of the constitution of the subject. What are the origins and nature of the immunity that account for resistance to social suggestions? If the "ways of self-immunization" come from past experiences, in social relationships, is not immunity socially constructed? Why should novelty, flexibility, and inconsistency appear as immunity/resistance to social suggestion? Are they not socially constituted as well? And last, can the role of social environment be reduced to "suggestion" or "contamination"?

In this broad discussion of the relationship between individual and society, Valsiner (1994) is engaged in an effort to preserve the subject, to free him or her of a threatening theoretical model that might challenge the existence or survival of the subject. This concern is made explicit by the author when he states that in the coconstructionist framework, the notion of person survives in this context of theoretical discourse.

The problem, however, is not that the "notion of person" must/ should survive, but *which* notion of person survives in *what* frame of reference and how a theoretical model actually explains the person's constitution process.

Such difficulties and dilemmas simply show us that the debate remains open concerning the social nature of the individual subject/person/thinking agent. Within this debate, another line of theoretical expansion can be found in the contributions offered by authors who attempt to conceptualize communicative and interactive processes in connection with the notion of intersubjectivity.

Intersubjectivity and individual processes

In the case of sociogenesis, we have concentrated on the elaboration of one author, as a representative (and reviewer) of that approach. In relation to intersubjectivity, we find it necessary to bring in elaborations of different authors, since an analysis of the diversity of formulations will be helpful to our discussion of the conceptual links between interindividual functioning and the constitution of the subject.

Several studies on interindividual functioning have alluded to Rommetveit's interesting and productive ideas on intersubjectivity in verbal communication, which are founded on the assumption that language is "a thoroughly and genuinely social phenomenon" and that interlocutors in a dialogue reach a "state of intersubjectivity" as they share the same focus of attention. Moreover, interlocutors in a dyadic interaction might reach a "perfectly shared social reality" if, besides focusing on the same object or topic, they assume the same point of view concerning that object or topic (Rommetveit, 1979). He also mentions that "states of intersubjectivity" are reached in a dyadic communicative movement depending on the "speaker's privilege" and the "listener's commitment," which brings up the question of symmetrical and asymmetrical relationships, acknowledging that symmetry exists only if there is an "unlimited interchangeability of dialogue roles," that is, an (inter)regulation between speaker's and listener's roles.

Rommetveit (1979, 1985) discusses other very relevant ideas for the understanding of "verbal interaction," particularly in dyadic situations.

Among them, he highlights the pluralistic character of the social world, fragmentarily known and partially shared. He emphasizes the vagueness, ambiguity, and incompleteness of ordinary language, which makes it a flexible and versatile means of communication, allowing for interpretation and negotiation. He stresses that reality, being complex and multifaceted, has multiple meanings – what makes each interlocutor a possible "inhabitant of multiple worlds" in a diversity of perspectives. Yet the multiplicity of meanings and the incompleteness of knowledge of the world lead to transcendence of different "private worlds" in communicative encounters. Communication, then, "sets up what we might call 'states of intersubjectivity' " (1979, p. 94). Each communicative encounter constitutes a unique and enigmatic "state of affairs" because of the multiplicity of meanings. According to Rommetveit, the enigmas are "subjectively" solved by a comparative process.

Thus, intersubjectivity becomes a condition for, or characteristic of, true human communication, implying for the interlocutors a "reciprocal faith in a shared experiential world." This allows Rommetveit to state that "intersubjectivity must in some sense be taken for granted in order to be attained. This semiparadox may indeed be conceived of as a basic pragmatic postulate of human discourse" (1985, p. 189).

Such interpretations of intersubjectivity are taken over by Wertsch (1985a, 1989) when analyzing the movement concerning the internalization of social forms of action through semiotic devices. In one of his earlier attempts to trace the transition from the inter- to the intrapsychological plane, and to make explicit the Vygotskian construct of the zone of proximal development (ZPD), Wertsch analyzes young children's joint activities (puzzle assembling) with their mothers, identifying levels in the children's path to autonomous performance.

Wertsch (1985a) draws his analysis of the inter-/intrapsychological functioning based on Vygotsky's genetic law of cultural development, also taking into account Rommetveit's arguments on verbal interaction. He uses the notion of situation definition – "the way in which objects and events in a situation are represented or defined" – to delineate and to characterize not just states, but increasing levels of intersubjectivity: "Intersubjectivity exists when interlocutors share some aspect of their situation definitions" (Wertsch, 1985a, p. 159).

This articulation of interpsychological functioning, from Vygotsky, and intersubjectivity, from Rommetveit, is seen as possible because the latter author's position "is compatible with the Vygotskyan approach to interpsychological functioning" (Wertsch, 1985a, p. 159). If contemporary authors who assume and/or develop Vygotsky's ideas have been using the term "intersubjectivity" related to his perspective, we can actually trace uses of the concept of intersubjectivity, in the past two decades, from different sources, especially research in the field of language acquisition and verbal or nonverbal communication (Rommetveit, 1979; Trevarthen, 1979) with no reference at all to Vygotsky. Many of these authors who had earlier elaborated on the concept have lately taken into account Vygotsky's works incorporating principles and ideas. What are, thus, the current assumptions underlying the uses of the term? How has it been used? What are the possible variations of its theoretical status?

For Rommetveit, as we have seen, intersubjectivity "must be taken for granted in order to be achieved," thus referring, at the same time, to a *tacit assumption* between interlocutors as well as to *circumstances* – space of encounters, time for sharing – of a "dialogue state."

As for Wertsch, when he examines instances of "states of intersubjectivity" in relation to Vygotsky's ZPD notion, thus determining *levels* of intersubjectivity in the analysis of adult–child interactions, it seems that intersubjectivity acquires the feature of an *emergent human capacity*.

A different use of the term appears with Trevarthen (1979) in his studies of early mother–infant relationships, when he proposes an *innate intersubjectivity* and talks about the "rudiments of individual consciousness and intentionality" as an attribute of acting agents that he calls "subjectivity." Trevarthen and Logotheti (1987) state that infants are born "communicators," soon developing "forms of sensitivity and expression that lead to 'acts of meaning' oriented to other people" (p. 66). The newborn baby has, thus, the capacity actively to seek out response, support, and appreciation. Trevarthen defines intersubjectivity as "both recognition and control of cooperative intentions and joint patterns of awareness" (Trevarthen, 1979 Rogoff, 1990), distinguishing between primary (shared focus of attention between people) and secondary (shared focus of attention between people, including objects or events) intersubjectivity. In this perspective, intersubjectivity is a specific *property* of the human species.

Yet another connotation for intersubjectivity has been stressed by Tudge (1992), as he studies peer interactions and cognitive develop-

ment, analyzing a partner's impact on each other's thinking. Tudge
states that his

use of the term [intersubjectivity] is based on the view that individuals come to a task,
problem or conversation with their own subjective ways of making sense of it. If they
then discuss their differing viewpoints, shared understanding may be attained. . . . In
other words, in the course of communication, participants may arrive at some mutually
agreed upon, or intersubjective, understanding. (p. 1365)

According to Tudge, if there is an already existing "intersubjectivity" or shared understanding between working partners, it is less likely
that a change in thinking will happen in the dyadic communication.
On the other hand, differences in thinking perspectives and competence
levels lead to cognitive changes, although these changes might not necessarily imply advance and may also include developmental decline.

When Tudge mentions "already existing intersubjectivity" between
or among peers, this is, nonetheless, a result of previous interactions.
What seems to be emphasized in his argument concerning intersubjectivity is the feature of an *objective* or a *result* of shared activity or
cognitive work.

Rogoff (1990) presents and discusses conceptions and positions related to intersubjectivity. In analyzing processes of guided participation
between children and their more skilled partners, she takes intersubjectivity (shared understanding based on a common focus of attention
and some shared presuppositions) as a crucial concept, assuming that
it underlies such processes and that communication between partners
presumes intersubjectivity. In her investigative work examining learn-
ing/thinking processes, from joint activity to individual regulation, in
diverse cultural settings as well as many different situations, Rogoff
speaks of a variety of forms and arrangements of intersubjectivity, depending on innumerable possibilities of communicative encounters, in
both symmetrical and asymmetrical relationships.

As presented, it seems that Rogoff brings together some of the meanings discussed earlier; taking intersubjectivity as a presumed or *preexisting condition* for communication and shared thinking, which give
rise to individual appropriation.

Hence, all these meanings – result, objective, assumption, condition,
circumstance, property of species, emerging capacity – pervade the uses
of intersubjectivity, which becomes, nonetheless, a quite homogenized,
extensive, and unspecified term in current usage.

These multiple elaborations, although contributing to the conceptualizations of intersubjectivity, may involve us in a conceptual circularity, created by assertions such as the following: "Communication *aims at* the transcendence of 'private worlds' of the participants" (Rommetveit, 1979, p. 94). "By its nature, communication *presumes* intersubjectivity" (Rogoff, 1990, p. 71). "Communication *sets up* 'states of intersubjectivity' " (Rommetveit, 1979 p. 94). "The mutual understanding that is *achieved* between people in communication has been termed intersubjectivity" (Rogoff, 1990, p. 67). Since intersubjectivity is assumed as shared or mutual understanding, this sharing/mutuality is, then, presumed, set up, aimed at, or achieved by communication.

There seems to be an ambiguity in relation to the theoretical status of intersubjectivity. When it is taken as assumed or presumed, it has the character of a precondition; when it is seen as something achieved or a circumstance, it has the character of an event. The uses of the term might imply one, the other, or both aspects. Does it stand, broadly, as a synonym for the term "social," or does it refer to specified instances of social functioning?

Despite this diversity of meanings, there are convergent references to a harmonious nature of intersubjectivity. This is revealed by expressions such as "mutual understanding," "symmetrical dialogue," "smooth and fair turn taking," and "sharing of focus and meanings." But is harmony the essence of intersubjectivity? In fact, there have been arguments for the expansion of social interaction or interregulation to encompass instances of disagreements, conflicts, misunderstandings (Elbers, Maier, Hockstra, & Hougsteden, 1992), and active nonparticipation (Valsiner, 1994).

We tend to agree with these arguments in the sense that divergent perspectives, opposition of ideas, resistance to communication, and other disharmonious instances will not fit nicely in the aforementioned models. From this, we can ask how deregulations can be conceived. Are they to be taken as intersubjective disfunctioning or as functioning that is not intersubjective? Another possibility is that they are *part* of intersubjective functioning. The difference is not subtle. It seems to us that a harmonious–disharmonious conception will involve not only an addition of elements, but an effort to modify current conceptualizations of intersubjectivity.

These problems are related to the selection, by investigators, of the situations and processes empirically studied. Given that conceptual elaborations determine and are also determined by methodological options, some limitations at the level of discussion are linked to the fact that intersubjectivity has been analyzed as implying communicative instances, involving dyadic face-to-face relationships, and has generally been restricted to cognitive development.

These considerations about the theoretical status, nature, and methodological approach of intersubjectivity indicate that, within this perspective, the process whereby the subject is constituted is, at most, only indirectly addressed. The models do not pose specific questions about the status or constitution of the subjects in relationship and often seem to refer to already constituted subjects who enter into relationship. The scarce references to the subjectivity implied in intersubjectivity suggest that several clarifications are needed to advance the study of the process of social constitution.

Is this process to be explained by intersubjectivity as a broad principle, or does it also encompass instances of nonestablished intersubjectivity? In each of these cases, how should different empirical situations be methodologically approached? In either case, how can nonharmonious processes be assimilated in the nature of the constitutive process?

The constitution of the subject: elements for an inquiry

Our preoccupations in the face of discussions on sociogenesis and intersubjectivity are rooted not only in the study of theoretical work, but also in attempts to undertake empirical analyses. To illustrate our concerns, we will briefly describe and comment on an episode involving 4-year-old children in a preschool setting.

The episode

Four 4-year-old children (Joana, Raquel, Fernando, and Flávio), sitting at a table, are getting ready to play a memory game. Fernando distributes the cards among the other players, keeping for himself the larger amount. They start putting the cards face up on a

board to observe them before turning them face down. Fábio approaches the corner of the table, between Fernando and Flávio:
Fábio calls out:

1. Fernando!
2. Fernando!
3. Fernando!
4. Fernando!

Small pause while Fábio observes Fernando's movement arranging the cards on the game board.

5. Hey, Fernando!
6. Fernando!

Another small pause and observation.

7. Fernando!
8. Fernando!

Flávio imitates Fábio, teasing him:

9. Fernando! (Same rhythm and tone)

Fábio goes on:

10. Hey, Fernando! (Fábio touches Fernando's arm)
11. Hey, Fernando! Let me play with your dog. (Touching Fernando's arm)
12. Fernando!
13. Hey, Fernando! (Pushes and pulls Fernando's arm)

Fernando (as they finish setting the cards):

14. . . . the frog (male) and the frog (female). Now let's turn everything down.

Fábio:

15. Fernando! (Touches Fernando's arm)

Flávio, teasing Fábio again:

16. Fernanda? (Uses feminine ending and laughs)

Fábio:

17. Fernando, let me play with your dog!

. . . (Continues up to turn 25)

This small episode lasts for 2 minutes, during which Fábio calls Fernando's name 25 times, touches or holds Fernando's arm 11 times, and asks 3 times if he can play with Fernando's dog. He is twice teased by Flávio, and gets from Fernando (at turn 23) an answer: No! He tries calling and asking Fernando a couple of times more and gives up, walking away. The four children continue to play.

One methodological option in examining the situation could be to select, or highlight, in the interactive process, instances of dyadic relationships. But this would not account for the whole dynamic of the game. Another option, then, would be to work with nondyadic, but polyadic relationships, including in the analysis the four participants. In this case, the focus of interest in the analytic effort would be the course of interactions among children, during the game as a whole.

At first, we can observe four children getting together as they have a common objective – to play the memory game. One could say that according to the criteria and models presented earlier, there is intersubjectivity among these children who are getting ready to play. Their past experiences support a "common faith" in a shared world, and they share a focus of attention. The situation could be seen as quite favorable or ideal for the achievement of a "state of intersubjectivity."

Yet, if we examine the course of the game beyond the described episode, we can observe that at certain moments in this interaction, during the preparation for and within the actual game, the children argue and dispute about who is going to start, who is winning, and so on, thus configuring a "shared world" concerning the conditions of the game, but not a "perfectly shared understanding" concerning the rules, results, and individual perspectives. Given these circumstances and methodological choices, one could say that "states of intersubjectivity" are achieved among some or all of the children at different levels in different moments of the interactive process, which can be characterized as a symmetrical relationship.

However, a fifth participant comes and "intrudes" into the scene. What happens? How does he relate to the other participants? Should we disregard this moment in the analytical procedure? How do we analyze this disruptive moment? Can we include it in the analysis of the "intersubjective" relationship?

When Fábio enters the scene, the configuration of the group changes.

He has a specific purpose that does not fit or belong to the game. According to some of the theoretical positions, we could say that intersubjectivity is not presupposed or achieved between Fábio and the other children since there is not a shared focus, shared intentions, or shared objectives.

In fact, if we analyze the speaker–listeners relationship in this situation, we observe that if Fábio "has the word" (calling Fernando 25 times), he doesn't "get to the floor." Fábio calls Fernando, but there is not an answer, less yet commitment from the listener. The four children (getting ready to play) seem to ignore him totally, although they certainly hear him.

Fábio calls Fernando 11 times, waiting for (at least a sign of) his assent before saying what he wants, asking permission to play with Fernando's dog. He shortly stops calling (2 or 3 times) to observe briefly the children setting the cards on the board. After turn 10, Fábio insistently touches Fernando's arm as he continues calling his name.

At turns 9 and 16, there is a form of reply, but not commitment, from Flávio. The first time (turn 9), Flávio imitates Fábio, echoing and teasing him. The second time (turn 16), Flávio transforms Fábio's words, teasing both, Fábio and Fernando (using the feminine ending and laughing). Here, we could ask who is Flávio talking to? To nobody? To anybody? To everybody? To himself? To the camera (the situation is being videotaped)? How do Flávio's comments fit into the analysis of such interactions? Can we speak of "intersubjectivity"? Flávio's focus is on Fábio's words, more specifically on the way Fábio is talking. Fábio's focus is on Fernando's attention.

At turn 25, Fernando finally answers, quite abruptly, Fábio's insistent calling (and question) with a "No!" Fábio cannot play with his dog. This no, however, does not end Fábio's attempts.

At this moment, and only at this moment, one could say that a shared focus of attention was established. But in what terms? Contact was reached, or at least made explicit by Fernando's answer, even though marked by negation, disagreement, and disregard. There seems to be instant, fugacious, mutual understanding concerning an issue: Fernando knows what Fábio is saying and what he wants; Fábio knows that Fernando knows that. Nonetheless, Fernando hasn't the slightest interest in paying attention to or considering Fábio's talk. There is no syntony, reciprocity, shared focus, sustained conversation, or negotiation. Hence, we should say, intersubjectivity does not happen, although there is a short moment of communication.

Our point is that if intersubjectivity does not happen in the sense of a "state" contingent upon certain specific conditions, there is, nonetheless, a relationship between subjects. There is *intersubjective relationship*, as well as a simultaneous process of subject constitution, which is not included or taken into account in the notion of intersubjectivity reviewed before.

The issue acquires an even greater complexity when we look at the position of individuals in the dynamic interaction. In fact, 4-year-old children already bring a history of relationships with others that configurates a singular process of individual formation – they are (considered) *subjects:* They are each given a name, they are referred to and called, they are recognized, they can recognize themselves, they can attend when called, they can even not attend when called. What positions do they assume in relation to each other? How do others configurate the position of an individual subject? For example, when Fernando refuses to answer or pretends not to listen to Fábio's insistent calls, or when Flávio teases, or when the girls keep quiet, how do they circumscribe Fábio's position? In this same movement, how is Fernando's position configurated?

We can identify a not so subtle power relationship: Fernando (unequally) shares the cards among the players; he gives the orders and sets the rules (as in turn 14); he has the dog, which he may or may not share. Yet Fábio's persistent calls seem quite empowering to Fernando, as does the girl's silence. Flávio's teasing might be challenging, but it is also ignored. In this interactive movement, Fernando is the boss; he controls the situation. Fábio appears totally subjected to the group and to Fernando's power, as Fernando leads the group.

So, the initial (apparently) "symmetrical" relationship among 4-year-old peers gains other contours, not strictly determined by age or by competence – the usual, implicit criteria for characterizing symmetrical or asymmetrical relationships. How does one determine competence, for example, in this case? Concerning what matters? So, if we take into account implicit power relations, we must face and examine an intricate *drama* that necessarily changes, as it makes more complex, the focus of the analysis. It seems, then, that symmetry and asymmetry categories should include other criteria for the analysis of the interactive dynamics.

Still, if in the texture of human relations we cannot always find the ideal or desired "symmetry" and "harmony," we can certainly identify simultaneous, even *reciprocal*, process whereby subjects are constituted in relation to some definite or assumed social positions. This reciprocity does not, however, have the same harmonious meaning as "mutuality," which pervades the notion of intersubjectivity. Here, "reciprocal" is used in the sense of being *inversely related*, as the empowering of one subject *disempowers* the other. But yet, in a deeper sense, we can say that reciprocal means "constitutively related." The process of individual consciousness formation, or subject constitution, happens not only "intersubjectively" but also dialectically in interpsychological functioning.

This point can be made explicit as we highlight one aspect in the analysis: Fábio, as speaker, calls Fernando's name and, in this very act, constitutes himself and the other as protagonists in the event. The *proper* (main) name, when enunciated, configurates (the place of) a specific subject in this scene. As Fernando listens to Fábio but does not answer, he also constitutes Fábio as a subject, recognizing him while negating him, denying him an answer, or making this answer shortly explicit: "No!" (turn 23). Through Fábio's multiple calls and insistent voice, as well as through Fernando's silence, lack of answer, and denial, an asymmetrical (power) relationship is established – each action sustaining the "I" while constituting the other.

The constitution of the subject: revisiting perspectives

Considering the preceding discussions of recent conceptualizations and the questions posed in relation to the empirical material presented, we could say that in different approaches within the historical-cultural perspective, when intraindividual functioning is focused on, there is a concern with the risk of a "dissolution of the subject" or of a "dictatorship of the other" in the interindividual functioning; on the other hand, when interindividual functioning is focused on, the question of the subject constitution is not directly addressed.

Wertsch's work can be identified as an important attempt to establish an articulated view of "the two sides" of subject formation; within this attempt are explicit concerns for the risk of a predominance of either inter- or intra-individual processes. After having explored the relationships between these processes at the levels of ontogenesis and microgenesis (Wertsch, 1985, 1987), he has turned to what could be called a sociogenesis of mind formation (Wertsch, 1991). In these efforts, the semiotic and dialogic nature of human actions and development have been emphasized, in analyses predominantly inspired by Vygotsky and Bakhtin.

Such emphasis on semiosis and dialogicality appears as a promising line of theoretical refinement. In agreement with this position, we suggest that as a further articulation of inter- and intraindividual functioning, some important clues can still be found in the classic works of Vygotsky, Bakhtin, and Wallon.

In Vygotsky's interpretation, human development involves mutually constitutive processes of immersion in culture and simultaneous emergence of singular individuality in the context of social practice. The conceptual nucleus of this perspective is *semiotic mediation* – as those processes that allow for an understanding of transformation of actions realized in the interpsychological or intermental level into internalized, intramental actions.

When Vygotsky formulated the general law of development postulating that "any function in a child's cultural development appears twice – first between people and then inside the individual" (1978, p. 57), one of his fundamental issues was, in fact, the question of the formation of the person, that is, the individual consciousness. This development of the individual was taken as a semiotically mediated process, with signs playing an essential role in the encounters of the person with others and in the construction of intrapsychological functioning.

In his formulations about the social genesis and nature of development, Vygotsky speaks of the relationships with others as the context of the formation of the individual. The role of social mediation in development is configured in strong terms: "The path from object to child and from child to object passes through another person" (Vygotsky, 1978, p. 30). Vygotsky (1981) makes insistent assertions about the role of the other, stating that "it is through others that we develop into ourselves" (p. 161). The development of signs happens through the meanings attributed by others to the child's actions. At the same time, the formation of the individual is related to the production of signs for others, so that the person becomes "what he/she is through what he/she produces for others" (p. 162).

The ontogenetic unfolding of the relationship between the subject and the other is analyzed by Wallon (1975, 1979). According to him, there is an initial symbiotic relationship of the child with the other (mother). Reciprocal relationships will then develop within situations for which there are alternations of two roles: agent and recipient of gestures. The experience of reciprocal roles allows for the emergence of I and other as distinct individualities; these existences are complementary – one cannot exist without the other – and antagonistic – for an individuality to exist, there must be an opposition to the other.

These dialectical movements, in a course of fusion–differentiation, also characterize the process of imitation, which is situated between fusional participation with and opposition to the model: In trying to be like the model, the child distinguishes himself from it, from the other.

The participation of the other implies an attribution of meaning to the child's actions from early on. The infant's needs can only be satisfied by the other, who completes, compensates for, and interprets the infant's actions, so that it is in the movements (handling, manipulation) of others that the infant's first attitudes will take form.

In this framework, the other is conceived as "a perpetual partner of the I." however, as we have seen, this partnership does not consist of a harmonious linkage. The formation of identity is presented as a complex process whereby the child starts to posit him- or herself as an individual by opposition to others; the formation of the I involves an affirmation of an identity and an expulsion of the other out of that identity.

In this interplay of adhesions and oppositions to the other, as movements of emergence and transformation of the individual consciousness, we identify what can be interpreted as the dramatic texture of social relationships. This interpretation of Wallon's ideas can be approximated to those of Vygotsky, for whom the key for understanding individual formation lies "in the *drama* that takes place among people" (Vygotsky, 1981, p. 163, italics added).

This idea of drama also pervades Bakhtin's theoretical elaborations, as he inquires about and analyzes instances of language in everyday life and in works of art. Bakhtin (1984) is deeply concerned with the constitutive, dialogic, and dialectical character of the I–thou relations, stressing that consciousness begins to operate only when individuals begin to participate in the texture of human communication. In his latest works, Bakhtin states that "as the human body is originally formed into the mother's womb, the individual's consciousness awakens involved into the other's consciousness" (1984, p. 358, our translation). Yet Bakhtin argues that "at the bottom of man we find not the Id, but the other" (as quoted in Todorov, 1984, p. 33).

This *alterity* principle, which constitutes the anthropological basis of Bakhtin's thinking (Todorov, 1984), is inescapably linked to, and happens only in the material reality of, the linguistic sign. This implies the individual's inevitable immersion in a territory populated by others. Indeed, "no human event unfolds or is decided within a single consciousness" (Bakhtin, as quoted in Todorov, 1984, p. 105).

Bakhtin's crucial contribution is, though, the *dialogical* principle, which is inherently related to the alterity principle and gives the I–thou relation a new status. Bakhtin expands the usual notion of dialogue to encompass not only the actual face-to-face verbal interaction, but every type and situation of "voices" coming into contact. Indeed, "words are, initially, the other's words, and at foremost, the mother's words. Gradually, these 'alien words' change, dialogically, to become one's 'own alien words' until they are transformed into 'one's own words' " (Bakhtin, 1984, p. 385), which enter into dialogue again with other words, other voices, and so on. This dynamic dialogical movement results in processes of the "monologization of consciousness," in which appropriating the words of others leads to missing the origins of one's own words (in not just an individual, but a socioideological sense). This dialogism is, therefore, deeply polysemic and always polyphonic.

It is in the core of the dialogic movement that individuals become *subjects*, configurated by the *other*, by the *word*. As Bakhtin states:

There is no such thing as abstract biological personality, this biological individual that has become the alpha and the omega of contemporary ideology. . . . To enter into history, it is not enough to be born physically. . . . A second birth, social this time, is necessary as it were. A human being is not born in the guise of an abstract biological organism, but as landowner or a peasant, a bourgeois or a proletarian . . . Russian or

French . . . in 1800 or 1900. Only such a social and historical localization makes man real and determines the content of his personal and cultural creation. (Bakhtin, as quoted in Todorov, 1984, p. 31)

From our view, the main contribution of these theoreticians for the present discussion lies in their interpretations of the reciprocal constitution of the subject and the other, related to the thesis of semiotic mediation.

The constitution of the subject: final remarks

The highlighted points from the works of Vygotsky, Wallon, and Bakhtin allow us to reframe the question of the constitution of the subject. From our point of view, if the sociogenetic perspectives leave the question of the formation of the individual consciousness unresolved, this same question seems to be dissolved in approaches that thematicize intersubjectivity.

The problem found in these theoretical approaches seems to concern the ways in which the social nature of the formation of mind is conceptualized while assuming the historical–cultural principle of its origin. It seems that a more radical (in terms of basis, or roots) exploration is needed concerning the thesis of semiotic mediation.

In fact, the Vygotskian postulate of the social origins cannot be restricted to a mere genetic sequence: "first inter, and then intra psychological," as it cannot be accepted independent of the related thesis of semiotic mediation. We believe this argument needs special attention.

The sign emerges in interindividual relationships, mediating encounters of the subject with others while (trans)forming mental functioning. As a privileged sign, the word constitutes the interface of social and individual processes, in either speech for/from others or inner speech. Yet, as historical product and production, the word evolves in its meanings, involving multiple senses. This multiplicity of senses and meanings characterizes the polysemic nature of the sign. The notion of polysemy, implying constitutive diversity, brings strong consequences to an analysis of words uttered by individuals in dialogues.

Indeed, the category of the *other* – the principle of alterity – and that of *sign/word* – the dialogical principle – as proposed by Bakhtin, seem to delineate the drama of the social texture, the *locus* of the constitution of the subject. The notion of an individual consciousness configurated by and in relationship with others, populated by many different "voices" or words of others, makes possible for the subject a quite singular constitution – unique "place" of articulation of such voices. The subject populated by many voices speaks his or her "own" voice in the "chorus": a polyphonic nonharmonious concert characterized by synchronic movements, as well as by distinct, conflicting, and dissonant voices.

Yet, if the subject is semiotically constituted – by the other or by the word – and if the sign is fundamentally polysemic, the nature of the constitution process must imply what is different, not just identical.

Although some authors have pointed in this direction, there is a general tendency to consider movements from the chaotic to the clear, from misunderstanding to shared understanding, from the irregular to the regular, as if the achievement of the latter pole in each case was, in fact, what characterizes the nature of the process. Thus, its dialectical character becomes neutralized.

The Wallonian ideas on partnership as participation–opposition in I–other relationships allow us to think of an interplay of processes of recognition–negation, and of resistance–adhesion, with respect to the reciprocal formation of the identity of I and other.

The polysemy of the sign, the polyphony of the voices, and the conflicts and encounters of I–other, constitute the *drama* of human relationships. All these notions may suggest or bring other elements to this debate and thus seem to delineate a challenge: to elaborate and articulate such notions in further conceptualizations about the constitution of the subject. And so, the question persists.

References

Bakhtin, M. (1984). *Esthétique de la création verbale*. Paris: Gallimard.

Elbers, E., Maier, R., Hoekstra, T., & Hoogsteder, M. (1992). Internalization and adult-child interaction. *Language and Instruction, 2,* 101–118.

Lawrence, J. A., & Valsiner, J. (1993). Conceptual roots of internalization: From transmission to transformation. *Human Development, 36,* 150–167.

Rommetveit, R. (1979). On the architecture of intersubjectivity. In R. Rommetveit &

R. M. Blakar (Eds.), *Studies of language, thought and verbal communication* (pp. 93–108). London: Academic.

Rommetveit, R. (1985). Language acquisition as increasing linguistic structuring of experience and symbolic behavior control. In J. V. Wertsch (Ed.), *Culture, communication and cognition* (pp. 183–204). Cambridge University Press.

Todorov, T. (1984). *Mikhail Bakhtin: The dialogical principle.* Minneapolis: University of Minnesota Press.

Trevarthen, C. (1979). Comunication and cooperation in early infancy: A description of primary intersubjectivity. In M. Bullowa (Ed.), *Before speech* (pp. 321–347). Cambridge University Press.

Trevarthen, C., & Logotheti, C. (1987). First symbols and the nature of human knowledge. In *Symbolism et connaissance.* Geneva: Cahiers No. 8, pp. 65–92.

Tudge, J. (1992). Processes and consequences of peer collaboration: A Vygotskian analysis. *Child Development, 63,* 1364–1379.

Valsiner, J. (1988). Ontogeny of co-construction of culture within social organized environmental settings. In J. Valsiner (ed.), *Child development within culturally structured environments: Vol. 2. Social co-construction and environmental guidance of development* (pp. 283–297). Norwood, NJ: Ablex.

Valsiner, J. (1994). Bi-directional cultural transmission and constructive sociogenesis. In W. de Graaf & R. Maier (Eds.), *Sociogenesis re-examined* (pp. 101–134). New York: Springer-Verlag.

Voloshinov, V. N. (1973). *Marxism and the philosophy of language.* New York: Seminar Press.

Vygotsky, L. S. (1978). *Mind in society: The development of higher psychological processes* (M. Cole, V. John-Steiner, S. Scribner, and E. Souberman, Eds.). Cambridge, MA: Harvard University Press.

Vygotsky, L. S. (1981). The genesis of higher mental functions. In J. V. Wertsch (Ed.), *The concept of activty in Soviet psychology* (pp. 144–188). New York: Sharpe.

Vygotsky, L. S. (1987). *The collected works of L. S. Vygotsky* Vol. 1 (R. Rieber & A. S. Carton, Eds.). New York: Plenum.

Wallon, H. (1975). *Psicologia e educaçao da infancia.* Lisbon: Estampa.

Wallon, H. (1979). *Do ato ao pensamento.* Lisbon: Moraes Editores.

Wertsch, J. V. (1991). *Voices of the mind.* Cambridge, MA: Harvard University Press.

Part IV

**Sociocultural settings:
design and intervention**

8 Socio-cultural-historical psychology: some general remarks and a proposal for a new kind of cultural-genetic methodology

Michael Cole

Preliminary remarks

Before focusing on the main theme of this chapter, I feel it necessary to say a few words about the current circumstances confronting psychologists who take the social and cultural foundations of human nature as the starting point for their analyses.[1] While such approaches to psychology remain distinctly minority viewpoints within our discipline, it is my impression that they are receiving more attention than at any time since the 1920s and certainly in my professional lifetime. This situation offers pleasant prospects of increased support and recognition. But it also poses dangers: Nowhere are these ideas so highly developed that it is possible to refer to them as a mature scientific paradigm with generally accepted theoretical foundations, a methodology, and a well-delineated set of prescriptions for relating theory to practice. It is my hope that the first meeting of the Society for Sociocultural Research will further the goal of formulating an ecumenical and broadly useful approach to the inclusion of culture and the social world in our theories and practices.

Assuming I am correct about the increasing popularity of the ideas discussed herein, it is possible to identify many causes for this interest: Disenchantment with positivist social sciences more generally, the ero-

An earlier version of this chapter was presented at the Conference for Socio-Cultural Research, Madrid, Spain, September 15–18, 1992. The preparation of this chapter was made possible by grants from the Carnegie Corporation and the Mellon Foundation. Vanessa Gack helped materially in its production.

sion of support for Piagetian theory among developmentalists, skepticism about the terms in which the study of artificial intelligence is being pursued, despair at the fractionation of psychology, and the search for viable alternatives to various kinds of social learning theory would be some of my candidate factors, but many others could be offered.

One of the leading indicators, if not causes, of this state of affairs is the extraordinary interest that has been shown in the work of L. S. Vygotsky by non-Russian psychologists since the publication of his selected essays in 1978 under the title *Mind in Society*. Despite (or perhaps because of) the well-documented shortcomings of the scholarly work that produced that volume (Bakhurst, 1986; Van der Veer & Valsiner, 1991), the ideas expressed therein seemed to catch the imagination of North American and Western European psychologists. Presently, research characterized as Vygotskian or neo-Vygotskian can be found in dozens of monographs and hundreds if not thousands of journal articles. Vygotsky's classic *Thought and Language* has been retranslated twice, and additional early works are appearing all of the time.

It is something of an irony that just when North American and Western European psychologists were latching on to Vygotsky as a "leading Soviet psychologist," his legacy was the subject of a bitter dispute in the USSR. There, students of A. N. Leont'ev and S. L. Rubinshtein were disputing the origin of, and correct approach to, what they called "activity theory." Although translations of this work also became available to English-speaking and European readers (see Payne, 1968; Wertsch, 1981; and many issues of the journal *Soviet Psychology*), activity theory did not become a general fashion in North America, as Vygotskian ideas did at the time. However, it did attract a significant following in Northern Europe, especially in the version promoted by Leont'ev and his students, eventually becoming an intellectual presence in North America and Japan, where it has captured the interest of psychologists involved in the domains of work and education.

For the past several years I have been striving, with rather limited success, to understand the intellectual issues that divide the Vygotskian and activity theory approaches, as well as the division between activity theorists who follow Leont'ev and those who follow Rubinshtein. This task is complicated because, insofar as I can understand, contemporary followers of Leont'ev continue to adhere to the major principles articulated by Vygotsky, Luria, and Leont'ev in the 1920s and early 1930s, arguing in effect that Vygotsky was an activity theorist, although he focused less on issues of the object-oriented nature of activity than on processes of mediation in his own work (Engeström, 1987; Hydén, 1984). Followers of Rubinshtein, on the other hand, deny that Vygotsky was an activity theorist and tax him with "signocentricism," which in the overheated debates of the last decade of Soviet power seemed to be roughly equivalent to "idealist," a sin at that time (Brushlinsky, 1968). At the same time, they criticized Leont'ev for placing too much emphasis on activity as external conditions, likening him to a behaviorist (Abulkhanova-Slavskaya, 1980).

I do not want to minimize the possible scientific benefits to be derived from attempting to understand these disagreements more thoroughly, although I am not certain how productive such attempts will be for non-Russian psychologists. From existing historiographical evidence, debates among Russian adherents of these various positions appear to have been tightly bound up with the wrenching political upheavals that racked the Soviet Union repeatedly between 1917 and 1991 (and which are by no means over) (Van der Veer & Valsiner, 1991). What I am almost positive of, however, is that it would not be productive for adherents of the various positions to carry those battles into the international sphere except insofar as they have international intellectual merit.

What most concerns me is that for whatever combination of reasons, there has not yet been close cooperation on an international scale among psychologists who work under the banner of activity theory and those who use some version of the concept of sociocultural psychology as their conceptual icon. At the first Activity Theory Congress in Berlin in 1986, there was only one major address that took the work of Vygotsky and Luria to be coequally relevant to the proceedings with that of Leont'ev, and individual talks that proceeded from a more or less Vygotskian perspective were relatively rare. At the second Activity Theory Congress in 1990, there was a far richer mix of viewpoints, but many of the people prominent in organizing the current meeting in Madrid were preoccupied with preparatory work for the current meeting and did not contribute.

It would be most unfortunate if adherents of the various streams of psychological thinking whose history I have sketched were to continue their work in isolation from each other. The common intellectual issues facing different streams of cultural-historical, sociocultural, activity-based conceptions of human nature are too difficult to yield to piece-meal efforts. It is time for those who have come to questions about the socio-cultural-historical constitution of human nature to join in a cooperative search for their common past and to initiate coopera-tive efforts to address the difficult intellectual issues and staggering national and international problems facing humanity in the post–Cold War era.

The common starting point

I take the common starting point[2] of all socio-cultural-historical viewpoints about which I have been speaking to be the as-sumption that the species-specific characteristic of human beings is their need and ability to inhabit an environment transformed by the activity of prior members of their species. Such transformations and the mechanism of the transfer of these transformations from one gen-eration to the next are the result of the ability/proclivity of human beings to create and use artifacts – aspects of the material world that are taken up into human action as modes of coordinating with the physical and social environment. The idea that the mediation of activ-ity through artifacts (often referred to by the slightly reduced concept of tools) is the fundamental characteristic of human psychological processes and the human environment can be found in the scholarly traditions of many countries as the following examples are intended to illustrate:

If we could rid ourselves of all pride, if, to define our species, we kept strictly to what the historic and prehistoric periods show us to be the constant characteristic of man and of intelligence, we should say not *Homo Sapiens* but *Homo Faber*. In short, *intel-ligence, considered in what seems to be its original feature, is the faculty of manufacturing artificial objects, especially tools for making tools, and of indefinitely varying the manufac-ture.* Henri Bergson (1911/1983, p. 139)

Experience does not go on simply inside a person. . . . In a word, we live from birth to death in a world of persons and things which is in large measure what it is because of what has been done and transmitted from previous human activities. When this fact is ignored, experience is treated as if it were something which goes on exclusively inside an individual's body and mind. It ought not to be necessary to say that expe-rience does not occur in a vacuum. There are sources outside an individual which give rise to experience. John Dewey (1938/1963, p. 39)

Man differs from animals in that he can make and use tools. [These tools] not only radically change his conditions of existence, they even react on him in that they effect a change in him and his psychic condition.

[Now] instead of applying directly its natural function to the solution of a particular task, the child *puts between that function and the task a certain auxiliary means . . . by the medium of which the child manages to perform the task.* Alexander Luria (1928, pp. 493, 495)

While the animal learns something in its individual life, this always remains his own property but the creations and achievements of man have a lasting existence and transmit themselves from one generation to the next. This fact is the reason for man's immense development, the fact that each generation did not always have to begin anew, but could continue its work where its predecessor left off. . . . Society consists not only of those living now, it also reaches into the past and the future. Eric Stern (1920/1990, p. 18)

Implicitly or explicitly, these early formulations emphasize the double-sided nature of artifact-mediated actions. On the one hand, there is the tool/auxiliary means, but such means are themselves defined with respect to the goals of behavior – the task. The inextricable link between these two moments of human activity are neatly summarized by Vygotsky as follows:

All processes forming part of that method form a complicated functional and structural unity. This unity is effected, first, by the task which must be solved by the given method, and secondly, by the means by which the method can be followed. . . . It is precisely the structure which combines all separate processes, which are component parts of the cultural habit of behavior, which transforms this habit into a psychological function, and which fulfills its task with respect to behavior as a whole. (1929, pp. 420–421)

The remaining central postulates of this paradigm flow necessarily from the premise of artifact mediation. Historical (genetic) analysis is an essential methodological tenet of this paradigm because culture (the synthesized totality of artifacts available to a group) and mediated behavior emerged as a single process of hominization. To understand the workings of culturally mediated behavior, it is necessary to understand processes of change and transformation that, by definition, take place over time. A *full* theory demands simultaneous analysis on several temporal levels (what Wertsch, 1985, refers to as genetic domains) because any psychological phenomenon emerges from interaction of processes occurring at all the levels of the human life system: phylogeny, cultural history, ontogeny, and microgenesis.

The emphasis on social origins of human psychological functions arises from the same source. As Dewey emphasizes in the fragment quoted earlier, every child is born into a world transformed by the activity of prior generations. It is only enculturated human beings who can organize children's environments and thus afford them the opportunity to appropriate the existing pool of cultural resources. It is only through interactions with other human beings that newcomers can become old-timers.

The overall perspective sketched here is summarized quite succinctly by Vladimir Lektorsky, who wrote the following using activity theory as his point of departure:

Practical activity itself must be understood in its specifically human characteristics, namely as joint or collective activity in which each individual enters into certain relations with other persons; as mediated activity in which man places between himself and an external, naturally emerging object other man-made objects functioning as instruments of activity; and finally, as historically developing activity carrying in itself its own history. (1980, pp. 136–137)[3]

The result of accepting these propositions is to commit oneself to charting difficult and poorly understood territory. It means, to use Valsiner's term, that human psychological processes are *coconstructed*. It renders problematic standard psychological research methods without specifying their replacements.

It is difficult to overemphasize the fact that the problems we are facing are old problems. They were not generally or satisfactorily solved by those who promoted socio-cultural-historical activity approaches at the turn of the century, and they continue to confront us today. This point is brought home in a thoughtful review of two volumes of research in this tradition edited by Jaan Valsiner. The reviewers, Sharon Lamb and Robert Wozniak (1990), point out that the views promoted by authors in the Valsiner volume are similar to those promoted at the turn of the century by James Mark Baldwin, who turned away from psychology to philosophy, in part because he despaired of reconciling the complex object of analysis with the inadequate tools of analysis at his disposal. They go on to comment that, like Baldwin, Valsiner and his colleagues find themselves severely hampered by the limitations of traditional method.

Lamb and Wozniak offer several criteria for good research that adopts a coconstructionist theoretical approach:

1. dynamic analysis of the flow of events over time
2. interactional analysis of dyads, triads, and larger units
3. pattern analysis of the interrelatedness of variables
4. transactional analysis of person–environment interactions
5. multicultural and historical analyses
6. willingness to deal with the messy interactions outside of laboratories

This list strikes me as an excellent starting point for formulating a broad agenda for research by those concerned with the issues of this volume. The remainder of my chapter will be devoted to one modest effort in this direction. One theme of my remarks will be that the task confronting us is even more complex than Lamb and Wozniak's list recognizes because there is a third partner in the coconstruction process – the cultural past reified in the cultural present in the forms of the artifacts that mediate the process of coconstruction.

A "mesogenetic" method for the study of culture and thought

The idea that to understand behavior means to understand the history/genesis of behavior has long been acknowledged as a fundamental tenet of cultural-historical approaches to the study of human nature. The actual representation of this idea in the practice of cultural-historical psychologists has, however, been restricted to implementing only parts of the overall paradigm. In place of research programs that include phylogenetic, cultural-historical, ontogenetic, and microgenetic data within a single, integrated field of inquiry, scholars have focused entirely on a single genetic domain (ontogeny or microgenesis, for the most part) or the relationship between two neighboring domains (e.g., ontogenetic changes in microgenetic processes).

The reason for this state of affairs is obvious: phylogenetic and cultural-historical change generally take place at rates so slow with respect to the ontogeny of the investigator that integrated research is impossible. In the relatively few cases where the goal has been to study the relation between phylogeny or cultural development and ontogeny, the "cross-species" and cross-cultural methods, with all of their attendant methodological problems, have been used.

In the research to be described here, my colleagues and I have adopted what might be called a "mesogenetic" approach to cultural mediation, one whose time scale falls between the microgenetic scale employed in classical studies, where children are confronted with a difficult problem and their use of new mediational means is studied, and the macrogenetic scale implied by the historical difference between peasant and industrialized societies. The basic strategy for this research has been to create a system of activities with its own standing rules, artifacts, social roles, and ecological setting, that is, its own culture.[4] Since it was formed almost a decade ago, this cultural system has sustained and replicated itself through many "generations," and it now exists in a variety of institutional environments in several geographic locales. This cultural system goes through a yearly cycle of growth and decline that divides naturally into four "seasons," each with its own typical properties of growth and interactivity. Because of its cyclic nature and the fact that new members enter the culture at specified periods throughout the year, it gives us an unusual opportunity to investigate the dynamic relationship between cultural change, ontogenetic change, and microgenetic change, all within a single setting.

From individual artifacts to culture

In the classical statements of cultural-historical psychology given earlier, culture is represented only in a restricted, abstracted form designed to highlight the crucial property of mediation through artifacts. Artifacts do not, of course, exist in isolation. Rather, they are interwoven with each other and the social lives of the human beings they mediate in a seemingly infinite variety of ways. Considered in the aggregate, they constitute the unique medium of human life, the medium we know as culture.

In attempting to bridge the prototypical examples of artifact mediation embodied in experimental setting where a child confronts a difficult task that can be solved by the appropriation of a readily available tool or mediation through an adult to contemporary notions of cultural systems, I have found it helpful to adopt Marx Wartofsky's (1979) three-level hierarchy of artifacts. The first level consists of *primary artifacts,* those directly used in production (as examples, Wartofsky gives "axes, clubs, needles, bowls"; my examples will include computers, telecommunications networks, and mythical cultural personages). This level corresponds closely to the concept of tool as it is ordinarily used.

The second level, *secondary artifacts*, consists of representations both of primary artifacts and of modes of action using primary artifacts. An important kind of secondary artifact are *cultural models*, which "portray not only the world of physical objects, but also more abstract worlds such as social interaction, discourse, and even word meaning" (D'Andrade, 1984, p. 93).[5] Secondary artifacts play a central role in preserving and transmitting modes of action.

The third level is a class of artifacts that "can come to constitute a relatively autonomous 'world,' in which the rules, conventions and outcomes no longer appear directly practical, or which, indeed, seem to constitute an arena of non-practical, or 'free' play or game activity" (Wartofsky, 1979, p. 208).

Wartofsky calls these imagined worlds *tertiary artifacts*. Such imaginative artifacts, he suggests, can come to color the way we see the "actual" world, providing a tool for changing current praxis. In modern psychological jargon, modes of behavior acquired when interacting with tertiary artifacts can transfer beyond the immediate contexts of their use. Wartofsky applies this hierarchical conception of artifacts to works of art and process of perception; I want to generalize his conception for use in designing activities for children that will promote their social and cognitive development. To make that link I must now turn to a second key concept, that of culture as a medium.

The garden as a metaphor for culture-as-medium

The notion of culture as a special medium of human life is certainly familiar to cultural-historical theorists, but here I want to draw on its interpretation within the history of Anglo-Saxon thought, whose metaphors appear especially useful in dealing with critical methodological problems facing the field.

Raymond Williams, who has traced the English concept of culture back to its connection with Latin roots, notes that the core features that coalesce to produce modern conceptions of culture refer to the process of helping things grow. "Culture," Williams wrote, "in all of its early uses was a noun of process: the tending of, something, basically crops or animals" (1973, p. 87).

Sometime around the sixteenth century, the term "culture" began to refer to the tending of human children, in addition to crops and animals. From the beginning, the core idea of culture as a process of helping things grow was combined with a general theory for how to promote growth: Create an artificial environment where young organisms could be provided the optimal conditions for growth. Such tending requires tools, of course, and it is somehow provocative to learn that one of the early meanings of culture was "plowshare."

Although it would be foolish to overinterpret the metaphoric parallels between the theory and practice of growing the next generations of crops and growing the next generations of children, the exercise, I will argue, has particular heuristic value for thinking about the processes of development and for designing new activity systems to promote development. Broadly speaking, like gardeners, theorists must attend simultaneously to two classes of concerns: what transpires inside the system ("garden") they study (or design and study) and what transpires around it. These issues can often be addressed independently of each other. But, as I will attempt to show, both the putative object of analysis and its context must be considered simultaneously. To continue the metaphor, inside the garden, for every kind of plant, there is the quality of the soil to consider, the best way to till the soil, the right kinds of nutrients to use, the right amount of moisture, and the best time to plant and nurture the seeds, as well as the need to protect the growing plants against predators, disease, and so on. Each of these tasks has its own primary and secondary artifacts to draw upon. The theory and practice of development at this level will be focused on finding exactly the right combination of factors to promote life within the garden walls.

Gardens do not, obviously, exist independently of the larger ecological system within which they are embedded. While it is possible to raise any plant anywhere in the world, given the opportunity first to arrange the appropriate set of conditions, it is not always possible to create the right conditions, even for a short while. And if what one is interested in is more than a short-run demonstration of the possibility of creating a development-promoting system, but instead the creation of conditions that sustain the needed properties of the artificial environment without much additional labor, then it is as important to attend to the system in which the garden is embedded as the properties of the garden "itself." In the extended example given in the next section, I will treat the garden-as-culture metaphor as a way of specifying a particular kind of cultural system, constituted jointly by artifact-mediated practices that occur within its walls and by the nature of its ecological setting. A schematic rendition of this idea is contained in Figure 8.1. Note that there is a close conceptual affinity between this diagram and various versions of Bronfenbrenner's (1979) ecological approach to psychology.

Applying the garden metaphor: from tertiary artifact to the Fifth Dimension

We have applied the notion of artifact and culture-as-garden to a particular cultural system we have been using to develop a cultural-historical theory of mind. We call this system of activities the *Fifth Dimension*. In terms of the garden metaphor, the Fifth Dimension is a specially designed cultural medium for promoting the all-around intellectual and social development of 6- to 12-year-old children. In Wartofsky's terms, the system is a tertiary artifact – a bounded alternative world with its own social norms, tasks, and conventions. This artifact is a tool designed to address certain long-standing problems in American education, in particular, the distressingly low academic achievement of a great many American children, the widely perceived need for them to gain a qualitatively richer experience with new information technologies, and the failure of apparently successful educational innovations to survive beyond the period of innovation and external funding.

To transform this tertiary artifact into a material system of activity, we needed, of course, to provide participants with primary and secondary artifacts as crucial mediational means. We also needed to identify likely social institutions that would serve as environments for our proposed innovation. For this purpose we have worked with youth clubs, day-care centers, libraries, churches, and schools.

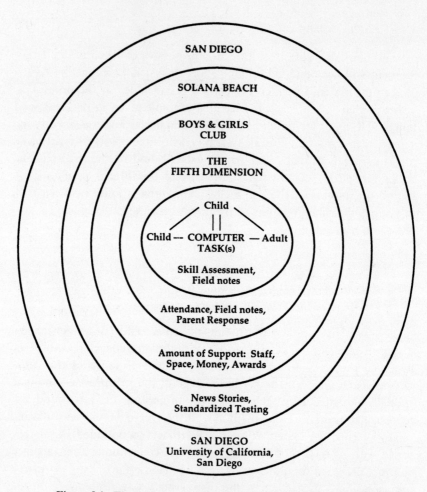

Figure 8.1. The "culture as garden" metaphor applied to an artificially created system of activity, the Fifth Dimension. The innermost circle corresponds to the level of face-to-face interaction between adults and children engaged in computer-mediated activities. The next circle represents the activity as a whole. Successive circles represent higher levels of context. Note that each level of context is evaluated according to criteria specific to it.

An overview of the Fifth Dimension

Figure 8.2 provides a schematic overview of the Fifth Dimension. The central coordinating artifacts at the heart of the Fifth Dimension are shown at the top of Figure 8.2 in the form of a cardboard maze approximately 1 square meter in area divided into twenty or so "rooms," each of which gives access to two activities. About 75% of the time these activities are instantiated as computer programs that include computer games and educational software, some of which also have gamelike qualities; the remainder are noncomputer activities that include board games, arts and crafts, and physical exercise. According to the rules of the system (enshrined in a constitution, a printed copy of which each child receives upon entering the system), children can make progress through the maze by completing tasks set out by the Wizard. "Graduation" from the Fifth Dimension occurs when children have achieved the excellence level prescribed for the activities in all the rooms of the maze.

In addition to the local goal of completing a task, the rules of the Fifth Dimension provide for a variety of other goals designed to appeal to a variety of children. For example, every child is given a very plain looking token figurine upon beginning the program. By traversing a path that takes them in one door and out another, they may "transform their cruddy creature" and obtain more desirable figurines. Or they may choose to complete all the rooms in the maze, thereby attaining expert status and access to new activities. In Leont'ev's (1981a) terms, the Fifth Dimension provides a variety of possible effective motives, in addition to motives (such as the need to master new information technologies) that are merely understandable to the children.

Two other features of the life-world of the Fifth Dimension require mention. First, it is maintained that once upon a time a Wizard appeared when the adults working with children could not cope with all of the problems of running and maintaining computers, software, and the computer network that unites children in different after-school programs around the world where telecommunication is available. The Wizard is said to be the author of the constitution, provider of the software, arbiter of disputes. The Wizard is known to enjoy corresponding with children and to have a terrible sense of humor. Because

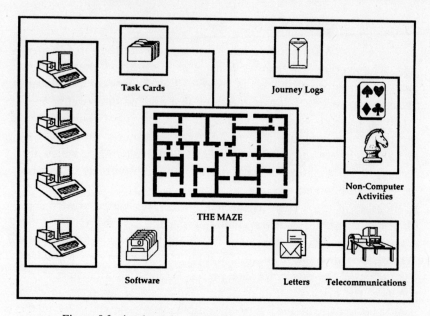

Figure 8.2. A schematic representation of the artifacts that constitute the activity system called the Fifth Dimension.

the Wizard is very forgetful, necessary tasks (such as keeping up with needed repairs of computers) are neglected and things go wrong. In such circumstances, the participants in program activities (with full justification) criticize the Wizard and send her or him (the Wizard changes sexes to fit its mood) sharply worded letters of complaint.

The Wizard is also a secondary artifact for reordering power relations between adults and children in the Fifth Dimension. This rearrangement comes about in part because when conflicts arise in the system, it is the Wizard, not the human participants, who has the power to adjudicate disputes. In such cases, adults as well as children write to the Wizard to decide how matters should proceed. It is also important that by subordinating themselves to the Wizard, the adults can collude with the children in the pretension of the Wizard's existence and thereby enter into playful relations with them. Finally, since computer technology is not especially reliable and programs or computers often fail to work, adults can off-load responsibility for breakdowns onto the Wizard at strategic moments, a possibility that has endeared the Wizard to all adults who have worked in the system.[6]

Second, it is an important feature of the Fifth Dimension that it is staffed primarily by undergraduate students who participate in the activity as part of a course in such departments as psychology, education, and communication. These undergraduates have generally not worked with computers before and often know less about the specific game activities than do the children. Their enculturation, which intertwines with the enculturation of the children, is an important feature of the culture of the program. Their assignment is to work with the children in the activities in the role of "Wizard's assistants."[7] After every session, they write detailed field notes about their interactions with the children, the Wizard, the software, and the life of the system. These field notes are primary data about the workings of this cultural system.

Fifth Dimensions spring to life in the fall of every year when children and college students return to school. At UCSD, which divides its academic year into three 10-week quarters, the Fifth Dimension goes through three 8-week sessions that children attend from 1–4 days a week, depending on local circumstances. Undergraduates are allowed to take the course three times, and children are allowed to attend year after year. Consequently, at any given time, participants include a mix of "old timers" and "newcomers" with varying amounts of experience and knowledge about the activities. Among the interesting features of this arrangement is that cultural knowledge and age are not tightly linked: Very often the children have more knowledge about the computers, games, and norms of the program than the undergraduates, a situation that helps reorder everyday power relations with important consequences for the dynamics of the interactions that take place.

To summarize, the Fifth Dimension can be viewed both as a tertiary artifact and as a cultural system. As a tertiary artifact it is a system of activities infused with primary and secondary artifacts, participation in which is designed not only to be satisfying in itself, but to provide the participants with experiences that can influence their lives in the community and at school. As a cultural system it is an activity infused with norms, goals, meanings, and esoteric knowledge that provides the medium for learning and development.

Sample findings

The following sample of empirical findings substantiates our claim that we are dealing with a cultural system and illustrates the way in which principles of cultural-historical psychology can be investigated within it.

The process of enculturation.   One way in which it is possible to discover the existence of a culture is at its borders, one of which is marked by the difference between (enculturated) old timers and (unenculturated) newcomers. Our best evidence about the process of enculturation (and hence, the existence of a distinctive culture associated with the Fifth Dimension) comes through the field notes written by undergraduates. Routinely the undergraduates initially express their conviction that they are entering a system of shared understandings that is mysterious to them, a condition that generally evokes anxiety and an expressed desire to figure out what it takes to become a member:

As I looked into that room through the windows I had many questions running through my head. How does this program work? What am I supposed to do here? How can I possibly be a leader here when I don't know the first thing about computer games? (JG, field notes, January 20, 1992)

I was anxious about today because it would be the first day with the children. I understood the orientation but had the feeling that the only way to fully understand it was to actually play the games and spend time with the children. I expected to make a lot of mistakes, mostly in not directing the children well since I really had no direction! (AO, field notes, October 4, 1991)

It was really odd having a young adolescent guiding us through the game. I sort of felt helpless in a way, considering that knowledge is power in this society. Here we were, elders who would soon take on the challenge of helping children develop their minds and to help them get through the fifth dimension and we couldn't even finish the first round! Boy was I humiliated in a fun way! (CM, field notes, October 4, 1991)

A second, slightly more subtle indicator of the process of enculturation can be found in a predictable shift in how artifacts of the system are used by newcomers interacting in the system. Participants typically reference fundamental artifacts like the Wizard, maze, constitution, and task cards in their field notes of daily interaction as they learn to become functioning citizens. Analysis of the field notes reveals the presence of the two "coordinates" of mediation emphasized in cultural-historical theory. These two coordinates are discussed by Leont'ev (1981b):

Vygotsky identified two main, interconnected features (of activity) that are necessarily fundamental for psychology; its tool-like [instrumental] structure, and its inclusion in a system of interrelations with other people. It is these features that define the nature of human psychological processes. The tool mediates activity and thus connects humans not only with the world of objects but also with other people. . . . But it is impossible to transmit the means and methods needed to carry out a process in any way other than in external form – in the form of an action or external speech. (p. 56)

What makes this distinction particularly interesting in the present circumstances is that there is a shift in the relative use of interrelational and instrumental mediational patterns that reflects participants' enculturation into the cultural system. When they first enter the system, Fifth Dimension participants hear about artifacts like the constitution, Wizard, task cards, and maze from other people. But they are confused about their functions and how they fit into the overall pattern of activity. Then, as they acquire knowledge about the workings of the system, they appropriate them in unique ways to accomplish their goals.

This enculturation process is reflected in the way artifacts are discussed in the field notes. At first, field note references to the artifacts are primarily oriented toward interpreting and understanding "their inclusion in a system of interrelations with other people." As participants become more comfortable in the culture, they begin to view these objects more like tools, and the instrumental function appears in their field notes.

Typical examples of interrelational uses of the lexicon referring to cultural artifacts in the system come when a participant mentions some element of its cultural artifacts as a means of gaining understanding:

Scott proceeded to tell us more about the program: what our role with the children would be, how to use the maze as a guide, the taskcards. . . . We then split into small groups in order to use the computers and different games. (LA, field notes, October 1, 1991)

Here, we learned about the task cards, the hint box, the journey log, the all knowing Wizard and his Wizard's assistants, the 5th Dimension map, the constitution. . . . Even the Task Cards didn't give you that much advice. (JG, field notes, January 14, 1991)

Later, participants used the task cards in an instrumental fashion. A variety of such instrumental uses can be distinguished:

Since he didn't read the instructions, I read him the task card and then asked him to tell me the objective of the game and what he needed to do in order to finish the game successfully. (LA, field notes, October 31, 1991)

The Task Card mentions that you should start off with all levels at five and gradually increase one of the variables to see which level they belong to, to eventually reach the requested growth of 100cm (Botanical Gardens) (CM, field notes, December 5, 1991)

I asked if Isabel would read the task card out loud so that we would know what to do in the game. Isabel had some difficulty in pronouncing some of the bigger words that appeared on the task card, but I helped her with these words. One of the words that she had difficulty pronouncing was Island, but she knew how to pronounce it upon finishing reading the task card because it was used a lot and hence, she was forced to repeatedly pronounce it. (EB, field notes, October 24, 1991)

An analysis of the frequency and usage of references to various key artifacts shows changes in vocabulary usage over time. References to task cards illustrate this trend. As shown in Figure 8.3, in the first weeks of their participation in the Fifth Dimension, students' references to task cards are primarily of an interrelational kind, but toward the end of the 8-week session, instrumental uses came to outnumber interrelational uses. Current analyses suggest an additional result. When students continue in the program for two or more "seasons," the third kind of incorporation of such artifacts into their conceptual systems emerges – a reflective/critical function in which they comment on the way that novices understand (or fail to understand) their uses and ways in which the artifacts could be improved through modification:

The day began with a visit from Romy; she wanted me to tell her whether the task card for Golden Mountain was a good one or a bad one. [Later she wrote:] I think that if I had read him the task card straight through I would have lost him. . . . The task card was not challenging for the children. (CM, field notes, November 5, 1991)

The relationship between culture and its ecological setting.   It is a truism of anthropological research that cultures represent qualitatively distinct, historically specific adaptive systems that form over generations of interaction between social groups and their environments. It is equally true, but less generally recognized, that context means more (or other) than "that which surrounds"; "text" and "con-text" are mutually constitutive of each other, and when used in this way, context is a *relational* concept (Bateson, 1972). Our experience with the Fifth Dimension has made this relational aspect of context too salient to overlook.

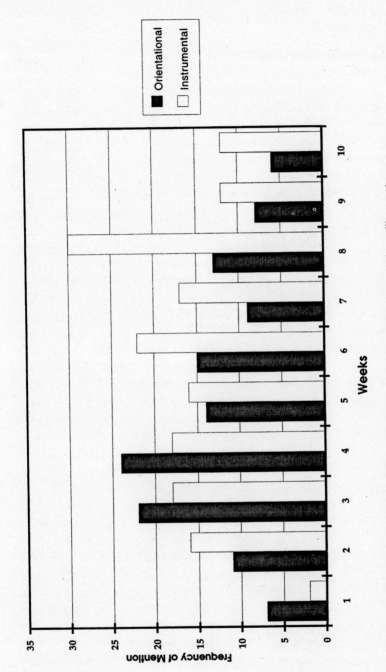

Figure 8.3. The frequency of orientational and instrumental uses of the term "task card" over the course of a 10-week season in which the Fifth Dimension operated.

In a recent paper, Ageliki Nicolopolou and I compared the cultural systems characterizing two Fifth Dimension programs located in the same town, one in a Boys and Girls Club, the other in a library (Nicolopolou & Cole, 1993). These two cultural systems each used the same set of program artifacts, ran at the same hour of the day, involved undergraduates from the same course, and served children from the same socioeconomic background. Given this commonality of mediational means and institutional purposes, it might be thought that similar, if not identical, cultures would emerge in the two settings. Yet the two systems were remarkably different from each other. Whenever people who participated in one of the systems for a while journeyed to the other, they invariably remarked on the difference. The Fifth Dimension at the Boys and Girls Club seemed loud and chaotic as children came and went for reasons that were difficult to fathom. The children worked with undergraduates and played games, but there seemed to be a more contentious atmosphere and a good deal of byplay. By comparison, the library group seem intimate and concentrated; children came on time and stayed to the end of the session, often having to be dragged away by their parents or pushed out the door by the librarians. Intense friendships grew between undergraduates and children, and concentration on the games was often intense.

A key to accessing the difference between the two cultural systems is to step outside of the system (beyond the walls of the Fifth Dimension–as–garden) to examine its local ecology. Outside the room that houses the Fifth Dimension program it is clear that the Boys and Girls Club is a boisterous place with rock music blaring and pool games usually in progress nearby. Elsewhere children are playing basketball and tag, or gossiping with their friends. The library, expectedly, is a quiet place where decorous behavior is expected at all times; education, not play, is the leading activity of the library. When children left the Fifth Dimension program in the Girls and Boys Club, as they were free to do at any time, there were many different activities to engage in; they could even go home if they liked. But when the children left the program at the library, they were expected to read quietly and wait for their parents, who expected them to spend the full 1½-hour session there.

When we investigated the relationship between the two programs and their institutional settings, we immediately grasped how the culture of each activity (text) is coconstituted with its context (Figure 8.4). Using the crude variable of "noise level" as a proxy for the qualitatively complex differences between the two locations, we found that while the program in the Boys and Girls Club was noisier than the one in the library, the program in the library was noisier than its institutional ecology while the one in the Boys and Girls Club was quieter than its setting.

The qualitative features of each Fifth Dimension are created in the relationship of text to context. Each of the programs mixes two main kinds of activity – education and play. In an institutional context where play dominates, the educational features of the Fifth Dimension render it relatively more serious and education-like, while the play features make it noisier and more playlike than a serious educational setting such as a library. Each is a compromise, a synthesis of the properties of the objects and their contexts.

The relation between cultural "level" and cognitive achievement. A long-standing issue in the study of a culture's impact on the development of thought is the relationship between the level of knowledge characteristic of that culture and the cognitive achievements of its members. As a way of testing the cognitive correlates of these apparent cultural differences, Nicolopolou compared the degree to which each of the two cultural systems fostered the development of shared knowledge using the evidence provided by field notes gathered when children were playing a particular computer game. Figure 8.5 shows the changes in performance on one of the Fifth Dimension games over the course of the year in the two settings. Note that in the Boys and Girls Club there is no overall increase in the level at which the game is played; performance at the beginning of the year is actually better, on average, than at the end of the year. By contrast, performance improves with the growth of the culture of shared knowledge achieved in the library. A number of measures of the density and growth of the cultures of the two programs confirmed that there was little growth during the year at the Boys and Girls Club, but marked and sustained growth in the library.

Effectiveness of the tertiary artifact. A good deal of our current research is devoted to developing ways of evaluating the impact of participation

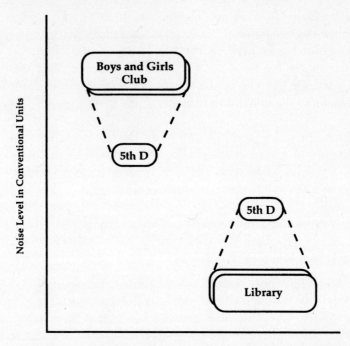

Figure 8.4. A schematic representation of the relationship of Fifth Dimension programs to their institutional contexts in the library and the Boys and Girls Club. Note that the program is quieter than its context at the Boys and Girls Club, but noisier than its context in the library, indicating the way in which properties of an object and its context are mutually constituted.

in the Fifth Dimension on individual children. There is not space to go into the complex issues of evaluation, but in closing I want to mention an unusual line of investigation that this line of work makes possible. Because the Fifth Dimension has been in existence for several years in a locale with a more or less stable population, we have had the opportunity to observe children for extended periods of time. However, owing to the institutional timetable of the university, the undergraduates who have interacted with the children and provided the field notes are constantly changing. Consequently, as the children grow older and the culture of the Fifth Dimension continues to evolve and deepen its roots in the institution, the age and experience of the observers does *not* change. This unusual circumstance permits a new kind of longitudinal study of individual children.

MYSTERY HOUSE GAME SCORES

Library (M/W): Fall 1988 — Spring 1989

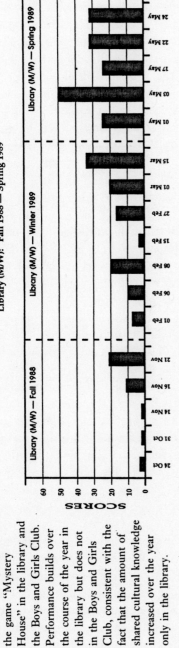

B & G Club: Fall 1988 — Spring 1989

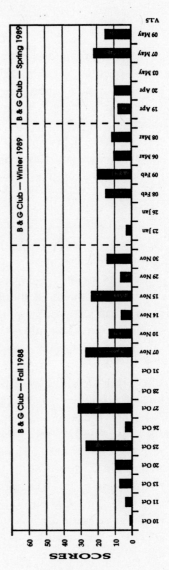

Figure 8.5. Performance levels for children playing the game "Mystery House" in the library and the Boys and Girls Club. Performance builds over the course of the year in the library but does not in the Boys and Girls Club, consistent with the fact that the amount of shared cultural knowledge increased over the year only in the library.

A single example of a child I will call Chet illustrates the potential of this method. Chet was classified by the personnel of the Boys and Girls Club as a "special needs" child. In this case, the special need arose from a difficult home situation and the suspicion that Chet was mildly retarded. The director of the program for special needs remarked that, in his opinion, during the past year Chet had made excellent progress in the cognitive and social spheres. Chet seemed more confident of himself and less self-conscious, a change that the director attributed to his accomplishments in the Fifth Dimension. As an exercise, we went back over the field notes of interactions involving Chet between 1987, when he first entered the program, and 1992. There we noted a remarkable change. From a child who had difficulty paying attention and dealing with the tasks of the program, Chet had become adept at many of the games, helpful to teach undergraduates not only how to be members of the Fifth Dimension, but how to use the computers that were baffling them. Instead of remarking on his lack of abilities, the undergraduates working with Chet reported him to be an intelligent and socially accomplished young man.[8]

It is, of course, extremely difficult to separate other influences in Chet's life from those of the Fifth Dimension. However, I am impressed with two facts. First, Chet has clearly made advances in his ability to engage in joint activity with undergraduates around computers and games, advances that were not predictable from his behavior several years earlier. Second, both Chet and the adults around him attribute his current satisfaction and accomplishments to the experiences of the Fifth Dimension. At least in the perception of these participants, the program is fulfilling the task of a tertiary artifact as defined by Wartofsky – providing its users with tools for dealing more effectively with their everyday lives because of the time they spend living imaginatively in it.

The sustainability of change.   One of the central issues highlighted by the garden metaphor is the importance of creating *sustainable* environments. By its very nature, research on sustainability requires that the research be continued long enough to determine if the newly created activity system will continue to exist in a steady state. It is of course important to demonstrate that it is possible to create a useful environment for nurturing children's intellectual and social abilities; this was the focus of our research at the outset of this project, and it remains an ongoing concern (Cole, Quan, & Woodbridge, 1992). However, our experience has taught us that proving the effectiveness of an innovation such as the Fifth Dimension is difficult. This lesson was brought home to us most poignantly in a comparison of the fates of the programs at the Boys and Girls Club and the library.[9]

At the very start of the project, we made it clear that at the end of a 3-year period, the project would come to an end. We promised that at that time we would be prepared to continue staffing the program with eager undergraduates who would be given course credit at the university. The university would also continue to provide telecommunications facilities so that the children could communicate with children in other parts of the country and the world. But we would no longer provide the computers, software, and the labor of a site coordinator: This would be the responsibility of the local institution.

During the project we worked with the staffs of the local institutions to develop expertise in running the programs and we helped them raise money locally to begin the process of replacing hardware and software. We created special activities within the program that required the children to acquire library skills, and we met with staff periodically to review progress in the program, which they seemed to support. However, when the time came for a shift to shared responsibility, the library staff decided that they did not want to continue the program. There were many reasons for this decision: The library was short of space, there were administrative difficulties in handling the money needed to pay a site coordinator, they did not have time to train people to work with the children, and so on. Each of these problems could have been solved, but the fact of the matter was that even if the money was available and volunteers stepped in to help, the librarians had come to the conclusion that the Fifth Dimension did not fit closely enough with their main goals. And that was the end of that.

By contrast, the Boys and Girls Club not only accepted their new role; they supported the diffusion of the Fifth Dimension into two neighboring clubs. They gave the program an award and embraced it as an important new addition to their program.

This situation will be recognized as paradoxical from the perspective of a developmental psychologist. There is no doubt in my mind that the library club was a better "garden" for cultivating cognitive and social development, but it was not sustainable and no traces of it remain. On the other hand, the very properties that weakened the developmental impact of the program in the Boys and Girls Club, especially the freedom that children felt to come and go as they pleased, made it an easy-to-assimilate activity from the institution's point of view.

In this context, the relationship of activity to setting depicted in Figure 8.4 takes on added significance. The fact that the library program, while quieter and more studious than the Boys and Girls Club program, was noisier than its setting turned out to be a major factor in its eventual demise at the same time that it was a major factor in being desirable from a psychological perspective. By the same token, the relative quiet of the Boys and Girls Club program confirmed its (relatively) educational nature (relative to the other activities at the club) and made it a feather in the program's cap.

This story is still in progress, of course. At the time of writing these remarks, we have just completed an experimental summer program at the Boys and Girls Club that has been conducted in a more structured manner, with regular, scheduled attendance. The institution *liked* the more structured approach and for the coming year proposed that we introduce it into the regular activities of the club in a somewhat modified form that allows drop-in participation when children fail to turn up for their scheduled appearances in the program. We cannot be certain that this innovation will be a success, of course; only time and continued effort will tell.

Notes

1. In the chapter title I have used the awkward convention of referring to socio-cultural-historical psychology to emphasize my theme of commonality among approaches designated by the elements of that hyphenated phrase in isolation. In an earlier paper (Cole, 1988) I used the term "sociohistorical" to refer to the work of Leont'ev, Luria, Vygotsky, and their students as it was appropriated by American scholars. In part this decision was based on my belief that since cultural phenomena are necessarily historical, the social nature of cultural-historical phenomena needed to be emphasized. It might also be noted that Leont'ev (1981a) used this term in his well-known monograph on development. Subsequently, after many discussions of the issues involved, I have come to the conclusion that such a change in terminology does a disservice to the historical record and fails to add conceptual clarity,

since cultural-historical phenomena are also necessarily social. Consequently, I will use the term "cultural-historical," or "cultural-historical activity theory" throughout this chapter.

2. It should be clear that in the paragraphs to follow I am saying nothing original; rather, I am attempting to summarize what I take to be generally accepted background knowledge that can serve as a foundation for further discussion.

3. Lektorsky identifies this as a conclusion from Marxist philosophy; the same conclusion follows just as readily from American pragmatism.

4. Yrjo Engeström (1987) refers to this as "activity-genesis."

5. Dorothy Hammond and Jaan Valsiner (1988) note the close correspondence between cultural models and what they call "mediational devices." They prefer to limit the notion of mediational device to "circumscribed, tangible activities or objects of sensory dimensions." I prefer to think of cultural models as systems of artifacts so as to emphasize the dual material–ideal nature of both cultural models and artifacts with more obvious sensory dimensions.

6. The function of the Wizard is distributed among undergraduates and research staff in such a manner that the best way to state what the Wizard *really* is, is to characterize it as the collective will of the adults to promote the children's welfare.

7. The normative rule of thumb that guides their participation is that they should provide as little help to the children as possible, but as much as necessary so that the children have a good time (this heuristic will be recognized as an operationalization of the notion of a zone of proximal development; Vygotsky, 1978).

8. This analysis was carried out by Amy Olt.

9. For a fuller account of research on the sustainability issue, see Cole and Nicolopolou (1991).

References

Abulkhanova-Slavaskaya, K. A. (1980). The category of activity in Soviet psychology. *Psikhologicheski Zhurnal, 1*, 11–28.

Bakhurst, D. (1986). Thought, speech, and the genesis of meaning: On the 50th anniversary of Vygotsky's *Myshlenie i rech*. *Studies in Soviet Thought, 31*, 102–129.

Bateson, G. (1972). *Steps to an ecology of mind.* New York: Ballantine.

Bergson, H. (1911/1983). *Creative evolution.* New York: Henry Holt.

Bronfenbrenner, U. (1979). *Experimental human ecology.* Cambridge, MA: Harvard University Press.

Brushlinsky, A. V. (1968). *The cultural-historical theory of thinking.* Moscow: Vyshaya Shkola.

Cole, M. (1988). Cross-cultural research in the sociohistorical tradition. *Human Development, 31*, 137–151.

Cole, M., & Nicolopolou, A. (1991). *Creating sustainable new forms of educational activity in afterschool settings.* San Diego: Laboratory of Comparative Human Cognition, University of San Diego.

Cole, M., Quan, S., & Woodbridge, S. (1992). *A mixed activity setting for the promotion of cognitive and social development.* San Francisco: American Educational Research Association.

D'Andrade, R. (1984). Cultural meaning systems. In R. A. Shweder & R. A. LeVine (Eds.), *Culture theory: Essays on mind, self, and emotion* (pp. 88–122). Cambridge University Press.

Dewey, J. (1938/1963). *Experience and education.* New York: Macmillan.

Engeström, Y. E. (1987). *Learning by expanding.* Helsinki: Oy.

Hammon, D., & Valsiner, J. (1988). Cognition, symbols, and Vygotsky's developmental psychology. *Ethos, 16,* 247–272.

Hydén, L-C. (1984). Three interpretations of the activity concept: Leont'ev, Rubinshtein and critical psychology. In M. Hedegaard, P. Hakkarainen, & Y. E. Engeström (Eds.), *Learning and teaching on a scientific basis* (pp. 33–41). Arhus: Psykologisk Institut.

Lamb, S., & Wozniak, R. (1990). Developmental co-construction: Metatheory in search of method. *Contemporary Psychology, 35,* 253–254.

Lektorsky, V. A. (1980). *Subject, object, and cognition.* Moscow: Progress.

Leont'ev, A. N. (1981a). *Problems in the development of mind.* Moscow: Progress.

Leont'ev, A. N. (1981b). The problem of activity in psychology. In J. V. Wertsch (Ed.), *The concept of activity in Soviet psychology* (pp. 37–71). Armonk, NY: Sharpe.

Luria, A. R. (1928). The problem of the cultural development of the child. *Journal of Genetic Psychology, 35,* 493–506.

Nicolopolou, A., & Cole, M. (1993). The Fifth Dimension, its playworld, and its institutional contexts: The generation and transmission of shared knowledge in the culture of collaborative learning. In E. A. Forman, N. Minnick, & C. A. Stone (Eds.), *Contexts for learning: Sociocultural dynamics in children's development* (pp. 283–314). New York: Oxford University Press.

Payne, T. R. (1968). *S. L. Rubenstejn and the philosophical foundations of Soviet psychology.* New York: Humanities.

Stern, E. (1920/1990). Problems of cultural psychology. *Zeitschrift fur die gesamte Staatwissenschaft, 75,* 267–301. Translated and reprinted in the *Quarterly Newsletter of the Laboratory of Comparative Human Cognition, 12,* 12–23.

Van der Veer, R., & Valsiner, J. (1991). *Understanding Vygotsky: A quest for synthesis* Oxford: Blackwell.

Vygotsky, L. S. (1929). The problem of the cultural development of the child, Part 2. *Journal of Genetic Psychology, 36,* 415–434.

Vygotsky, L. S. (1978). *Mind in Society.* Cambridge, MA: Harvard University Press.

Wartofsky, M. (1979). *Models.* Dordrecht: Reidel.

Wertsch, J. (1981). *The concept of activity in Soviet psychology.* Armonk, NY: Sharpe.

Wertsch, J. (1985). *Vygotsky and the social formation of mind.* Cambridge, MA: Harvard University Press.

Williams, R. (1973). *Keywords.* New York: Oxford University Press.

9 Tossing, praying, and reasoning: the changing architectures of mind and agency

Pablo del Río and Amelia Alvarez

"E pur, se muove!" ("In spite of everything, it moves!")

Quotation attributed to Galileo, who whispered it immediately after he had declared that he accepted the immobility of the earth before a panel of inquisitors

Those of us who try to understand humankind have become entangled in a tension between the illusions of modernity and progress, the legacy of the past two centuries, and the ironic caution of postmodernism, offered as a bridge into the next century. Located between these two positions is what Alvin Toffler (1970) referred to more than 20 years ago as "the furious storm of change." No one questions the inevitability of change, but in the scientific community it seems that there is little consensus about whether it is prudent to allow it to go beyond the "defense belt" of paradigms, and if so, there is little consensus about how to deal with it.

Neither among scientists nor among citizens is there unanimity on the perception of change. In general, it could be said that a state of uneasiness has arisen over a whole series of events occurring in societies throughout the world. It seems that there is no easy way to respond to this state of affairs. There is the increasingly rapid disappearance of relatively stable traditional societies and long-standing contexts that have been essential for humans' well-being. And the new conditions

We gratefully acknowledge Natalie Mello Acuña and Jim Wertsch for their invaluable collaboration and inexhaustible patience in the task of putting our words into English. What in the text is understandable is undoubtedly due to their efforts. The possible obscurities and inaccuracies are entirely our responsibility.

215

replacing these contexts bring their own set of problems. These problems include the increasing number of cultures and social groups in which unemployment and inactivity, with all their psychological consequences, have become the norm; a pattern of an extended period of schooling followed by unemployment and inactivity; urbanization; mass migration; individual isolation; and instability and other disruptions of families. One must also mention the disappearance of old belief and identity systems; social rootlessness and associated patterns of irresponsibility, mental illness, moral disintegration, delinquency, and drug dependency; difficulties in intercultural integration and the conflicts of national, cultural, and generational identities; changing patterns in the practices of integrative thinking by academics; and new developments in mass communication and technology.

All of these conditions and problems give rise to psychological issues that were taken into consideration in earlier applied formulations of psychology. However, these issues now need to be revisited in light of the theoretical and epistemological dimensions of recent massive social changes. The bottom line of all these considerations is whether the ensuing changes will be only skin deep or will be more fundamental. In particular, will the changes involve the redesign of psychological functions that are more appropriate for humans in their current context? We now need formulations of psychological functioning and consciousness that take into consideration unforeseen trends of historical change and have the capacity to explicate and allow for patterns of incoherence. The question that remains at the center of all the human sciences concerns the definition of human nature or the essence of humans. This is a question that is still open in anthropology (Winkler & Schweikhardt, 1982), paleontology (Donald, 1991; Lewin, 1987), philosophy (Toulmin, 1972), and, of course, psychology, and it allows us to turn to the issue of explicating mental functions.

We would argue that psychological accounts of human nature keep vacillating between two tendencies that Vygotsky tried to address in the first third of this century. On the one hand, there is a tendency toward viewing psychological processes in universal terms. On the other hand, there is a tendency toward cultural relativism that accepts cultural differences in the construction of mind. Approaches under this heading accept differences across cultures and historical changes within them. Vygotsky did not manage to resolve this dichotomy (see Sutton,

1988). Even so, he did provide relevant suggestions for addressing change as a means of theoretical and empirical investigation (Vygotsky, 1929).

Vygotsky's thesis (1982a, b, c, 1983, 1984) about the human mind and about the science of mind – psychology – postulates an object in transformation and suggests that methods adequate for studying this must themselves also constantly undergo transformation. From this perspective, cultural activity systems and the complexes of symbolic mediation they incorporate are simultaneously the effect and the cause of the design and construction of the architecture of the mind. Sociocultural and historical changes in these activity systems and psychological tools are viewed as provoking correlated changes in this architecture; that is, they modify our object of study.

But psychology is concerned not only with mental changes in the subjects it studies. It must also be concerned with changes in psychologists themselves. That is to say, at the same time that everyday, or popular, mental tools are undergoing change, we can also witness change in the mental tools used in science. Therefore, the object as well as the methods of psychology undergo a continual process of historical change, which must be to a large degree articulated. The only realistic alternative in this view would be to develop a science of the structure of change for a changing object. Although the sociopolitical trajectory of sociohistorical or cultural-historical psychology involves ambitious tasks in many areas of psychology, our opinion is that no other orientation in psychology is better prepared to take on the issues of change.

If we examine the new problems on the agenda of psychologists – the problems that society must address – we see that accelerated historical, social, and cultural changes are raising a whole new layer of issues, especially for the development of new generations. These are the problems that many consider the direct causes of serious disturbances in human nature (see, e.g., Bronfenbrenner, 1989). We can tabulate this set of problems with a simple list of "alarms" or "indicators" of change that will allow us to put them provisionally on the list. However, it is another matter to establish a viable methodology for dealing with the list of "shoulds." It is this list of changes that is most obvious, and this is for good reason.

A whole series of theoretical and methodological developments is in order for psychology in general and for the sociocultural approach in particular (e.g., Bruner, 1990; Cole, 1990; Scribner, 1985; Valsiner & Winegar, 1992) if we are to capture this change in an objective manner. It is equally necessary to develop the theoretical instruments and the techniques that will make it possible to intervene constructively in this change. But this is not easy. The monograph by Todorova et al. (1993) includes a discussion of the overwhelming methodological and social difficulties encountered when trying to investigate historical and ontogenetic changes in an articulate manner.

Investigators who assume the universality of mental architecture need examine only one subject or any sample of human subjects, which they can then convert into a normative model. If one assumes different cultural architectures of mind, it is necessary to confront the need to investigate all the cultural groups that range across history and across the planet. This latter option would allow us to examine universal as well as culturally specific theses. The first approach, in contrast, is much less expensive, but it is probably incapable of examining either set of issues. It would seem to be justified only in the absence of the problems that seem to be afflicting the planet so seriously today. Pursuing it has resulted in a psychology that is today immobile and incapable of discussing major issues. It is a psychology that is immune to criticism, as was the geocentric model for astronomy in Galileo's time. The risks are gargantuan.

To continue overlooking this contradiction, therefore, is dangerous. As was the case with the idea that the earth's ecology and natural resources are inexhaustible – an idea that is contributing to the destruction of our planet – we should not think that human nature is inexhaustible. We should not think that human resources can be maintained in a stable and biogenetically guaranteed way. This contributes to the social and political indifference to changes that continue to occur, that we ourselves go on producing in our context and cultural framework.

Going back to the need for methodological development, only by investigating cultural systems in historic and social change can we do justice to the change. This obliges us to concentrate our investigations on the external processes, which are cultural and contingent, on the *popular designs* and sociocultural situatedness of the mind. To that end, we must suppose that most of the architecture of mental functioning is accessible to investigation in an *implicit* form and that we have only explicated some of this architecture, the part adapted more to the logical and discrete operations of the rational subject and of today's psychologist. It is better to understand this in terms of the conditions of the tasks and the cultural instruments and practices of our particular context in the West.

In our view the agenda for systematically approaching the problem of change includes:

1. the axioms, heuristics, or *positions in psychology* that justify the investigation of change;
2. a formulation of the *types of changes* on which investigators focus: *cognitive changes*, or changes in mental technology; *directive changes*, or changes in the affective-moral action of consciousness and conduct; changes in the *actual systems of activity*, especially changes within *learning and development*;
3. the introduction of new methods, both at the level of *assumptions and methods of investigation*, that will be required to provide an empirical account of human change; and
4. a discussion of new *methods of intervention*, based on the assumption of changing and self-designing human nature. This modifies the agenda of psychology and presents alternatives and new tools for intervening in human development.

The flexible mind: a psychology for a changing object

Our first concern is that by presupposing a rigid division of the models of mind when dealing with change, we have arrived at the dead-end of the opposition between universalism and relativism. Our second concern is that this opposition has been conflated to a great extent with an opposition between a psychology focused exclusively on meaning and one that recognizes the exigencies attached to sense.

To address our first concern, we must be able to locate "universals" of the mind. In this connection, three paths offer themselves to us. Two of them are extreme and epistemologically simpler, and amount to bypassing or suspending the problem of explicating human nature: First, universals are innate and we must look for them in biological and genetic endowment (i.e., we do not know and we do not need to know what human nature is); second, universals do not exist, and the essential functions of the human mind are culturally relative (we do not and cannot know what human nature is). The third alternative is to consider constructing "universals about universals." That is to say, one could consider constructing higher or more human mental functions and distinguish those that are innate from those that are "universals of culture." This would permit very diverse, though restricted, cultural architectures of psychological functions and would therefore facilitate many diverse functional designs.

Human sociocultural organization always facilitates a few common structures that will guarantee that there will be some kind of cultural construction of consciousness. These are socially and technically organized labor, language and other symbolic mediators for regulating behavior, systems of collective memory, and the cultural organization of social and instrumentally distributed activity. These structures also include the possibility of instrumentally mediating the regulation of intentions, emotions, identity, and social relations. In addition to what is common to these structures, there are important differences in mediational means and the systems used for developing them. Cultural and biological continuity will be relative, and relations will be dynamic, as Cole has noted:

The invention of new ways to exploit energy or new media of representation, or simple changes in custom, may disrupt sufficiently the existing cultural order to be a source of significant developmental discontinuity. (1992, p. 28)

These changes in cultural structures can be contemplated from the perspective of a model of unilinear development, of permanent historical progression (like that in the traditional perspective of Soviet psychology), or they can be considered from the perspective of cultural-historical relativism. In the latter case historic progression is recognized, but without the commitment to a homogeneous or a stable and unique line of development (something that will be more to the liking of those formulating sociocultural psychology such as Cole, 1992, or Wertsch, 1985).

It has to be admitted, nevertheless, that both a psychology that presupposes the same mind for all subjects (universal mind as the point of departure) and a psychology that presupposes a unique line of historical progress, which has been characteristic of the cultural-historical perspective (the universal mind as the end point), are more economical for science. Both make it possible to define a unique repertoire of mental functions. The third alternative, the one in which changes are neither totally determined nor linear, obliges us to create a methodological and theoretical perspective with the capacity to capture in dynamic relations both what is common and what is different and to characterize what is stable and what is changing.

We are confronted with the need for methodological innovation, as well as for parsimony of another sort. The sociocultural program must take on the study of psychological functional systems as historical and cultural constructions involving external systems and coconstructions, as well as the issue of how these systems interact with biological universals. It must also examine various designs of aptitudes and regulative systems, distinct architectures of consciousness, and the representation and management of action. This involves a very arduous and extensive task: investigating all humanity (or all humani*ties*) so we can make legitimate affirmations about one humanity. But at the same time we arrive at a methodological philosophy that will allow us to approach the study of the mind with efficacy. It allows us to suggest *a path between the internal and the external.* This is the measure in which those external systems of activity and behavioral regulation, of representation and consciousness, are externally anchored and distributed and are, therefore, *directly available to the investigator.*

In dealing with models of consciousness in our own culture, and even more so in other cultures, there are structures that cannot be apparent to us. We are not talking about something being biogenetically implicit, as is supposed in many aspects of cognition analyzed from the perspective of information processing, but of something that is *culturally implicit.* And its explication will not be viable using isolated tasks or proofs involving isolated individuals, but only when we examine functioning in real, culturally situated activities. And if we assume the existence of distinct systems or functional architectures flexibly constructed in distinct activity systems or cultural architectures with their recourse to mediation, changes in these activity systems or cultural architectures imply changes in cultural designs of consciousness, in systems of psychological functions.

Starting from the concept of *activity systems* taken from the biology of Jennings, Vygotsky (1983) saw the history of development as the construction of *psychological systems,* as the interaction between natural functions and activity systems. The latter are enriched by modes of artificial-cultural action that have developed historically. Luria (1978) proposed *functional systems* as constructions in which external cultural mediation (the name Vygotsky and Luria gave extracortical connections) converge with internal neuropsychological circuits. The psychological systems are supported by natural neurological systems, but they cannot be defined properly or systematically without taking into account the activity systems and cultural operators of consciousness which are distributed externally in these systems of activity (see del Río, 1995). In this connection we wish to discuss and extend Gardner's metaphor of "cultural modules" (del Río, 1986).

In place of a supposed mental model and unique internal functioning or the plasticity of cultural relativism and total indeterminacy, the cultural systemic approach presupposes the existence of external cultural architectures with which functional systems are constructed. These functional systems are internally and externally distributed. The methodology implied here is one of establishing for each functional model (of a single subject or a group) *a form that is contingent on the cultural means.* For this same reason, intervention is flexible and accessible.

At this point it is impossible to gather even a set of diverse examples of this program of sociocultural investigation. However, we do have indications that we can arrive at a viable alternative, starting from our initial work on the historical and culturally flexible mediation of aptitudes (del Río, 1986, 1990) and of activity systems and systems for regulating action in various generations and cultures (del Río & Alvarez, 1992).

Our second concern is that psychology has focused on the analysis of mind, and even of culture, exclusively from the perspective of processes of representation and meaning, and has neglected processes of sense and agency. It was the old goal of uniting both aspects of the human that de Unamuno was pursuing when he pointed out that consciousness of agency is the field of the consciousness of knowledge. In his view, one oneself is the principal problem of cognition, and one's own action is the principal challenge to knowledge. The problem, then, is to reconcile the mechanistic model of humans with the narrative model, that is to say, the "clock" character with the novelistic character of the religious individual, to continue using the expressions of the Spanish philosopher de Unamuno (1927). The models of mind that should be relied on more heavily in psychology must attend to both agency and *sense*, as well as representation and meaning (Bruner, 1990; Wertsch, Tulviste, & Hagstrom, 1993). We will give some very brief considerations to conscious systems for *managing cognition* or *representation* to get to what we wish to undertake more specifically: the systems for managing *emotion and directive action*, at least as they can be addressed in cultural-historical psychology.

Cognitive changes in the management of meaning

One can include among the assets of mechanical approximations and universals of knowledge the attempt to deprive psychological experiences of their original traits of animism and subjectivism, the deletion of all references to the subject "who knows" and his or her mental processes and intentions, and the deletion of mental verbs and subjects, until they are converted into what Rivière (1993, p. 69) calls "doubly de-mentalized propositions." But, if we approach these issues from the cultural-historical perspective, these processes have been achieved not by depriving the mental of the external and nonmental, but precisely *because of* the use of the external mediation of intentional and intensional processes of behavior, because of the use of psychological instruments in the extended space of external representation.

From a historical perspective, computational rationalism, the Turing machine, and computers are by themselves cultural instruments, created thanks to the mechanism of cultural mediation, that make possible external and cultural psychological computation. That is, they convert actions or situations into discrete facts and symbolic contents, thanks to which the continuity of action is broken up, made discrete, and mediated by an object or psychological instrument, by signs that permit the constitution of sequential, computational, symbolic contents within the confines of a natural system organized for action in the physical world.

In effect, the Vygotskian perspective contemplates functions and symbolic intelligence as *properly artificial or psychotechnical*. This cultural *product* has over time been converted into a "natural model" by the strand of cognitive psychology (Chomsky, 1980; Fodor, 1975) that seeks to be valid not only for culturally mediated psychological processes, but for all human psychological processes. The natural is thus reified and confounded with the artificial-cultural, reducing the significance of both the natural and the cultural.

Cultural constructions have been elaborated to serve two grand watersheds of mental life: the *cognitive* subject or the functions of processing (where cognitivists with strong artificial orientations view the mind as a computer system) and the *pragmatic* subject (concerning the intentional system of Brentano or the directive system of Luria). This latter system emotionally regulates action. Historical changes that affect the cognitive subject (or, more properly speaking, the cognitive *psychologist*) would imply modifications in cultural artifacts of information processing. Those that affect the pragmatic subject would imply the cultural means for regulating intentions, affect, and meaningful action. It can be argued, however, that this distinction may not be useful at all in the external territory in which cultural behavior is organized.

To be coherent, the cultural-historical approach must conduct intensive synchronic (transcultural) and diachronic (historical) empirical studies of psychological functions such as attention, perception, memory, self-regulation, and thinking designated as "higher." That is, it must explain cognitive functions in a cultural-historical way. The classic study by Vygotsky and Luria examined the effects of schooling in Uzbekistan (Luria, 1976) and has not been sufficiently followed up in psychology. Although for political reasons Luria could not examine his hypotheses empirically, he planned to study whether ideographic languages of certain peoples from various cultures in the USSR are associated with the structure of neuropsychological functioning. Tsunoda's studies have provided unanticipated support for this thesis (Tsunoda, 1985; Chapter 5, this volume).

There are also other investigations of the effects of cultural activity systems and languages or other psychological instruments on mind. We give special mention to Scribner and Cole's (1981) recovery of the earlier research agenda, and we mention here only the basic issues of thinking (Scribner, 1984; Tulviste, 1991), memory (Middleton & Edwards, 1990), and mental instruments (del Río, 1986), as well as changes in the competencies in children resulting from the use of technology (Salmon, 1979). In general, the problems remaining for this research far outweigh what has been accomplished, and although the point of the thesis of change is correct, it is far from being a sufficient functional alternative when investigating the *flexible mediation of psychological functions.*

We therefore confront a very paradoxical situation: Rigid ideas about aptitudes do not provide an account of change and trivialize it by reducing it to "learning" or superficial modification. The sociocultural thesis (in both its unique line and its flexible construction versions) respects change as authentic development, but it has not provided an adequate account of either change or the instruments for measuring it. Such accounts are scarce and scarcely utilized.

In this framework of change in the cultural tools of knowledge, the very epistemological emphasis on artificial intelligence seems to be an effect of change. Rivière (1993) argues:

Man has, in the last years, the strong impression that he is producing mental functioning with these techniques. Or, at the very least that he is producing "cogito," thinking that has been the mark of the mental at least since the origin of modern epistemology beginning with Descartes. (p. 48)

This *impression,* which is pervasive among cognitive psychologists, would do justice to the facts if we were to view things socioculturally: The "cogito" would be the result of the construction of external, social, and cultural systems, of re-presentation, or of mediated communication with others and oneself. Cultural artifacts are like "external programs" for directly computing the incomputable. In this view, intelligence is a cultural, that is, higher, constructed function not only in a metaphorical or methodological sense, but in a *genuinely artificial* sense. This is in tune with most cognitivist theses.

But this agreement on the artificial character in the final "product" obscures an important disagreement with respect to causal explanation: From the cultural-historical perspective, it is not the natural brain that imitates the computer or vice versa, but the *cultural brain,* the new formations that support acquired functions, that produce mental functions through incorporating cognitive tools of culture, including the computer. It is precisely the computational claim expressed in the Turing machine that offers a way to resolve the old problem of natural and cultural functions. Certain natural actions are culturally mediated by sequences of stimulus mediators organized in discrete, step-by-step procedures. This applies both to social communication and to computation and is what constitutes the "artificial." For this reason, these actions are reducible to procedures and hence can be computed or simulated by a Turing machine.

We have argued that psychological functions are the consequence (of course, based on the foundation of powerful natural functions) of sociohistoric construction and the appropriation of operators and externally distributed cultural processes. Therefore, these functions are readily *accessible* to the investigator. For example, if argumentation and reflection are viewed as artifacts proceeding from dialogue and social, external discussion, or if Euclidean space is viewed as learned mechanisms deriving from the external manipulation of cultural frames and operators, the assessment (and eventually the teaching and development) of such functions would be much more approachable for psychologists. We could say that together with a new problem we receive new and more powerful methodological possibilities for directly and externally accessing the constructive processes of mental functioning, at least of "higher," culturally acquired forms of this functioning.

Measuring aptitudes or functions implies knowledge of past and present cultural constructions. Instead of a fixed and universal ideal mental model, we must address models that are specific to generations, cultures, groups, and individuals – that is, flexible models. This makes it possible to cross easily from the mental level to the cultural level and from research to intervention. The objective is not so much to postulate individual or cultural differences, to defend cultural relativism, as it is to know and comprehend the *architecture* of past, present, and future versions of consciousness, the changes in phylogenesis, history, and ontogenesis in the cultural construction of mind (of *minds*).

This path is based on the joint work of anthropology, ethnology, sociology, and psychology. It also includes the engineering of knowledge and forces us to undertake a great deal of field work with more ambitious empirical structures and theoretical formulations. The possibility that *the same unit of analysis* may account for actions that are cultural and mental, as well as external and internal, could be propitious for an articulation of cognitive and sociocultural forces involved in establishing this functional architecture.

The flexible measurement of aptitudes and functions implies finding methodological possibilities for analyzing cultural variability. In addition, it implies finding ways to carry out constructive demonstrations (where cognitive psychology and sociocultural studies converge) for simulating psychological functions (Johnson-Laird, 1988) or constructing them culturally (Luria, 1979; Vygotsky, 1984). Thus, we are proposing the theoretical and methodological possibility of obtaining a convergence between what Garfinkel (1967) calls the *etic* level (the scientific description) and the *emic* level (the level of popular, everyday descriptions or distinctions that, according to Garfinkel, should be the subject for ethnomethodology).

Cultural-historical formulations of the psychological management of sense

Historically, cognitive and directive processes, on the one hand, and social relations, on the other, have been integrated. Socially shared psychological action has been very difficult to separate into distinct procedures by dividing off psychological processes. It is fairly simple to distinguish between operations and mediation by *instruments* (knots, stones, notches, tokens, or numbers as operators for memory or calculation) and *social* operations or mediations (the mother who guides the hand of the child, the member of the tribe that always remembers who is related to whom, the colleague who remembers mathematical formulas, etc.). There is social management in the social sphere and cognitive management in the cognitive sphere. Nevertheless, in functional terms there are not clear divisions – sometimes there is cognitive management of social actions and sometimes social management of cognitive actions.

The Egyptians developed a form of instrumental mediation – geometry – to record the properties of the land after the Nile's flood, but as Schousboe (1986) notes, memory was distributed in feudal systems. It was the distributed memory of domestic serfs that maintained records for the lords of the land that they owned. To dismantle the functioning of this system of activity and the consciousness of its components into isolated elements would result in an enormous impoverishment of the understanding of psychological functioning. To reduce this functional system epistemically to instrumental operations would hide a problem that has not been resolved. To recoup the system of mediation, social representation, and intention for psychological functioning, it seems that one essential and urgent task is to repair the totality of the psychological system and guarantee its flexible cultural measurement.

Having considered animism as something that disturbs psychological processes (and consequently something to be got rid of), Western psychology, with rare exceptions, has arrived at a curious theoretical as well as practical paradox of two-sided decontextualization. While historical progress in cognitive tools has provided positive effects in the abstraction and decontextualization of meaning, changes in tools and mechanisms that culturally control action have also produced a negative effect in the form of the social and affective decontextualization of sense.

But a very elaborate external and cultural construction of symbolic computational processes that provides formally powerful cognitive architecture of higher functions will lack functionality if a subject is not inserted as an agent in situated behavior. We are thinking of a curriculum designer who wishes to produce an impeccable architecture of external cultural mediators, instruments, and symbols necessary for making representationally easy and accessible the acquisition of competencies in mathematics or language. This specialist could perhaps be proud, but not at all confident. It may very well be that children will not get involved in the perfect external mental mechanism, that they will be like children prohibited from touching presents under the Christmas tree. A good design of external and internal processes must rely on the whims of the child, who is not a computer, or is not only a computer, and who may refuse to "process."

The cultural-historical perspective not only asserts the cultural construction of *cognitive psychological functions* through the appropriation or internalization of certain operators and activities such as writing, multiplication tables, commands, plans, discussion, argumentation, and so forth. It also postulates the cultural construction of psychological directive functions. There is evidence that the manner in which motives, affect, and values are constructed is realized by the entire sociocultural architecture of intentions and emotion and by all *the cultural and external operators which guarantee that these intentions materialize in effective conduct.* From the start, Vygotsky understood the connection between the cultural management of representation and that of action, and he did not neglect in the least the role of the latter:

It is an exceptional fact that humans have great freedom for intentional action, even for foolish acts. This freedom that characterizes civilized humans, and to a lesser degree children and probably primitives, distinguishes humans from their close animal relatives much more than their higher intelligence. (1983, p. 120)

The thesis of de Waal (1993) about the "political" chimpanzee, the thesis of Premack and Woodruff (1978) about the intentional expertise of the chimpanzee who possesses "theories of the mind," and the thesis of Leslie (1988) about the existence in children of these same "theories of mind" all raise the same basic problem. Given the basic competency for cooperation, deception, and administering actions on the basis of intentions and vice versa, how can we arrive at the organization of general cognition and some cultural dispositions for the interregulation of intentions and actuation?

If anthropoids and humans stand out by virtue of having "theories of mind," by virtue of having the power to distinguish between the inanimate objects of reality and object-subjects (i.e., "objects with a mind"; Rivière, 1991), the problem is to know whether cultural dispositions to mediate and represent actions and intentions essentially change the natural processes regulating action. This is something that has been investigated to a much greater extent for basic cognitive processes such as memory, attention, and reasoning. The fact that chimpanzees demonstrate this richness of socially calculated behaviors and deception is probably an indication that the capacity for episodic behavior (Donald, 1991) or the control of "theories of the mind" was decisive in philogenesis. However, the distance between the conduct of the chimpanzee and human animism, religion, or judicial-bureaucratic organization is very great and raises an explanatory challenge. Rivière (1993) has grounds for maintaining that the mere description in the formal computational terms used by Leslie of the metarepresentations that support theories of mind give us the (possible) informational *form* of these representations, but they do not provide us with information about semantic genesis. In our opinion, it is precisely at this point where one must revert to more dense concepts such as consciousness and intersubjectivity (e.g., Rommetveit, 1992; Trevarthen, 1992). The study of these cultural forms of consciousness and intersubjectivity, or the design or implicit architecture of intentional regulation of behavior, is one of the areas most neglected by psychology, including cultural-historical psychology.

At this point psychology confronts a problem for which it is poorly engineered. While humanity has, over its history, constructed very powerful cultural architectures for managing intentional action and behavior, ethnography and cognitive anthropology have usually dealt with these. However, psychology has generally ignored the implicit architectures involved. It has done so for the same reasons that it has ignored the problem of intentionality (a mechanist does not require that an organism *tries* anything, for it is simply a process and a reaction). From that perspective, all organisms are supposedly governed by the same laws of "voluntary conduct" that can be analyzed in a decontextualized way in the laboratory. While psychologists analyze voluntary behavior deprived of all traces of culture and of the architecture of "voluntariness," the principal accomplishment of a culture has possibly rested on the development of situated modes of voluntary control of behavior.

If we wish to maintain the hypothesis of flexible consciousness, we cannot neglect, in addition to the analysis and the continued and open mediation of cognitive functions, the analysis of the historical architectures of voluntary (cultural) control of action in daily life. A brief look will permit us to verify the enormous wealth and variability of these socially implicit designs of the "motives," the "will," the intentions, and the programs for executing action.

In an investigation recently initiated in Spain, we are comparing the psychological architecture of regulation in three "cultures," or cultural systems of consciousness, through the analysis of their cultural operators. The first of these is a traditional town in Castile, the second is a monastery of a traditional religious discipline, and the third is an urban, mass culture system. This last one is perhaps largely homologous with other transnational cultures, with a certain normative context that seems to be emerging all over the world.

Both the monastic and the traditional rural Castilian architectures are of what we can call a life "under the eye of God," a life inserted in a fluid scene and narrative, in a certain "encultured nature." It is a life dictated by the sun and the bell, presided over by rain and the crucifix, articulated by the tasks of farmers and by religious festivals, stitched together by sayings for regulating activity and by prayers and religious phrases or songs, by the "commandments" or precepts of "catechism" learned by heart in childhood and associated with the appropriate occasions. This is a life in which culture defines actions and situations: what to wear on every occasion; how to deal with your spouse, children, and parents.

Two of the pillars supporting a good part of the historical development of humanity and the enormous diversity of cultural systems for guiding behavior are magic and religion. These two architectures coexist in us, and we would like to address the psychological qualities of these architectures for the construction of the mind. What is next is not so much intended to outline this psychological analysis as perhaps to provide an initial pass at this agenda for psychology.

The animistic management of situation and activity

The Spanish philosopher Ortega y Gasset has said that humans carry within themselves a machine to confront the irresolvable issue of action: the fact that "each person's authentic life consists of doing that which needs to be done and avoiding doing anything else" (Ortega y Gasset, nd). Combining decisions with action has been the key problem, from the scholastic perspective, in the psychology of human action. To say that one must act but has no capacity to act would be equivalent to having an incomplete intentional architecture, an architecture that rests on only one leg. It is something that in religious traditions is expressed in sayings such as "The road to hell is paved with good intentions."

From a historical perspective, both deciding what to do and doing it have a natural, or biological, as well as a cultural architecture. In action guided by what Premack calls "theories of mind" (we are distinguishing here *natural* theories of mind), action and intentions are regulated from the biological context on the visual-motor plane. But in the cultural mind, the problem of intention is transformed by mediation – generally verbal mediation. That is to say, it transcends the situation (exporting the intention to the appropriate situations) by means of accompanying the saying with the doing or vice versa. And the problem of action is converted to that of the regulation or self-control of one's own conduct through the use of external sociocultural tools. This involves a process whereby culturally based operators shaping decisions supercede other stimuli present in the situation.

Because the structure is mediated, or "extracortical," to say is to do. As Bruner notes, "Saying and doing represent a functionally inseparable unit in a culturally oriented psychology," and "The relationship between action and saying (or experiencing) is, *in the ordinary conduct of life,* interpretable" (1990, p. 19). Hence, the interpretation of biological action in terms of reaction, an interpretation implicit in the term "behavior," would be changed to active intentional conduct, to situated action in a cultural context, to symbolic action. From a biological context, where intention and action are hardly distinguished (intentions are utilized expressively for interaction and the regulation of action), a cultural context emerges in which the development of cultural systems results in decisions becoming a kind of symbolic action. We can legitimately consider these new psychological designs based in the cultural operators to be "*cultural* theories of mind."

It is not without interest that when Vygotsky (1984), building on the ideas of Levy-Bruhl (1927), proposed the first examples of psychological instruments utilized in the "vestigial" functions (the cultural constructions that are more primitive than superior functions that we can observe in today's humans, modern or traditional), he focused fundamentally on the problem of decision making. The philosopher Buridan's problem of how the donkey died of hunger standing before two equal mountains of hay, immobilized by the two similar, simultaneous stimuli served for Vygotsky as a way to think about the vestigial function that is present in primitive people when solving this problem (a problem that is not at all vestigial, but affects us all everyday when deciding between competing and simultaneous objects or courses of action, from the time in the morning that one decides which shirt to put on).

If a subject cannot decide between two actions, the primitive human transfers the decision to two mediators (e.g., two bones or other kinds of token are used in a magical or symbolic plane) that break the equilibrium at this new plane of mediation. In one of his novels, Robert Louis Stevenson magisterially characterizes the protagonist by his style of making decisions of all sorts, from trivial to major ones. He threw money to the wind, a genuinely vestigial procedure that today maintains its efficacy. Tarot cards, the stones of the Viking oracles, or opening the Bible or Koran to a page at random are similar formulas. Not only does the significance of the object get transferred to a plane of mediation (situation 2, or Sit 2) but the subject's intention is transferred to a plane from which the decision of the "sign" is clearer than that which occurs in the external situation (Sit 1).

The classic triangle that Vygotsky exemplified in memory tasks reflects a neutral mediational architecture, one that is relatively aseptic if we describe only the informational level. The stimulus (Stim 1) – say, a colleague who asks to borrow a book – merits a negative response in this situation (Sit 1) if I don't have the book at my disposal. My response (Res 1), noted in my date book (Stim 2), travels in the pages of this psychological instrument, which, like a vehicle, is brought happily to my desk at home, where every morning I open it before going to work, and from where (Sit 3) the annotation (Res 1) is already constituted (in Stim 2). It reminds me to take the book (Res 2), which is available here (in Sit 3), and put it in my briefcase . . . and so forth. This articulated system of situations and interconnected mediators, which permits me to transcend the dictatorial control of the primordial animal context, is perhaps what the majority of investigations of sociocultural mediation have considered to be their essential object of inquiry. It is probably the point at which the relations of continuous regulation in the environment enters to constitute discreet, discontinuous, and interrupted relations that Vygotsky called "stimulus-means."

The Vygotskian account of Buridan's problem nevertheless shows us mediation of a much more embodied form in the architecture of human action and permits us to understand the act of initial representation as the action of re-present-action (*re-present-acción* in Spanish). Animal behavior is governed by the situation, by what is "present" to the subject in it. Vygotsky viewed the human mechanism as making present artificially (culturally) that which interests the group or subject, that which makes present (re-presents) by means of psychological instruments. We are no longer confronted with a subject governed by the natural context (i.e., a direct relation between that which is present and action). Instead, we are confronted with subjects who present that context which interests them, a context that is artificially built, or mediated (re-present-action).

This process, which is tied to the action of sociocultural and historically constructed representation, has been neglected because we have deprived symbolic representation of its animistic vestiges. But in the service of conventionality and formal purity, we have perhaps thrown out the baby with the bathwater, forgetting the eminently pragmatic character of mediators in the psychological architecture of representation. There is no value in simply saying that there are two types of cognitive processes – one guided by computability and the other by intentionality or theories of the mind – because both (the latter in its most developed forms) are products of the same cultural structure and cannot be analyzed separately without losing their meaning.

The essence of animism and of the vestigial systems of re-present-action is that they incorporate primitive mediators. For the same reason, however (i.e., because of their unmediated connection with reality – something that Frazer (1905, quoted by Caro Baroja, 1988, p. 23) formulated as its law of "sympathy"), these mediators are powerful. Psychologically, for the user, the operators are not merely intermediaries that make it possible to break immobilization or the dictatorial control of direct stimuli. The intermediary operator not only distances itself from the stimulus; in addition the stimulus is tied to the operator, and paradoxically in this way the stimulus is made closer and more manageable.

Hence, subjects are not only opening the way to using representation; at the same time they are manipulating acts. The operators – the bone or the rune stone, the use of spells to cure, and so on – have a direct connection with acts. Thus, when we make them act, we open access to a plane of vision and action about future acts or facts that are not present.

This "primitive" mechanism has never ceased to play a role. Consider the stage actor today who refuses to wear yellow clothes on stage because bad luck would occur (a practice incredibly resistant to change), or consider the housewife who makes sure she leaves the house by taking a step with her right foot. Do not these practices remind us of primitive tribes? The tie between the most primitive animism and everyday life has never been broken (Caro Baroja, 1988).

It can, of course, be debated whether we have managed to destroy the residuals of animism in our psychological system that is constructed around material action. Of the catalogue of animistic practices criticized by the Church of Spain in the sixteenth century, most are still in force today in one form or another, not only in Spain, but in most of the modern world. Early psychological instruments that make missing objects be present (not symbolically, but in pragmatic action, like the stick used as a pretend horse that Vygotsky spoke about) constitute an extreme and initial case of mediation in which these psychological "handles" reveal an intimate tie not only with representation, but with action.

In regulating themselves as they are regulated from outside, as Vygotsky (1984) pointed out, primitive people were in reality the "first domesticated animals" utilizing language and gestures as mediators to establish forms, although still primitive, that were conditionally guided by social signals. The investigations by Luria (1961) of the ontogenesis of voluntary conduct clearly outlined the complex emergence of the word or external signs until they are constituted as instruments for "giving orders to oneself."

Ethnographic and anthropological examples of animistic mediation do not differ in kind from the mediators used by Luria and his collaborators in experiments on the control of action. Neither do the living and accessible examples from everyday life (from the alarm clock to the book that we read to fall asleep).

Technical and social procedures, along with mechanical and intentional "know-how," are intimately locked together in ritual and are very difficult to disentangle. Rites order the world by assuming a union of ritual operators with deeds. In providing psychological order and in making things present and manageable to the mind, rituals make it possible for humans to act in certain ways and also to order their action, transcending the physical zone of present-action. This is often overlooked by cultural-historical analyses of animism, where animism must be understood as the primary symbolic architecture and is for this reason a genuine representational means for intentionality and directionality. It would be useful to reread the work of disciplines that stand in contrast to the neglect in psychology of cultural operators, especially those involving "sense."

Along with Caro Baroja (1988), we believe that beyond its importance for anthropology and ethnography, one must recognize that animism is fundamentally *psychological* and crucial for explicating the architecture of the human mind. In this architecture it seems that decision making and action, as well as action and representation, are inextricably interconnected with the processes of knowing: Action on a mediator and on a space (magic) of re-present-action is perceived as real action "by means" of magic. Magic is the presumed generator both of acts and of the phenomena of consciousness, and the deeds produced with symbolic operators are real in the degree to which they are psychological, that is, to the degree that they are attributed to the order of the universe because they are present in consciousness. The architecture of rituals and myths is not, in this view, a superficial fact, a simple "superstructure." The folk psychology of more primitive functions, or the vestiges in Vygotskian terminology, are the best, and perhaps the only, way to investigate simultaneously the directive and cognitive architecture of initial forms.

From animism to moral and religious engineering

The boundary between animism and religion – like that between religion and rationalism – is weaker than it may appear. In effect, we are not looking at two alternative systems, but at complements. We see two threads that knit together the fabric of consciousness: One concerns situations and actions with objects, and the other concerns social situations and action. The elements of each cross over and are lent to the other.

In the cathedral museum in Segovia, Spain, a "relic," a bone, of Saint Benito has been preserved. He is the saint who created one of the Christian monastic models that were to contribute a great deal to the construction of a careful psychological and religious architecture for organizing conduct, for setting out what must be done and assuring that it is done. The use of relics such as Saint Benito's bone is an animistic reminder, and it is only one example of the widespread appeal to animistic mediators in religions. It is quite visible in Catholicism (bread, wine, relics of saints, images), but we can find it as well in Protestantism (bread, wine, books), Islam (the Koran), and Judaism (the Torah, phylactery), and in Zen Buddhism (gardens). But the monastic design of mind engendered by Saint Benito marked a shift in the psychological structure of cultural management in the Christian world, going much further in using resources from the previous history of animism.

The principal psychocultural heritage of Saint Benito to his followers was not his bones. The medieval monastic architecture of oration plus activity (*ora et labora*) constitutes a powerful, elaborate, and systemic psychological construction. The connection of practical and productive activity with the "novel" (in the terms of de Unamuno, 1927) or religion, is one of the most historically steeped designs of the cultural architecture of action that offers an external cognitive-affective articulation. The equilibrium between the enactive and the symbolic, the physical and the "spiritual," the objective and the subjective, the dialogic and the narrative, is so strong that it survives to this day in certain communities. Cathedrals and monasteries are not impressive empty constructions, but a living part of the essential resources of this psychological architecture. These are constructions in which an agenda of situated actions has developed, where the actions are systematically scaffolded with a precise technology and with the power of cultural operators of the mind for "living in communion with God."

What is of interest here are the psychological differences between animism and religion with respect to their directive character. Since the first studies were done comparing magic and religion, it has been pointed out that magic has a character that is grounded purely in objects. It is mechanical and intends to influence reality directly by its *operators*.

The resources of animism, which are based on the *instrumental operation* of magic, will be historically complemented and in part replaced by the resources of *narratives and dialogues* of religion. These two grand cultural constructions have perhaps been largely ignored by psychology proper, possibly because they are assembled and distributed in daily life and informal education. Nevertheless, they have attained a purer level and have been constituted in an authentic corpus of "ancient technologies of consciousness" through the work of their professionals: magicians and priests. The hostility between these groups of professionals that Durkheim (1915) has pointed out reflects the basic opposition between the instrumental character of the one and the narrative-dialogic nature of the other. At the level of popular practice, nevertheless, users tend to utilize both rituals syncretically.

What is characteristic of all religions is that they achieve a certain "purge" of syncretic animism thanks to the use of three major and very powerful cultural mediators. In contrast to the case of myths, nature and instrumental mediating objects remain relatively marginal, and the natural scene is relegated to the role of background in the drama. The powerful *narrative* architecture allows myths to be constructed that are much more specifically human and social, and these constitute a model and reference point for the daily activities of life. In the words of Ortega y Gasset (1940), "We can not choose whether or not to fantasize. Man is condemned to be a novelist" (p. 405).

Along with narration, the other grand pillars of the religious architecture of the psyche are mental or "spiritual" dialogicality (prayer) and the external organizers of activity (rituals and liturgy). Above these three there is an edifice of one of the most powerful systems of the implicit construction of consciousness yet achieved by humanity. This construction distributes in everyday situations – authentic "enclosures of consciousness" – a psychocultural architecture, a system of the consciousness that is perfectly integrated with the activity system.

Prayer, the construction of a direct *dialogue* with the ideal or absent subject – the divinity, saints, and loved ones "in heaven" accessible through a "spiritual path" – is systematically organized. It allows the construction of a psychological world in which the presence of a "divine order" and of a "father" or powerful personage presides and provides a scene, an argument, and a stable base of mental activity. It supplies a system of distributed consciousness and a system of organized knowing around a group of consciousness that is internalized but culturally situated.

Weakness in this system of consciousness operators would be perceptible to a prepared observer. During our childhood in Spain in the 1950s, when teachers spoke of some especially unaware or inconsistent child, they would say that he or she has "a poor internal life." To religious professionals, such consciousness or internal life was a result of the external processes of prayer (dialogicality) and of omnipresent and systematic narration. In effect it is almost impossible not to extract consciousness from these resources.

The interior and rational consciousness that psychologists are accustomed to taking for granted would involve modes of construction that are negotiated in very diverse ways by external, cultural architectures but are considered by science alien, irrational, and peripheral to mind – modes like animism or religion. If, as Vygotsky (1982a) said, to discover the spirit it was necessary to be able to discover the psyche, will it not be necessary in another manner to construct a religious spirit to be able then to count on a good psyche or a scientific mind? Will it be possible to create consciousness with the same strength and structure in any cultural field? Is it possible to design rational alternatives for the construction of the cultural architecture of consciousness? Have social models of bureaucratic-rational and audiovisual construction of the mind developed an adequate consciousness or internal life?

This state of emotional attachment and cognitive analysis with "divine" mediator-operators, having distinct characteristics in diverse religions, could come to have a profound and intense character of intersubjectivity – that is, of narrative implication and dialogic contact – at the cognitive and emotional level. This dialectic between the rational and the cognitive that permits the reciprocal development of both has been an essential attribute of humans for certain philosophers. Consider, for example, Spinoza's "algebra transformed in ecstasy," which Vygotsky (1982a) liked to cite, or de Unamuno's claims about the need "to think high and feel deeply" (1940, p. 102). The term "mind" is less extensive and rich than the Vygotskian "psyche." Action, intention, feeling, and social consciousness have no place in mind.

Religions are one of the richest reserves of the cultural directive architecture, of the implicit, historically generated models that we command. The abrupt and powerful emergence of recent constructions based on a dense external network of the rational bureaucratic action of institutional life, on a technologized process of internalization grounded in literacy and the media of mass communication are impelling a profound, systematic remodeling of the foundations of consciousness by promoting a *cognitive management of social life* in contrast to the religious option of the social management of the cognitive. Mass culture and the media of public communication can reestablish the equilibrium with its emphasis on the social and the intentional, but the formulas are still very tentative and inarticulate, and we are afraid that they are emerging as unconscious cultural constructions based strongly on immediate sensuous situatedness. Only the analysis of implicit directive models (together with competencies and aptitudes) will permit us to comprehend the actual mind and the possible alternatives of construction.

The speech or dialogue with oneself that Vygotsky (1982b) postulated as the avant-garde molding of thinking processes has been culturally fomented and designed by Christianity using a technology of psychological contact with an ideal "I" – in dyadic or private dialogue, as well as in communal dialogue. The basic human social group of the family – God is the father, the Virgin is the mother – and the community and primary forms of mediation coming from cultural-historic development – dialogue, narration, rituals – provide a simple and powerful architecture. For its part, Christianity has developed self-analysis as an extension of the feeling of being observed by the eyes of God, that is, an "I" that is external yet ideal and omniscient with regard to an internal level. This stands in contrast to the formula of treating yourself as if you were another person, which, as Ornstein (1991) has noted, is more like what one finds in Eastern religious practices such as Zen, Sufism, or yoga. In these traditions, one is encouraged to "observe yourself as if you were another person" (p. 243). Even though this detached observation of oneself emerged from Zen or Sufism and is a cultural technique in a very different narrative, it has structural elements in common with Christianity such as "simulating" or "taking the role of someone" that make it possible to achieve Being and, moreover, to construct the "theories of the mind" that have been of interest to many psychologists. In the view of Vygotsky and El'konin, this constitutes the axis of "cultural development" in children (El'konin, 1978).

To think in religious terms is to "meditate," which is a form of spiritual thinking oriented and therefore guided always by affective and connotative directions, by the personal implications of deeds and actions. To meditate is to situate any deed in "the plan of God." Independent of the type of paradigm utilized in Christianity to attain this, it is important to analyze the enormous sophistication of its architecture and its implications for the development of thinking. And like a good cultural industry of behavior, religious thinking not only constructs an architecture of consciousness at a general level of excellence; it produces one spirituality of a specialized, or "expert" sort (for the religious professional) and another that is for popular use (simple faith).

The "expert" spirituality has a design based on meditation and internal dialogue, with a cognitive and cultural rhetoric organized in macrostructures. In this case networks of mediational instruments, both concrete (a repertoire of objects) and abstract (a repertoire of symbolic signs), as well as internalization become very powerful. In addition, we see the massive use of psychotechnic and situated resources as rituals of consciousness in a scene (and the designing of scenes in accordance with what psychologists of memory know as the method of loci).

The second procedure is based on properties of an architecture that derive from its being enmeshed in social life: the emotional and cognitive protection that the affective dyadic relation between God and subject or between the Mother of God and subject provides occurs in encounters that are heavily mediated by communal situations and involve the distributed organization of everyday cultural operators of a religious sort in the "enclosures of consciousness." Also, these operators are encountered in external form, though they are adapted in order to be inserted into systems of everyday popular activity, making no pretense in general of constituting an activity system in and of itself. Consider public functions and popular fiestas, where rites and operators are routinely inserted in activities and prayers to begin and end these events. Consider also the short fervent prayers, signs, and gestures; calls to worship with church bells and crosses along the way; dialogic and narrative bonds, as well as visual or tactile bonds like carvings and images; catalogues of emotive situations and models that make it possible to attribute order and meaning to practical and social action; and so forth. While the professional and specialized scenes can, to some degree, be protected from change (the psychological architecture is still maintained in monasteries and among religious professionals), popular scenes will be much more exposed to destruction by massive sociocultural changes in systems of everyday activity.

One of the essential characteristics of religious consciousness involving animism is the construction of decision-making processes as emotional and as cognitively tied to identity and motivation. These issues are often inserted into a shared narrative in a social chronicle moving from past to future (e.g., a love story or a Christian narration of contrition and forgiveness). Another alternative, shared with animism, but acquired with an affective and narrative weighting of a new dimension, is the construction of external control of action. This is supported by a strong, dense, carefully and intelligently constructed network of attentional, mnemonic, and emotional operators distributed in this same network of the activity of everyday life.

This network is organized around a clear norm of education, adapted to the age of the child and inserted in the informal habits. For example, an 11-year-old or an adult will be told to reflect on something that is a "bad deed" (for universal religious reasons, for reasons of social reciprocity, etc.), but a child of 4 years can be told that "Baby Jesus is going to cry or it will make him very sad if you do that." This mode of directive consciousness can be maintained not only by adults or saints or spirits, but also by children, by simple people, and by various religions.

Recovering and designing: the exploration of new architectures

The notion of flexible mental architecture allows us to take up the issue of change, but it is more demanding than ideas about a unique line of progress and does not permit us to assume in an unquestioned way that a particular direction of change is always appropriate. It also does not allow us to demand of investigations that they unite the analysis of the past, the present, and the design of the future. Change is possible and almost inevitable. However, change is not always "progress," as supposed by the Whig mythology of "modernity" of the past two centuries.

All systems of organization and social control end up being systems that manage to guide the conduct of subjects and human groups with dexterity (even though their psychological structure is perhaps only partially known). In actuality, old systems are being replaced on a massive scale by others whose psychological functionality and effects on consciousness, though very evident in results, are not well-known in their internal structure. What are the structure and dynamics of this new cultural equipment of consciousness, and what is its product in terms of the mental architecture for new generations? Only a complete investigation will permit this to be determined. But the science of culture and of mind must be prepared to analyze implicit historical designs and the emergent properties in an even-handed way, regardless of the social power of the defenders of various designs.

It is accurate to understand social and technological change as the capital of the future, but ecological problems confront us with the necessity of not scorning that which was the capital of the past and present or condemning with thoughtless urgency all that is in scientific archives and museums. The attempt by certain religious and social groups to protect "irrationally," and sometimes without civility, their systems, should be understood as an attempt to protect their architecture of consciousness, perhaps following the maxim of Saint Augustine: "Guard the order and the order will guard you" ("Save your culture and it will save your mind" would not be an inadequate extrapolation). And this *consistency* of many of the cultural and historical cultural systems and their resistance to disappearing allows us, fortunately, as investigators to have access to many implicit historical designs that persist in various cultures.

It remains to be seen how mind will be produced by new cultural designs that attempt to substitute new for traditional mechanisms for the management of consciousness. The analysis of new cultural designs is not exhausted by the inventory of qualities for building *knowledge*. Their effect on the management of *agentivity* presents an additional agenda replete with problems for the human sciences. These are problems such as rationalism, schooling, and the bureaucratic organization of behavior. All these are equally worthy of analysis, as are the implicit traditional designs.

We trust that we have been able to communicate the urgency of the basic ideas that recur in this chapter. They are as follows:

1. There is a need to design the human mind not in a fixed, but a changing and flexible way. The psyche can be constructed from various cultural systems of activity and consciousness, as well as, with diverse architectures.
2. There is a necessity, therefore, to develop a comprehensive psychology of the *flexible architectures* and distinct properties of every design of consciousness. These architectures are in general *implicit* or not evident in principle either to the subject or to the investigator. This psychology will permit a convergence of concrete studies of mental, or internal, processes with cultural processes, provided that the functional systems are precisely defined at both levels.
3. If the foregoing point is resolved satisfactorily, it is possible for psychology to *act constructively* in education and the development of consciousness in an efficacious manner, since mental realities *can be approached and designed just as external cultural realities can be*. The recuperation, scaffolding, or design of activity and consciousness systems for social politics or the design of cognitive instruments in education would be instances of this.

The possibilities for human change are directly related to what is open to psychology, a discipline that must concern itself with such change. Dilthey (1977) recognized the role of culture in nourishing and guiding a new species in continual change in his "culturally based human science." When Vygotsky (1982a) finished writing his essay on the crisis in psychology, he expressed a very close idea, though perhaps one that was more ambitious. He attributed to science the role of advancing culture and professed an ardently scientific optimism, one that supposed that culture, after a stage in which it realized the design of consciousness in an implicit or nonconscious way, would realize another – illuminated this time by science. In this case things would be designed consciously and explicitly; consciousness would know itself already and for this reason could construct itself with complete capacity. In this process, the stage prior to such lucidity and scientific capacity would be in reality provisional, a prehistory leading up to the authentic cultural-historical evolution of the self-designed human, of authentic consciousness constructed from itself.

But perhaps the stage of lucidity and scientific human consciousness that Vygotsky considered as already having been attained is yet to be reached, and our highest stage of consciousness must be to recognize everything that is yet to be known, to recognize that change remains hazardous when we attempt to design it from the still primitive forces of our technology of consciousness. We do not wish to take away from Vygotsky anything of the ambition he had for the future, but his social enthusiasm must be tempered by the concrete investigation of implicit and explicit constructions of consciousness that remain, for the moment, in the set of tasks awaiting psychology.

References

Bronfenbrenner, U. (1989). *Who cares for children?* UNESCO, No. 188.

Bruner, J. (1990). *Acts of meaning.* Cambridge, MA: Harvard University Press.

Caro Baroja, J. (1988). *Del viejo folklore castellano.* Valladolid: Amtito.

Chomsky, N. (1980). *Rules and representations.* New York: Columbia University Press.

Cole, M. (1990). Cognitive development and formal schooling: The evidence from cross-cultural research. In L. Moll (Ed.), *Vygotsky and education: Instructional implications and applications of sociohistorical psychology* (pp. 89–110). Cambridge University Press.

Cole, M. (1992). Context, modularity, and cultural constitution of development. In L. T. Winegar & J. Valsiner (Eds.), *Children within social context* (pp. 5–32). Hillsdale, NJ: Erlbaum.

del Río, P. (1986). *El desarrollo de las competencias espaciales: El proceso de construcción de los instrumentos mentales.* Unpublished doctoral dissertation, Universidad Complutense de Madrid.

del Río, P. (1992). Knowledge in the media: Returning to an instant world. Paper presented at the First Conference for Socio-cultural Research, Madrid, September.

del Río, P. (1995). Extra-cortical connections: The socio-cultural systems for conscious living. In J. V. Wertsch & J. D. Ramirez (Eds.), *Explorations in sociocultural studies: Literacy and other forms of mediated actión* (pp. 19–31). Madrid: Fundacion Infancia y Aprendizaje.

del Río, P., & Alvarez, A. (1992). Tres pies al gato: Significado, sentido y cultura cotidiana en la educación. *Infancia y Aprendizaje, 59–60,* 43–62.

de Unamuno, M. (1927). *Cómo se hace una novela.* Madrid: Alianza.

de Unamuno, M. (1940). *Amor y pedagogía.* Madrid: Espasa Calpe.

de Waal, F. (1993). *La politica de los chimpancés.* Madrid: Alianza.

Dilthey, W. (1977). *Descriptive psychology and historical understanding.* (R. M. Zaner & K. L. Heiges, Trans.). The Hague: Nijhoff.

Donald, M. (1991). *Origins of the modern mind.* Cambridge, MA: Harvard University Press.

Durkheim, E. (1915). *The elementary forms of the religious life.* Glencoe, IL: Prentice-Hall.

El'konin, D. B. (1978). *Psikhologii igri* [The psychology of play]. Moscow: Pedagogica.

Fodor, J. (1975). *The language of thought.* New York: Harper & Row.

Garfinkel, H. (1967). *Studies in ethnomethodology.* Englewood Cliffs, NJ: Prentice-Hall.

Johnson-Laird, P. N. (1988). *The computer and the mind: An introduction to cognitive science.* Glasgow: Collins.

Leslie, A. M. (1988). Some implications of pretense for mechanisms underlying the child's theory of mind. In J. W. Astington, P. L. Harris, & D. R. Olson (Eds.), *Developing theories of mind* (pp. 19–43). Cambridge University Press.

Levy-Bruhl, L. (1927). *Lâme primitive.* Paris: P.U.F.

Lewin, R. (1987). *Bones of contention: Controversies in the search for human origins.* New York: Simon & Schuster.

Luria, A. R. (1961). *The role of speech in the regulation of normal and abnormal behavior.* New York: Irvington.

Luria, A. R. (1976). *Cognitive development: Its cultural and social foundations.* Cambridge, MA: Harvard University Press.

Luria, A. R. (1978). Funktsional'naya organizatsia psikhiki [The functional organization of mind]. In A. A. Smirnov (Ed.), *Estestvennonauchnie osnovi psikhologii* [The natural science foundations of psychology] (pp. 3–54). Moscow: Pedagogika.

Luria, A. R. (1979). *The making of mind.* Cambridge, MA: Harvard University Press.

Middleton, D., & Edwards, D. (Eds.). (1990). *Collective remembering.* London: Sage.

Ornstein, R. (1991). *The evolution of consciousness: Darwin, Freud, and cranial fire – The origins of the way we think.* Englewood Cliffs, NJ: Prentice-Hall.

Ortega y Gasset, J. (1940). Ideas y creencias. In *Obras completas* (pp. 403–405). Madrid: Revista de Occidente.

Ortega y Gasset, J. (nd). Alocución grabada. In R. Taibo & A. Ribas (Eds.), *España, años decisivos. 1920–1939.* Madrid: Videosistemas.

Premack, D., & Woodruff, G. (1978). Does the chimpanzee have a theory of mind? *Behavioral and Brain Sciences* 4(1), 515–526.

Rivière, A. (1991). *Objetos con mente.* Madrid: Alianza Editorial.

Rivière, A. (1993). Sobre objetos con mente. Reflexiones para un debate. *Anuario de Psicologia, 56,* 49–144.

Rommetveit, R. (1992). Outlines of a dialogically based social-cognitive approach to human cognition and communication. In A. H. Wold (Ed.), *The dialogical alternative: Towards a theory of language and mind* (pp. 19–45). Oslo: Scandinavian University Press.

Salomon, G. (1979). *Interaction of media, cognition and learning.* San Francisco: Jossey-Bass.

Schousboe, K. (1986). Panis et circensen: Orality and visuality in medieval Denmark. *Quarterly Newsletter of the Laboratory of Comparative Human Cognition, 8(1),* 10–17.

Scribner, S. (1984). Product assembly: Optimizing strategies and their acquisition. *Quarterly Newsletter of the Laboratory of Comparative Human Cognition, 6(1–2),* 11–19.

Scribner, S. (1985). Vygotsky's uses of history. In J. V. Wertsch (Ed.), *Culture, communication, and cognition: Vygotskian perspectives* (pp. 119–145). Cambridge University Press.

Scribner, S., & Cole, M. (1981). *The psychology of literacy.* Cambridge, MA: Harvard University Press.

Sutton, A. (1988). L. S. Vygotsky: The cultural-historical theory – National minorities and the ZPD. In R. M. Gupta & P. Coxhead (Eds.), *Cultural diversity and learning efficiency* (pp. 89–116). New York: St. Martin's.

Todorova, E. Schmidt, H. D., Kalmar, M., Beresneviciené, M., Lavzackas, R., Tyszkowa, M., Ruisel, I., & Smirnova, E. O. (1993). Developmental research in times of change: Comments from Central and Eastern Europe. *Newsletter of the International Society for the Study of Behavior Development, 23,* 2–4.

Toffler, A. (1970). *Future shock.* New York: Bantam.

Toulmin, S. (1972). *Human understanding: Vol. 1, The collective use and evolution of concepts.* Princeton, NJ: Princeton University Press.

Trevarthen, C. (1992). An infant's motives for speaking and thinking in the culture. In A. H. Wold (Ed.), *The dialogical alternative: Towards a theory of language and mind* (pp. 99–137). Oslo: Scandinavian University Press.

Tsunoda, T. (1985). *The Japanese brain.* Tokyo: Taishukan.

Tulviste, P. (1991). *The cultural-historical development of verbal thinking* (M. J. Hall, Trans.). Commack, NY: Nova Science Publishers.

Valsiner, J., & Winegar, L. T. (1992). Introduction: A cultural-historical context for social "context." In L. T. Winegar & J. Valsner (Eds.), *Children's development within social contexts: Metatheory and theory* (pp. 1–14). Hillsdale, NJ: Erlbaum.

Vygotsky, L. S. (1929). K voprosu o plane nauchno-issledovatel'skoi raboty po pedologii natsional'nykh men'shinstv [The problem of the plane of scientific research on the pedalogy of national minorities]. *Pedalogiya* [Pedalogy], *3*, 367–377.

Vygotsky, L. S. (1982a). Istoricheskii smysl psikhologicheskogo krizisa [The historical meaning of the crisis in psychology]. In *Sobranie sochinenie. Tom 1. Voprosy teorii istorii* [Collected essays: Vol. 1, Problems of the theory of history] (pp. 238–290). Moscow: Pedagogika.

Vygotsky, L. S. (1982b). Myshlenie i rech' [Thinking and speech]. In *Sobranie sochinenie. Tom 2. Problemy obshchei psikhologii* [Collected essays: Vol. 2, Problems in general psychology], (pp. 5–361). Moscow: Pedagogika.

Vygotsky, L. S. (1982c). *Sobranie sochinenie. Tom 1. Voprosy teorii istorii* [Collected essays: Vol. 1, Problems of the theory of history]. Moscow: Pedagogika.

Vygotsky, L. S. (1983). Istoriya razvitiya vyshikh psikhicheskikh funktsii [The history of the development of higher mental functions]. In *Sobranie sochinenie. Tom 3. Problemy razvitiya psikhiki* [Collected essays: Vol. 3, Problems of mental development] (pp. 5–328). Moscow: Pedagogika.

Vygotsky, L. S. (1984). Orudie i znak v razvitii rebenka [Tool and sign in the development of the child]. In *Sobranie sochinenie. Tom 6. Nauchniya nasledstvo* [Collected essays: Vol. 6, Scientific heritage]. (pp. 5–350). Moscow: Pedagogika.

Wertsch, J. V. (1985). *Vygotsky and the social formation of mind.* Cambridge, MA: Harvard University Press.

Wertsch, J. V., Tulviste, P., & Hagstrom, F. (1993). *A* sociocultural approach to agency. In E. Forman, N. Minick, and C. A. Stone (Eds.), *Contexts for learning: Sociocultural dynamics in children's development* (pp. 336–356). New York: Oxford University Press.

Winkler, E., & Schweikhardt, J. (1982). *Expedition Mensch. Streifzuge durch de Anthropologie.* Vienna: Ueberreuter.

Index